THE SOCIALIST CORPORATION
AND TECHNOCRATIC POWER

SOVIET AND EAST EUROPEAN STUDIES

Books in the series

THE SOCIALIST CORPORATION AND TECHNOCRATIC POWER

THE POLISH UNITED WORKERS' PARTY, INDUSTRIAL ORGANISATION AND WORKFORCE CONTROL 1958–80

JEAN WOODALL

SENIOR LECTURER IN POLITICS, KINGSTON POLYTECHNIC

CAMBRIDGE UNIVERSITY PRESS

CAMBRIDGE

LONDON   NEW YORK   NEW ROCHELLE

MELBOURNE   SYDNEY

Published by the Press Syndicate of the University of Cambridge
The Pitt Building, Trumpington Street, Cambridge CB2 1RP
32 East 57th Street, New York, NY 10022, USA
296 Beaconsfield Parade, Middle Park, Melbourne 3206, Australia

First published 1982

Printed in Great Britain at the University Press, Cambridge

Library of Congress catalogue card number: 82–1271

British library cataloguing in publication data
Woodall, Jean
The socialist corporation and technocratic power:
the Polish United Workers' Party industrial
organisation and workforce control 1958–1980—
(Soviet and East European studies)
1. Industrial organisation—Poland—History
I. Title II. Series
338.6'09438   HC337.P7
ISBN 0 521 24269 X

to my parents

Contents

vii

Preface

My initial interest in Poland was stimulated by the events that took place on the Baltic Coast during December 1970. At that time the fruits of several research projects on East European politics were just coming into print. As the discipline of Comparative Communist Politics was of relatively recent origin and begged for empirical investigations, these studies helped to fill the gap and draw attention to the very different identities of East European states and the contrasts between them and the USSR.

It was my own concern for that twilight area between political and economic science that led to the subject of a Ph.D. thesis on which this book was initially based. I felt that the analysis of the process of economic reform in state-socialist societies is never satisfactorily treated by either discipline alone. On the one hand the economist, while able to elicit the goals of economic policy and their achievement, makes a trite distinction between economic policy and reform and dismisses as exogenous to his analysis the recruitment of management and workforce and the articulation of their interests through a Marxist–Leninist party. On the other hand, the political scientist, while mindful of the interaction between industrial management, the working class and the Party, tends to reduce economic policy and reform to the simplistic dimensions of centralisation versus decentralisation, plan versus market and production versus consumption. It is my hope to forge a union between these two disciplines and to draw on the richness of both to study economic policy and reform in Poland since 1958.

The slow gestation period of this work reflects the many crises I encountered in attempting the task set. In the course of my research I have come to question many assumptions made by both political scientists and economists as to the nature of the Polish working class, industrial management, the Polish United Workers' Party (PZPR), and that basic unit of economic production: the industrial enterprise. Yet the recent events of July and August 1980, and the demise of Edward Gierek as First Secretary of the Polish United Workers' Party have provided a convenient point at which to break. So, in terms of chronology, the period 1958–80 covers the rule of two First Secretaries: Władysław Gomułka and Edward Gierek. Comment and conjectures on the events after the Eighth Congress of the PZPR in February 1980 have been left to a postscript at the end.

I should like to extend my thanks to several persons and institutions for their help and advice during the course of my studies on Poland. Firstly thanks are due to my former supervisor Professor Ghita Ionescu, Manchester University Department of Government and the Social Science Research Council for academic guidance and the finance of a Ph.D. programme between 1971 and 1974. Two trips to Poland during 1972–3, financed by the SSRC, provided the preliminary empirical data for this work, and I am particularly grateful for the help of Professor Włodzimierz Wesołowski and his staff at the Institute of Philosophy and Sociology at Warsaw University. A further trip to Poland was made during 1975, but the bulk of material dating from this time was made available by the Polish Library in London, by the British Library of Economic and Political Science at LSE and by the library at the Centre for Russian and East European Studies at Birmingham University. The opportunity to discuss my work with staff in the latter institution (especially Jane Cave, Dr R. Amann and Dr P. Hanson) plus access to their English language abstracts of Polish journals proved very helpful at an early stage of research. Special thanks are owed to George Kolankiewicz of the University of Essex and to colleagues at the School of Economics and Politics at Kingston Polytechnic for their encouragement and critical appraisal of earlier drafts of my work. Finally, I am indebted to Mrs Jane Jeffery for her painstaking and patient transcription of my execrable long-hand into immaculate type script. Nonetheless, despite the extensive help that I have received from all those cited here, I must in the customary way accept responsibility for all opinions expressed and errors of commission and omission.

JEAN WOODALL

Kingston Polytechnic
April 1981

Abbreviations

CODKK	Centre for Management Training (Centralny Ośrodek Doskonalenia Kadr Kierowniczych)
CPSU	Communist Party of the Soviet Union
CRZZ	Central Trade Union Council (Centralna Rada Związków Zawodowych)
FLT	Ball Bearing Plant (Fabryka Łożysk Tocznych)
GUS	Central Statistical Office (Główny Urząd Statystyczny)
IFiS	Institute of Philosophy and Sociology (Instytut Filosofii i Socjologii)
INP	Institute of Legal Science (Instytut Nauk Prawnych)
IOPM	Institute of Organisation for the Engineering Industry (Instytut Organizacji Przemysłu Maszynowego)
IP	Institute of Planning (Instytut Planowania)
JI	Pilot Unit (Jednostek Inicujący)
KCPZPR	The Central Committee of the Polish United Workers' Party (Komitet Centralny PZPR)
KERM	The Economic Committee of the Council of Ministers (Komitet Ekonomiczny Rady Ministrów)
KP	Planning Commission (Komisja Planowania)
KPSRK	Conference of Combine Self-Management Representatives (Komitet Przedstawicielski Samorządu Robotniczego w Kombinacie)
KSR	Conference of Workers' Self-Management (Konferencja Samorządu Robotniczego)
KSS–KOR	Committee of Social Defence and Workers' Defence (Komitet Samo-obrona Społeczna – Komitet Obrony Robotników)

KZ	Enterprise Committee (Komitet Zakĺadowy)
MKS	Inter-Factory Strike Committee (Między-Zakĺadowe Komitet Strajkowe)
NBP	National Bank of Poland (Narodowe Bank Polski)
NIK	Central Inspectorate (Naczelna Iżba Kontroli)
NOT	Chief Organisation of Technicians (Naczelna Organizacja Techniczna)
OOP	Sectional Party Organisation (Oddżiaĺowa Organizacja Partyjna)
PAN	Polish Academy of Sciences (Polska Akademia Nauk)
POP	Basic Party Organisation (Podstawowa Organizacja Partyjna)
PPS	Polish Socialist Party (Polska Partia Socjalistyczna)
PPR	Polish Workers' Party (Polska Partia Robotnicza)
PRN	District People's Council (Powiatowa Rada Narodowa)
PTE	Polish Economics Society (Polskie Towarżystwo Ekonomiczne)
PZPR	The Polish United Workers' Party (Polska Zjednoczona Partia Robotnicza)
RM	The Council of Ministers (Rada Ministrów)
RN	National Council (Rada Narodowa)
RR	Workers' Council (Rada Robotnicza)
RZ	Trade Union Factory Council (Rada Zakĺadowa)
SED	Socialist Unity Party (Sozialistische Einheistspartei Deutschlands)
SGPiS	Central School of Planning and Statistics (Szkole Gĺówne Planowania i Statystiki)
SCEP	State Commission of Economic Planning
TNOiK	Society for Scientific Organisation and Management (Towarżystwo Naukowe Organizacja i Kierownictwa)
VEB	(East German) Enterprise (Volkseigene Betrieb)
VVB	(East German) Association of Enterprises (Vereinigung Volkseigener Betriebe)
WOG	Large Production Unit (Wieĺka Organizacja Gospodarcza)

WRN	Regional National Council (Wojewodzka Rada Narodowa)
WSNS	Higher Party School of Social Sciences (Wyższa Szkoła Nauk Społecznych)
ZGZZM	Chief Executive of the Metalworkers Trade Union (Zarząd Główny Związki Zawodowej Metalowców)
ZMS	Socialist Youth Union (Związek Młodżieży Socjalistycznej)
ZMW	Peasant Youth Union (Związek Młodżieży Wiejskiej)
ZPA	Association of the Nitrates Industry (Zjednoczenie Przemysłu Azotowego)
ZPF	Association of the Pharmaceuticals Industry (Zjednoczenie Przemysłu Farmaceuticznego)
ZPO	Association of the Shipbuilding Industry (Zjednoczenie Przemysłu Okrętowego)
ZPSB	Association of the Joinery and Construction Industry (Zjednoczenie Przemysłu Stolarki Budowlanej)
ZSL	United Peasants' Party (Zjednoczone Stronnićtwo Ludowej)
ZSMP	Socialist Union of Polish Youth (Związek Socjalistyczne Młodziez Polskich)

1

Advanced industrialisation, the division of labour and the growth of bureaucratic power

The growth in size of the Polish industrial enterprise, and the acquisition of characteristics resembling Western corporations by some levels in the industrial bureaucracy, was chosen as the subject of this work because the author considers that this posed considerable problems for control by a Marxist–Leninist party: the Polish United Workers' Party (PZPR). What would be the implications for PZPR control over management recruitment into these 'socialist corporations', and how does the size of these units affect the legitimacy of the PZPR in the eyes of the Polish industrial working class? More broadly this raises the question of what particular forces in the Polish industrialisation process have led to these quasi-corporate structures: what are the political consequences of the pursuit of economic growth and in what manner has state bureaucratic power increased; is there an inevitable logic underlying the unfolding of the division of labour; are the 'forces of production' ideologically neutral? While conventional theoretical examinations of Communist polities are seen as inadequate to the task of answering these questions, the author feels that the more 'glamorous' theories of convergence and industrial/post-industrial society do not fit the bill much better. Rather, in the course of this chapter such 'grand' theory will be eschewed in favour of a more eclectic cluster of points, raised in the work of West European industrial sociologists and East European dissident intellectuals, which seem more germane to the major themes of this book.

We have taken as our empirical point of reference a country that emerged as a social and economic casualty of the Second World War: the People's Republic of Poland. The Potsdam Agreement of August 1945 had fixed a Western boundary just East of the Oder–Neisse rivers and, as a consequence, Polish territory was

1

shifted westwards with the loss of much land in the East. Moreover in 1945 there were two competing claims to the legitimate right to govern: the Polish Government in Exile under the leadership of General Sikorski and the Polish Committee of National Liberation. It was the latter, founded on the basis of the manifesto of 22 July 1944, that formed the nucleus of the Provisional Government called into existence by the Allies after the Yalta Conference of February 1945. Despite the call by the Western Allies for a broader basis for this government[1] and for the holding of nation-wide free elections, when the elections eventually took place on 13 February 1947, candidates fielded under the joint programme of the Polish Workers' Party and Polish Socialist Party (PPS) won 80.1% of the valid votes cast.[2] Power-sharing after the adoption of a constitution in February 1947 placed the PPR leader Bolesław Bierut at the Head of State and the PPS leader Jozef Cyrankiewicz was designated Prime Minister. By December 1948 a 'merger' of these two parties had taken place to form the Polish United Workers' Party (PZPR).

It was under the hegemony of the PZPR that Polish economic recovery took place, and (as will be outlined later in this work) by the early 1950s Poland was undergoing a rapid growth in national income.[3] However, since 1950 the comparative shares of industry and agriculture in contribution to national income have changed,[4] indicating the development away from an economy that was predominantly agrarian, to one based on manufacturing industry. It will be shown later that the spectacular growth rates in the early 1950s were followed by slower growth rates in the 1960s, especially in industry where the major barrier was seen to be the rising ratio of capital and labour to output. By the mid-1960s, the PZPR was calling for a change of economic policy away from extensive growth, towards 'selective sectoral development' and intensive growth. It was seen as necessary that the forces of the 'scientific-technological revolution' be harnessed to achieve these goals.

What exactly was meant by the 'scientific-technological revolution', and what exactly were the barriers to the achievement of intensive economic growth? The answer to the latter question will be left to Chapter 2, but here we will concentrate on the former. The irony of the argument that only under socialist relations of production could scientific research and technological innovation be more rational, speedier and more responsive to social needs, was that its articulation coincided with a slowing down of economic growth-rates in the Soviet Union and Eastern Europe after 1960.[5] Anxiety was masked by the expression of interest in 'prognostic science' and social and economic forecasting originally developed in the West. The 'Commission on the Year 2000' set up in the United States under the chairmanship of Daniel Bell[6] in the 1960s produced reports which focussed on the change in occupations, education and general lifestyle patterns taking place in the United States, as did the work of Kahn and Wiener.[7] The first significant emulation of such activity was published in Czechoslovakia, arising out of a symposium held by the Czech Academy of Sciences led by Radovan Richta.[8] He saw mankind to be on the threshold of a new revolution, the 'scientific-technological revolution', because existing rates of economic growth would suddenly take off with the entry of applied science into the production process and capital and labour output ratios would change 'intensively' as opposed to 'extensively'. Yet this 'scientific-technological revolution' would also be a cultural revolution that would change the nature of the work process (by releasing people from manufacturing for work in research and cultural and service sectors) and could provide the means of overcoming the remaining vestiges of alienation existing in a socialist society.[9] Such a revolution could only fail in capitalist societies and the most favourable conditions for its success were seen as present in socialist societies. With respect to Czechoslovakia, Richta proposed a programme of industrial modernisation focussing on the chemical and electronics industries, the elimination of unskilled labour, and the use of cybernetic management systems. His confidence of success was, however, tempered by reservations: on the one hand about the 'administrative–directive' system of management which could act as a disincentive to innovate and place restrictions on scientific and creative freedom;[10] and on the other hand that this would provide a free licence for the growth of planners' and managerial power. Unless there was the possibility for participation by all in this process, it would fail. Richta saw the conditions for success to be more likely in socialist states where the barrier between the working class and intelligentsia was seen to be dissolving, and a greater equalisation of opportunity was being achieved[11] (although certain sections of the working class such as the unskilled might be a source of 'conservative' pressure against scientific and technological progress). In any case this would necessitate a much closer integration of such groups into management decision-making and would involve, ultimately, a change in the structure and style of operation of the Czechoslovak Communist Party,[12] which would involve abandoning the model of a narrowly based revolutionary vanguard party, for a leading role that would involve the maximum integration of society.

It would be easy to label *Civilisation at the Crossroads* as a utopian product of the 'Prague Spring', but it does display a frank awareness that the survival of various phenomena from a capitalist society should be confronted and it was a serious attempt to propose a solution to the problem of a falling rate of growth. The symposium was greeted with interest by scholars in the Soviet Union and East European states, and in Poland a similar commission was appointed under the chairmanship of Professor Jan Szczepański and Kazimierz Secomski.[13]

However, this book is not concerned with the distant horizons of futurology, so much as the political consequences of economic growth and technological change in Poland. Hence there still remains the question of finding a suitable framework for analysis. While it is necessary to have a firm grasp of the economic mechanism, the tools used by economists are insufficient for our purposes. For them 'economic mechanisms' are understood as coherent (or incoherent) systems of commands and parameters transmitted from the central economic apparatus to the enterprise and can be grouped into models. However, the politico-institutional structure within which such mechanisms operate are considered only as a formal arrangement of central planning board and ministries on the one hand and constituent enterprises on the other hand. Generally, economists tend to ignore the problem of organisational structure, especially at the intermediate level between enterprises and central planning and management authorities. Economic reform is considered as a question of following an 'optimal sequence', and of the correspondence of policy objectives and policy instruments. The contradictions in objectives persist because reforms are introduced as a hurried response to political crisis, and the result is an eclectic and ill-conceived blueprint. A 'false policy of transition' arises because of mistiming and the failure to work out an optimal sequence of reform by, for example, co-ordinating the introduction of changes in the management mechanism with changes in the price system. Questions of class interest and recruitment into the labour force and management are considered to be exogenous to the analysis,[14] which occasionally poses problems when the evaluation of popular satisfaction/discontent with the economic system is considered, and can result in making what, to the political scientist or sociologist, can only be considered as outrageous claims.[15]

To be fair to the economists, political scientists cannot claim greater conceptual sophistication. Until the mid-1960s, the political systems of the Soviet Union and Eastern Europe were labelled as 'totalitarian'. The pedigree of this concept can be traced back to the 1920s, and has been used to cover Fascist as well as Communist forms of rule.[16] The best-known attempt to operationalise the concept is, of course, the syndrome first outlined by Carl Friedrich and later developed in collaboration with Zbigniew Brzeziński.[17] Yet this six-point syndrome was heavily criticised for being no more than a 'shopping-list' and for providing very little in the way of explanation of actual decision-making processes and regime dynamics.[18] This essentially static approach to the study of Soviet-type regimes was not immediately abandoned and attempts to revitalise the concept were made as late as 1969 and 1972; Leonard Shapiro, in particular, hoped that by distinguishing between the 'contours of the policy' and the 'instruments of rule' to introduce an element of flexibility.[19] Whether or not this is justified is still open to doubt. The impression remains that Shapiro has indulged in an exercise of conceptual 'stretching'.

As interest in the regimes of Eastern Europe and the Soviet Union increased during the 1960s, many political scientists abandoned the concept of totalitarianism and attempted to introduce the tools of comparative analysis and of the behavioural revolution.[20] A recent over-view of this effort, categorising the various methodologies comes out in favour of 'middle-range' theory but pin-points the gaps in knowledge of elite socialisation, policy innovation and implementation, and the responsiveness of the bureaucracy to popular pressures.[21] It was felt that a greater use of East–West comparison would generally improve the quality of analysis. This has yet to be achieved in the field of political science. In contrast, sociologists and economists have been busy for nearly 40 years with developing and refining theories of industrial society and convergence. The pedigree of these theories can be traced back to the works of Saint-Simon (and earlier Enlightenment *philosophes*), Durkheim and Max Weber.[22] Obviously convergence theory is related to development theory and ultimately to the developments in sociological thought that have examined the nature of the transition from traditional to modern industrial society. Thus the boundaries of convergence theory are very fluid, and the many writers who fall into this category have very little in common. While some may argue that there is a growing similarity between East and West in terms of social and economic organisation (Burnham and Galbraith),[23] others may be arguing that there is a uniformity of social and economic structure that underlies the transition from traditional to modern industrial society (Rostow and Schumpeter)[24] and yet others will argue that, while many societies in their industrial phase may have been very dissimilar, some are entering a post-industrial phase and display certain common features (Bell and Touraine).[25] Other theorists are slightly more difficult to place (Dahrendorf and Aron).[26] In a very comprehensive work, which attempts to verify the concept, David Lane uses the label 'convergence theory' to include the various approaches that observe similar arrangements for the performance of important social functions that are taking place in such ostensibly different societies as Britain and the USA, on the one hand, and the Soviet Union and Eastern Europe on the other. The evidence that is assembled to justify this convergence is seen by Lane to be located in four main trends. Firstly, the highly developed division of labour is seen as producing a hierarchy of statuses and political and social elites, which is similar in all industrial societies. Secondly, structural differentiation implies a declining role for the family as a structure of social integration, and its replacement by specialised institutions such as the industrial enterprise and the labour union. Thirdly, the value system of industrial society places increasing emphasis on the instrumental nature of work, a striving for the mastery of the environment, and for industrial advancement and status differentiation. Thus the utopian values of revolutionaries and radicals are displaced by instrumental values. Finally, the need for large-scale production implies the inevitability of central planning and the increased accumulation of power in the hands of technocrats. A bureaucratic system of organisation, bound by rules and promoting specific goals, has replaced the pursuit of profit and of the classless society. The growth of urban society breaks down the affective bonds of social solidarity and introduces greater anonymity into social relations.[27]

To probe behind this mainly economic and social theory for

political implications is difficult. However, as the main focus of this work is the political consequences of the pursuit of economic growth, one major concern will be whether there has been a growing need for large-scale production lodged in bureaucratic organisation that has increased the accumulation of power in the hands of the technocrats. Secondly, the implications of this for the division of labour and value systems must be examined. It is unfortunate, though, that some methodological problems must first be confronted. In the first place much convergence theory is couched in terms of a parody of historical materialism, and resembles the style of mid-nineteenth-century evolutionary theory.[28] Society is presented as passing through different stages and so there is an underlying theme of linear progression. The belief in an immanent teleology is not, however, to be derived from Darwinian evolutionary theory, but should be traced back to the common concerns of early sociological theorists to describe a transition from military to industrial society. Nonetheless, the general effect is to create a circular argument that presents problems for empirical verification: economic growth is both a precondition to and a consequence of new technological developments. The 'holistic' approach to explanation clearly in evidence in the work of Schumpeter and Rostow is precisely that element which is both appealing and extremely difficult to refute. As already mentioned, it is a mode of reasoning which has been seen to possess parallels to the approach of eighteenth-century *philosophes* who thought in terms of systems and drew analogies with the natural sciences in the form of laws of behaviour.[29]

Related to this 'holistic' approach is the employment of deductive reasoning, which despite the concern of convergence theorists to represent processes at work in the real world, in essentially non-empiricist. An example of this is the attempt by Bell to draw evidence of a transition from industrial to post-industrial society, by examining the changing profile of occupations in the USA. Notwithstanding the pit-falls of doing so, Bell blithely assumes that the greater percentage of GNP devoted to higher education and to research and development implies the growing centrality of theoretical knowledge.[30] Kumar casts serious doubt upon the existence of such an observable trend. He begins by challenging the assertion that employment in service industry has replaced manufacturing. This was based upon false assumptions about the process of industrialisation in Britain and the USA: rather, employment in service industry has displaced employment in agriculture. More-over, the actual development of service industries is nowhere examined. Secondly, to hail the increase in white-collar employment as indicative of a new work ethic which is also fostered by a more 'communitarian' spirit in the organisation of service industry, goes against evidence provided by studies of behaviour in large-scale technologically advanced organisations. Daniel Bell, in particular, is very lax in his definition of white-collar work and fails to appreciate that official employment statistics can mask a tremendous variation: the statistics he quotes suppress the fact that there are many manual workers employed in the service sector, and that many white-collar jobs attached to manufacturing industry such as management consultancy, marketing and general managerial work, are unlikely to be hostile or indifferent to the profit motive. A substantial share of white-collar jobs are the preserve of the semi-skilled, performing routine tasks not dissimilar to the tasks of the factory worker. These criticisms could apply equally to Schumpeter, Burnham and Galbraith: their fundamental mistake is to confuse the re-labelling of occupational activity with professionalism. Many of these indepen-dent professionals are in reality dependent upon public bureaucracy, and there is no reason to believe that they could be motivated to form either a 'new working class' or an enlightened humanitarian elite. Similarly the evidence that Touraine summons in defence of his arguments is both arbitrary and conjectural. The propensity of the highly skilled for a radicalism greater than that of the industrial working class is disputable, drawn from limited observations, and values and attitudes are imputed from the behaviour of individuals.

Leaving aside the general mode of empirical verification, the question of how convergence theorists account for the recruitment and beliefs of the emerging scientific and technological elite awaits a satisfactory answer. Their response is inadequately construed because their theory is 'anti-political'. There is no adequate autonomous theory of politics: politics is regarded as a category determined by economic and social factors, or as a distasteful disruptive activity. This can be traced back to an eighteenth-century tradition that sees the most distinctive feature of human relations as lying in the medium of *social* transaction (distribution, production exchange) and it is by this that political relationships are deter-mined. For Schumpeter it is the immanent logic of the rationalising spirit, for Rostow it is the sectoral patterns of growth, for Galbraith it is the imperatives of technology, that determine political relationships.[31] In general this weak sense of the 'political' causes theorists of convergence to reduce politics to the level of a synonym for administration (Schumpeter and Rostow) or to founder in their explanations of the *origins* of the forces for cohesion and protest in society (Bell and Touraine).[32] More specifically on the explanation of elite recruitment, in the main this tends to be based on no more than conjecture. Some theorists do not consider it to be at all problematic (Rostow and Schumpeter) while for Burnham it is explained in terms of an inevitable logic. Location in the socio-occupational structure is deemed sufficient by Bell, Touraine and Galbraith as an explanation of political consciousness. Furthermore, it is assumed that bureaucratic organisation in any society is but a mechanism that conforms to a common behaviour pattern, something that would not be easily accepted by those who have made a study of specific bureaucratic organisations in their specific socio-cultural environments.[33]

Leaving aside many other criticisms, perhaps the most damning is what Kumar sees as the fundamental misconception about the nature of industrial society itself. Most convergence theorists, and theorists of post-industrial society use as their model of industrial capitalism the conditions pertaining to the early stages of the British Industrial Revolution. There is a case for arguing that this is an inadequate model, as British industrialisation did not mature until the late stages of the nineteenth century when a process of bureaucratisation was already in evidence. Such an ahistorical approach means that the origins of the white-collar revolution are incorrectly ascribed to the twentieth century when, in Britain at least, their origin was much earlier. For Kumar, the essential blindness in this mode of theorisation lies in the failure to grasp the continuity of the industrialisation process.

Above all, it is striking how indebted convergence theorists are to the 'Founding Fathers' of sociology, in particular, Saint-Simon, Weber and Durkheim. It is also striking how reluctant they are to acknowledge their pedigree, and how intent they are to stress the novelty of their own work. On the whole these theorists tend to embellish (or pervert) the work of classical sociological theory and the novelty they claim emerges quite tarnished upon closer scrutiny.[34]

Convergence theory and industrial/post-industrial society theory raise many interesting questions for study in the context of a state-socialist society such as Poland, but they also raise as many problems in the field of methodological application and verification. This is faced but not resolved in a recent article by Tellenback.[35] He assumes that there exist different institutional ceilings under which common laws govern industrial society, and the intensive growth sought by the PZPR is only possible if political conflict is institutionalised. However, the PZPR is in conflict with civil society over the process of industrialisation, and, in the absence of a mechanism for gradual and piecemeal solution to conflict, two trends ensue. Firstly, a lack of alternative values creates an apolitical privatised society with a homogeneous value system stressing petty-bourgeois ideals, which can only be satisfied by the expansion of welfare. Secondly, the PZPR, to cope with the needs of industrialisation, becomes increasingly professionalised and its internal value system and legitimacy becomes increasingly tied to technical and administrative competence. The result is that a technological pragmatism is the only solution for mature socialist development, with the consequent dangers of consolidating a class-based system of power. The assumptions that value systems have changed in the manner specified, that mechanisms for conflict resolution do not exist, and that a new class power is emerging are not adequately verified, and Tellenback commits the same mistakes as the more illustrious exponents of convergence. David Lane, though, feels that criticisms of convergence can be attacking a 'straw man': namely that identity rather than similarity of societies is unjustifiably expected, but he does concede that the cultural filter through which technology passes into the factory system and the possibility of divergence in some aspects is under-emphasised.[36] Lane sees the major drawback of convergence theory to be its separation from a theory of social change that ignores the dynamic class character of society. While he chooses to supplement this gap by resorting to a Parsonian structural functional analysis of modernisation (an approach which we consider to be no great advance beyond the cultural constraints on convergence),[37] we shall turn in the opposite direction towards the contributions of the New Left.

It is to the credit of the New Left that they have always, in their analysis of the regimes of the Soviet Union and Eastern Europe, addressed themselves to the political consequences of economic growth, style of industrialisation and form of state power. These can of course be subdivided into several categories, but we have chosen two only. Firstly there are the well-rehearsed positions adopted by the Western Marxist Left. Secondly there are the less dogmatic analyses produced by dissident intellectuals in Eastern Europe.

To begin with the Western Marxist contributions, which purposefully challenge official Marxism–Leninism (society is made up of two classes – workers and peasants plus the stratum of the intelligentsia, in which non-antagonistic contradictions exist, and where leadership in the name of the working class is performed by a Leninist vanguard party), one of the oldest analyses is that of Cliff,[38] which views the process of constructing socialism in one country (the USSR) as having created state capitalism due to the low level of development attained in 1917. The Bolshevik Party and Soviet bureaucracy gradually assumed the tasks of the bourgeoisie in accumulating capital, and exploited the working class and became a new ruling class jealously guarding privileges and perpetuating inequality into the next generation. Until the late 1960s, the only major competition to this was provided by the Fourth International.[39] Trotsky saw the working class as able to carry out a programme of socialist industrialisation with the aid of the Party after 1917, but without passing through a capitalist stage, and the ensuing bureaucracy did not have the attributes of a ruling bourgeoisie (it had no compulsion to accumulate capital for its own ends nor did it pass private property and privilege on to its progeny). Thus, although the bureaucracy undoubtedly has power, the class relations characterise the Soviet Union as a 'degenerated workers' state'. Mandel developed this, arguing that, as the ruling bureaucracy is a privileged petty-bourgeois upper stratum of the proletariat, all that is needed is a political and not an economic revolution. Accumulation serves the production of use values, but under-development ensures that the Soviet economy has a non-capitalist mode of production, but a bourgeois mode of distribution, and hence is a transitional society. The sparring between these two contenders is of little interest here and continues with a regular monotony. More interesting for this analysis is the debate between Bettelheim and Sweezy.[40] Sweezy sees the introduction of many market phenomena in Czechoslovakia after 1965 (enterprise independence, material incentives, etc.) as presenting a contradiction to state capitalism and a regression back to capitalist relations of production. Bettelheim adds to this the argument that a capitalist restoration had taken place and the operation of the law of value and commodity production proved the existence of a state bourgeoisie which could only be overthrown by a revitalisation of the Communist Party and a cultural revolution. Although his earlier views on the survival of phenomena from a capitalist phase became hardened into a Maoist 'line', Bettelheim's ideas suggest several interesting channels of investigation into the development and composition of the working class and intelligentsia.

Indeed the class character of the intelligentsia and its relation with the working class under socialism has been of major interest to the Western Marxist New Left. While the more unorthodox approach of Hillel Ticktin[41] (to be found in the journal *Critique*) expresses a reluctance to embrace the concept of a technocratic class power, this is not the case for Serge Mallet.

Mallet's examination of changes within the working class under capitalism notes that the traditional manual working class has become a 'sub-proletariat' pushed into a position of technological marginality by the new technically qualified workers in the most advanced centres of production, with profound consequences for class unity and consciousness. In contrast to Touraine, Mallet feels that the revolutionary potential is not to be found in the whole of the young aristocracy of labour, but depends very much on the position of the workers in the technological process.[42] This embryonic 'new working class' goes beyond wage demands and challenges technocratic ways of controlling the economy in an attempt to recapture its professional autonomy. Mallet also looks at the way in which these divisions within the working class relate to the style of trade union activity. The growth of white-collar unionism ensures that technicians working in research institutes, with little contact with the process of production, as well as the more traditional working-class aristocracy of foremen and maintenance workers are likely to call for a greater participation in management. Thus for Mallet the changing nature of work under capitalism has blurred the distinction between manual and white-collar labour, and it would certainly be of interest to this work to consider whether similar developments can be traced in Poland. Indeed Gorz and Marglin have argued that organisation of production technology and the division of labour has remained essentially unchanged with public ownership, and yet there is nothing inevitable about technology and a hierarchical organisation of work.[43] To justify the argument that technology is socially and economically determined, Gorz looks at the function performed by scientific and technical personnel and sees their work as justifying not so much the technical efficiency of production, but rather power over the labour process and the extraction of a maximum surplus. Like Mallet he sees it as possible to divide this scientific–technical personnel into those who supervise and control, on the one hand, and those who do routine, repetitive work on the other. In contrast to Mallet, though, Gorz sees the former as possessing the greatest potential for challenging the existing division of labour and power structure within the factory, and as not being a working-class vanguard: the notion of 'new working class' tends to overemphasise the unity of these groups.[44] Thus, the capitalist industrialisation process can dequalify workers and erode their sense of professional autonomy. Does the same process occur in Poland, and what implications does this have for elite class power?

To return to Mallet, before his death he wrote a short monograph entitled *Bureaucracy and Technocracy in the Socialist Countries* .[45] In this he tries to relate current forms of rule and class power to the pre-socialist development of these countries. Firstly he argues that the roots of bureaucratisation can be traced back to the regimes existing in the nineteenth century and prior to the socialist take-over. Bureaucratic states emerged at a stage of proto-capitalist development and through an alliance with finance capital were able to industrialise while inhibiting the development of a capitalist market and the subsequent rise of a national bourgeoisie. As far as countries like Poland are concerned, this meant that there was low resistance to the creation of a bureaucratic stratum and no liberal democratic revolution. Thus the socialist revolutions have merely continued this development; but state control over the appropriation of surplus value presents an obstacle to the full development of the productive forces, and a technocratic stratum, perceiving the maintenance and extension of its privileges as founded on the uninterrupted development of the productive forces, becomes increasingly interested in adapting market phenomena to this end. Mallet sees strong parallels between this 'Soviet' technocratic class and the 'new working class' emerging in the West. It tries to win over the old bureaucracy to its ideas and also promotes worker participation in enterprises (albeit from an instrumental point of view) but also tries to redirect worker interests into demands for consumer welfare. In the struggle with this technocratic class, the bureaucracy is able to exploit the grievances of the old working class over the inequalities resulting from uneven economic development, and use them as a main support base. Mallet sees the outcome as forcing the technocracy to seek mass support from a new stratum of worker-technicians who challenge authoritarian socialism.

While it would certainly not be fair to attribute any greater degree of empirical accuracy to the work of the New Left than accorded to convergence theorists, the ideas of the more recent work of Bettelheim, Mallet and Gorz are of immediate relevance to our investigation of the political consequences of industrial growth. These themes of the interrelation between technical intelligentsia and old working class, plus the survival of pre-socialist value systems will be taken up later in this chapter.

Our search for a methodological framework necessitates that we look at some of the dissident literature emerging from Eastern Europe. The amount of this literature appearing in the West has increased markedly of late, but the 'open letter' of Kuron and Modzelewski written in 1965 shows that its origin is far from recent.[46] They argue that the central political bureaucracy is a ruling class exploiting a working class, from whom the surplus product is expropriated, and who can only rise up to pursue their interests by an alliance with the technicians. The starkness of the 'open letter' contrasts quite markedly with more recent works, which draw very heavily on Western ideas and are prone at times to obscurantism. Such an example is Rudolf Bahro's redoubtable book,[47] which draws very heavily for its inspiration upon ideas from Max Weber, Georg Lukács and Hegel. For him 'actually existing socialism' is not treated as a transitional stage between capitalism and true socialism: the inevitability of the Stalinist model of industrialisation ensured that the vertical division of labour became the basis of the new system of rule resulting in relations of alienation and 'subalternity' that are more oppressive than those experienced in capitalism. 'Surplus consciousness' has emerged amongst a population which secures its compensation in consumption, but can only be ultimately fulfilled by emancipation. A cultural revolution is necessary to achieve the political alternative of a new party that will absorb broader particular interests and will operate in a new way to bring the bureaucracy firmly under popular control.[48] An economic alternative will also be sought with the aim of abolishing corruption, piece-rates, centralised vertical control over the division of labour, and the administrative constriction of enterprises within industrial branch organisation, with the purpose of fostering growth based on a free association of enterprises. This theme of the unique nature of Soviet-type societies has been taken up in two other works by Hungarian dissident authors.[49] Rakovski sees Soviet-type societies to be class societies of a specific type that are different from and co-exist alongside capitalism. The interests of change and economic reform are not dictated purely by an economic rationale, but a heterogeneous group extending from segments of the ruling class to the cultural elite ensures that at different times different interests are aroused and, in particular, middle and higher economic management respond differently to the issue of economic reform. There is the possibility of a potential alliance between experts advocating economic reform that will introduce a self-regulating economic mechanism and the working class, but the working class is more interested in breaking up the reform movement, fearing an attack on its level of consumption. However, the political elite is able to play off the workers against the intelligentsia and even to divide the latter (as enterprise managers are interested in decentralisation, but fear the break up of the economic hierarchy), and thereby maintain its position of pre-eminence. The whole system is in a kind of unstable equilibrium: technological development is low but the imitation of Western consumerism, and especially working-class attempts to control autonomously their individual incomes, is a constant source of tension. The economic cycle tends to make this more acute as increased investment inputs usually coincide with the need to cut consumption. Rakovski sees this dynamic as continuing indefinitely until an East European Marxism develops that addresses itself to the needs and interests of the working class. That coalitions form and dissolve over the issue of economic reform is a point that should be pursued here.

Finally, Konrad and Szelenyi have some light to throw on the nature of the intelligentsia under socialism. They see it as a dominant class that is still in the process of formation, but in the context of the 'rational redistributive economies' of Eastern Europe becomes increasingly homogeneous basing its authority on the disposal of the social surplus. Despite the rather irritating and confusing tendency of the authors to substitute the terms 'technocracy', 'intellectual', 'bureaucracy' and 'individual redistributor', for the concept of intelligentsia without recourse to precise denotation, we acquire an impression of the intelligentsia that is historically relative. Its origins in the nobility and entry into state officialdom; its consequent absorption into the 'triple alliance' of great landed property, finance capital and the bureaucratic state – or its exclusion to the radical margin of society; its growing cohesion and self-awareness and the issue of redistribution and the ensuing friction with the working class, its penetration of the Communist Party to transform it into a 'mass party of the intellectuals and cadre party of the working class' – results in a new basic class polarity 'between an intellectual class being formed around the position of the redistributors, and a working class deprived of any right to participate in redistribution'.[50]

Although difficult to follow at times, Konrad and Szelenyi paint a picture of a complex and uneasy alliance between the ruling elite and intellectuals, based on favours and compromise. Occasionally the elite will make its counter attack to disrupt the class unity of the intellectuals and frustrate an alliance with the working class, but using its power over consumption to broaden its mass base through appeals to egalitarianism.

This excursion through convergence theory and radical and dissident evaluations of economic development certainly provides us with a theoretical *embarras de richesses*. Yet what sense, if any, can be acquired from this bewildering array of ideas? In unashamedly eclectic fashion certain questions drawing on these themes will be posed, and answers provided in subsequent chapters.

On the subject of Polish industrial policy and the division of labour, it is proposed first of all to consider the pre-socialist level and social determinants of economic development. What was the leading force for industrialisation: state or bourgeois entrepreneur? How did this affect subsequent economic development and in particular industrial policy? What are the implications of the relative balance between manufacturing industry, agriculture and foreign trade and service sectors for the growth of national income? Are common problems of industrialisation encountered, or does the Polish economy have to be classed among the '*sui generis*' Soviet-type economies?

In the second case, some consideration is necessary of how the constraints of economic planning and development in Poland have affected the division of labour and industrial production. It is often assumed that economic reform involves proposals for varying degrees of enterprise autonomy in business transactions. However, it will be noted that since the late 1950s there has been a marked increase in the size of the basic production unit. The enterprise statute of 1950[51] stressed that the industrial enterprise was the basic unit of the Polish economy. It was the basic unit of full cost-accounting (*rozrachunek gospodarczy*) and business was to be conducted according to the principle of one-man management, in a manner that was not substantially different from any other East European country (with the exception of Yugoslavia). The principles of enterprise management were coloured by a Stalinist view of the economy: a teleological distinction between production and distribution distinguished the enterprise as an organisational unit below the level of the central administration and the ministry, and separate from trade and procurement organisations. As early as 1956 the appropriateness of this enterprise law to the needs of Polish economic development was brought into question and, as we shall see, the conception of the enterprise as an executive agent of the central administrations and industrial ministries was difficult to reconcile with the role envisaged for Workers' Councils in 1956. The creation of various institutions (associations, combines etc.) between the enterprise and the central planning authorities obviously counteracted legal prescriptions for the role of the enterprise. Despite a recent observation[52] that the 'entrepreneurial function' was indeed shared between the enterprise and other levels of the industrial hierarchy, and the suggestion that a precise definition of the Polish enterprise should only be attempted in terms of the behaviour attributes constantly present (independent evaluation and informational freedom) whatever the style of management – it remains patently obvious that the theory of the socialist firm is undeveloped. This is not to say that Western economists can boast any greater superiority. Neo-classical economics generally proceeds to ignore the organisational structure of the firm. Inasmuch as it pays any attention to firm size this is examined from the point of view of competition in market structure. Theories of market concentration are based on the use of one or more indices (the structure of asset ownership, the size of value added, the volume of sales, the share of employment in an industry, the volume of turnover amongst the largest firms and the nature of interlocking financial ties).[53] It has only been the institutionalist tradition in economics stretching back to the work of Thorstein Veblen, and to which amongst others[54] Galbraith belongs, that has grasped the economic importance of corporate structures. Out of this approach has grown an awareness that corporate power and discretion is not confined to a merely economic realm (price control, demand management, etc.) but can also be located in an 'ownership alliance' of management and financial institutions. Although there is much interpenetration of government and corporate activities, the government retains only its policing functions in relation to the corporations.[55] The interrelation between nation state and corporate power has recently been accepted as a legitimate field of study for political science,[56] and the history of West European government ventures into promoting state enterprise has been of long-standing interest to political science[57] and is seen as presenting practical problems for political control and accountability. So, with the acceptance of the idea that the corporate structure has become a universal feature of industrialised society penetrating both public and private domains with political implications, is it necessarily unreasonable to expect that the changing status of the industrial enterprise and its merger into large production units might also carry political implications for Party control over management power in the People's Republic of Poland? Such notions might at first seem fanciful, were it not that such diverse writers as Galbraith, Brus and Rakovski have suggested it.[58] To take this beyond the level of conjecture will be the task of Chapters 3 and 4 by means of a chronicle of the organisational reforms affecting enterprise grouping since 1958, and by asking the question whether political implications arise from this.

Our preceding discussion provided a multitude of somewhat conflicting suggestions about the nature of class rule, and managerial and technical elite power in state-socialist societies. It now remains to disentangle these. First of all it should be clear that the class structure of a state-socialist society such as Poland cannot be meaningfully encapsulated by Marxist–Leninist formulae and that the polarisation of interests between the working class and the intelligentsia, *tout court*, cannot be so boldly stated. Hence, in later chapters, it is proposed that the impact of the division of labour upon the development of class structure in the People's Republic of Poland be considered. Has dequalification of the skilled working class and de-professionalisation of many intelligentsia jobs resulted in the creation of a 'new working class', whose revolutionary consciousness goes beyond the immediate satisfaction of its national needs? Or, is the impact of the division of labour upon both white-collar and blue-collar work, infinitely more complex? If there do exist divisions in outlook within the intelligentsia class, is it really possible to argue that a homogeneous technocracy is in the ascendant? Although the most obvious division exists between the cultural and technical intelligentsia, can the latter be differentiated between middle and higher economic management, or between enterprise management and experts? It is necessary to ask how firm are these divisions, do they tend towards a solid position or is all in flux? These questions are rarely asked by theorists of convergence or industrial society, and if they are, rarely receive verification.[59] Yet they must receive attention if meaningful statements are to be made about the political consequences of economic growth. It is only on the basis of this that the precise relations between intelligentsia and working class can be established. If the class consciousness of the industrial manual working class is only raised in the defence of collective consumption this must surely affect the role and operation of workers' self-management. If the only outlet for the interests of worker-technicians or experts is in pursuing a style of economic reform that aims at the decentralisation of autonomy to the enterprise may be this in turn has implications for the agenda and responsiveness of institutions of workforce representation. Finally we must ask whether, on the basis of the limited evidence available, it is fair to assume that attitudes are changing from upholding expressive and affective values, towards an instrumental outlook, and whether status based on ascription is giving way to that based on achievement and function. We must not ignore the survival of pre-socialist patterns of behaviour, lifestyles and values.

These many questions must be posed if the final issue is to be confronted: the 'leading role' of a Marxist–Leninist party in conditions of advanced industrialisation. It is all too easy to see a conspiratorial vanguard party being infiltrated and taken over by a 'technocratic pragmatism' that eschews all deference to the manual working class. It is too convenient to forecast an impending legitimacy crisis as the inexorable outcome of this trend. To assume that interests cannot be articulated and aggregated within the Polish United Workers' Party is not permissible without examining the response to and outcome of problems and crises. The issue chosen here is the quest for intensive growth, and the policy of industrial merger and concentration.

2

The building of a socialist economy: social and political limits to growth

We have already referred to the analysis of Polish economic reforms made by Zieliński, who attributed it to the contradictory objectives of planners (with consequent eclecticism) and a false policy of transition (with associated mistiming).[1] This chapter will try to illustrate these features and relate them to overall problems of Polish economic development since 1945. At the same time the author is not satisfied by a purely economic explanation, and will argue that post-war industrial growth is determined and constrained by political factors, both domestic and international, and by pre-war social structure and forms of property ownership. It is felt that there was no inevitable economic logic that led to the creation of a command model of planning and management after 1948, and that the structure of ownership and employment in agriculture is of crucial importance to comprehending the success of industrial growth strategy. The weight of history lies heavy on the Polish economy even today. Problems of the 1940s and 1950s were still to be resolved in the Fifth Five-Year Plan 1976–80. Rather than present a chronology of the medium-term plans, the period since 1945 will be treated in four sections: the capitalist heritage, the transition to a planned economy, the economic experimentation and reform 1956–70, and post-1970 prosperity. It is hoped that through this the reader will be provided with an understanding of the reasons why planners turned their attention to modifications of the structure of the enterprise along the lines of merger and concentration.

The capitalist heritage

Mallet, Konrad and Szelenyi[2] would have us believe that the manner in which the industrial revolution took place in Poland was

20

a determining factor in post-World War II industrial development: that the alliance between a bureaucracy and finance capital inhibited the development of a capitalist market and the subsequent rise of a national bourgeoisie; and encouraged the growth of an 'intelligentsia'. There is a substantial amount of truth in this assertion as will be demonstrated in the following account.

Industrial development in Poland did not take off in the mode of competitive entrepreneurial activity ascribed to the British experience. The history of Polish industrialisation can be traced back to the mid-nineteenth century, but domestic determination of its structure was precluded even at this early stage. Foreign capital came to dominate large areas of Polish industry: the French were subsequently dominant in the ownership of the textile industry, and Nazi Germany concentrated on stimulating those sectors associated with armaments, (mining, iron and steel, chemicals and the electrical industry). The depreciation of the Polish currency in the mid-1920s, and the impact of the world economic crisis that hit Poland after a brief period of prosperity during 1928–9, impeded economic recovery from the effects of the First World War, and provided an encouraging climate for the insinuation of cartels (both domestic and international) into industry. By 1930, 56 cartels controlled about 37% of total industrial production in Poland, and they continued to flourish during the depression years through a strategy of fixing production quotas, high prices and dumping abroad, and also because the Polish government erected a high tariff barrier to protect industry from foreign competition[3]. The cartels were not seen as exerting a wholly deleterious influence on the Polish economy, and it has been argued that Polish economic development would have proceeded at an even slower pace, had it not been for the influx of foreign capital, and that the cartels kept industrial plant in operation that would otherwise have been driven out of existence.[4]

The impetus from the foreign imperial powers, the lack of native capital, and the inheritance of some of the old state monopolies (salt, alcohol, matches, tobacco and lotteries) permitted the new government formed in 1919 to operate a number of public and mixed ownership concerns. During the 1920s there was a marked expansion of bureaucracy and office employment and by 1927 this public–mixed ownership comprised about 12% of the total, and in 1932–3 it was estimated that state enterprise turnover was around 17% of the total for industry.[5] This high degree of 'étatism' plus the favourable nature of state legislation towards cartels, made the prospects for successful small- and medium-scale private enterprise dismal. Although supply and marketing co-operatives were in existence, much small-scale enterprise was of a handicraft nature serving a very localised market. Foreign policy and trade during the 1920s and 1930s tended to discourage small- and medium-scale domestic private enterprise. Polish academics tend too readily to de-emphasise the role undertaken by the state in the inter-war period,[6] which is contradicted in particular, by the work of Douglas and Taylor,[7] who choose to apply the labels of mercantilism and state capitalism respectively to this period.

One reason for the lack of domestic capital formation and the role undertaken by the state can be located in the fate of Polish nationhood since the late eighteenth century. The three Partitions of Poland between Austria, Prussia and Russia divided the Polish nation, which did not achieve independent statehood until 1919. This independence was short-lived and by 1939 Poland was again under occupation, this time by the Nazis. Constant fear of expropriation provided a weak incentive to the growth of an industrial bourgeoisie. At the same time an intelligentsia class was in the process of formation. At its origins in the early nineteenth century it included people who were involved in intellectually creative occupations, the free professions, or who possessed secondary education and above. Unlike in most of Western Europe where the concept of intelligentsia acquired pejorative connotations, it was accorded a high status in Poland even though the control by the imperial powers ensured that entry into universities was limited, forcing many to study independently or to travel to France for enlightenment.[8] Despite the strong links between this intelligentsia and the minor land-owning gentry; and despite its involvement in the struggles for national independence in 1832 and 1863, it assumed values of cultural independence isolating itself in a coterie or 'social circle'[9] that scorned work in 'trade'. The growth of state bureaucracy, especially in the 1920s, provided employment in white-collar work for many of those from rural areas aspiring to the social cachet of intelligentsia status. The increased complexity of social stratification in the 1920s and 1930s and the entry of people from the working class and the peasantry into white-collar jobs, made the objective structure of the intelligentsia very ambiguous.[10] Thus the cultural and political conditions surrounding the construction of Polish nationhood deterred the formation of an independent bourgeoisie able to take a leading role in the process of industrialisation.

Finally no account of the pre-1945 Polish economy would be complete without reference to the position of agriculture. That the majority of the active population was employed in agriculture and that the latter was the major constituent of national income was of vital importance for the transition to collective ownership. The system of land ownership inherited from the three empires has been seen as the key to Poland's economic problems after 1945.[11] There was excessive rural over-population with high disguised unemployment in agriculture; the price of land was high; many of the large estates inherited from the imperial powers had been fragmented into minute land-holdings; and crop yields were low although foodstuffs accounted for about 40% of Polish exports during the inter-war years. Around 70% of the peasantry were independent land-holders but they enjoyed an extremely low standard of living. Social concern apart, their low purchasing power was in turn an obstacle to the development of the domestic market and an inadequate stimulus to industrialisation.[12]

It would be quite easy to see a parallel between the economic situation in Poland in 1945 and the USSR in 1917 but the differing political status was crucial, as will be evident from an examination of the transition to a planned economy.

The transition to a planned economy, 1948–50

The liberation of Poland from Nazi rule in 1945 had an immediate political impact: independent statehood was again acquired but over (yet again) a different territorial area involving a loss of territory amounting to 20% of the pre-1939 total. A large part of the post-war economic achievement has been interpreted as a direct consequence of boundary shifts that resulted in the acquisition of a greatly expanded industrial plant base and better agricultural land.[13] The loss of the poorly industrialised eastern territories neighbouring the USSR was offset by gains of highly industrialised Upper and Lower Silesia in the west which had an industrial production capacity greater than that for the whole of pre-war Poland. The legacy of the Nazi defeat was a much improved situation in natural resources (coal, lead, zinc, nickel and copper) and a well-developed extractive, heavy and light industry base along with railway and water transport networks.

It was however political considerations that determined the manner in which these resources were to be taken advantage of. Above all the way in which the Polish Workers' Party (PPR) acquired power during 1945–7, and was forced under Soviet pressure to consolidate power during 1948–50, ensured a key role for domestic and international politics in economic development. Competing claims to legitimacy meant that compromise was necessary during 1946–7 and during this period the PPR held only two-thirds of ministerial posts in the Provisional Government of National Unity, (though they included the strategic cabinet ministries of defence, public security, food and industry). The merger of the PPR and the PPS in 1948 to form the Polish United Workers' Party (PZPR) did not render it the sole political force: the remaining political parties realigned themselves into the United Peasants' Party (ZSL) and the Democratic Party (SD). Nonetheless, there was a shift in the balance of forces within the PZPR during 1948–9. This was provoked by the Soviet–Yugoslav dispute and by the Cominform decision to institute disciplinary action against Rightist-Nationalist elements in the European Communist Parties. In Poland it was expressed in the change of First Secretary of the PZPR from the 'nationalist' Władysław Gomułka to the Moscow sympathiser, Bolesław Bierut,[14] and in a debate over economic growth strategy. In the latter, Czesław Bobrowski (Chairman of the Central Planning Office and member of the PPS) was accused by Hilary Minc (Minister of Industry and Trade and a member of the PPR) of engineering a significant deviation from Marxist principles in the national economic plan for 1948: namely by inflating the importance of the non-socialist sector in final output. Minc argued that the rapid expansion of the producer goods sector was the only way of increasing consumption in the long run. Bobrowski advocated a more balanced pattern of growth, and was reluctant to base an economy on current sacrifice for the promise of future gains.[15] The immediate result was the resignation of Bobrowski and his replacement by Minc as Chairman of a newly formed State Commission for Economic Planning.

It is a commonplace to view changes of elite personnel as symptomatic of the shifting balance of power between factions within a Communist Party. However, the Minc–Bobrowski debate was tied up with the issues of the 'Polish Road to Socialism', and as we shall see, many of the issues raised were a recurrent theme in post-war industrialisation policy in Poland. Not only did the victory of the Minc faction imply that henceforth, Polish economic planning and management was to conform to a Stalinist model, but that the political control necessary to enforce this must be consolidated. The merger of the PPR and PPS took place against a background of uneasy relations between Eastern Europe and the Soviet Union. The repudiation of 'National Roads to Socialism', expressed in the change of PZPR leadership, coincided with a hardening of attitudes towards the private sector, a repudiation of UNRRA (Marshall) Aid and the eventual withdrawal of Poland from the IMF in 1950.[16]

From the above it might seem surprising that the private sector played a key role in the Polish economy in the mid-1940s. That the Polish economy shared many common characteristics with West European ventures into the 'mixed economy' at that time can be seen by an examination of agriculture, the process of industrial nationalisation and the development of planning.

In agriculture the predominant form of legal ownership remained private. Radical restructuring of the system of land-holding was prevented by political interests. Power-sharing with the PPS precluded wholesale expropriation of land by the PPR. Thus, in the land reform of September 1944 large estates of over 50 hectares were confiscated (over 100 hectares in the Western territories), but, on the whole, the former owners had the choice of fixed monetary compensation or resettlement. Land was redistributed into small-holdings generally around 12½ hectares in size, and state credit facilities were offered to farmers. Agricultural co-operatives were set up on a modest scale in 1949 (totalling 120 in that year) but by 1953 they covered only between 7% and 9% of the total farm land. State-owned farms accounted for only 8% of gross agricultural output in 1950, so at that time 85% of Polish farm land was in private hands, and this proportion has not changed significantly since then.[17] Even after 1948 in the move to a Stalinist command economy, the PZPR was unsuccessful in trying to encourage the peasantry to move into collective farms. The motives for this were as much due to considerations of political control as to economic efficiency. The high point in this campaign was reached in 1955 but only 10% of cultivated land was successfully collectivised, and the political resentment that this move generated amongst the peasantry culminated in the dissolution of the collective farms in the politically eventful year of 1956.[18] In 1968 such farms cultivated less than 11% of the land. The most that the Polish government could do was to set up agricultural circles to bring together individual land-holders for the purpose of agronomic advice and for the distribution of government investment credits after 1956.[19] The co-operative sector remained negligible in agriculture, and was only to become important in the retail trade and service sector. The existence of independent peasant proprietors has presented a continuous political problem for the Polish leadership. Disadvantageous price levels for produce, unattractive credit schemes, the absence of state social welfare benefits such as sickness insurance and the inability of peasants to transfer land to their families all meant that life on the land during the 1950s in the period of collectivisation and the Six-Year Plan 1950–5 (6YP) was sufficiently unattractive to induce a large-scale migration away from the villages to work in industry in the towns, where wages and conditions of work were better. Initially this helped to solve the problem of disguised unemployment in agriculture and to provide the necessary workforce for industrial expansion, but by the mid-1950s a slow or even negative rate of growth of agricultural labour productivity, accentuated by bad harvests, meant that in the 1960s, and increasingly so in the 1970s, the PZPR had to offer inducements to the peasantry. Not even changes in prices, social insurance and title to land have been able to raise productivity in agriculture, and food imports have acted as a considerable constraint upon investment and foreign trade policy in the 1970s. In 1970, 37% of the active population worked in agriculture, but agriculture only contributed 16% of GNP. By 1975 the figures were 30.7% and 11.3% respectively.

To return to the 1940s, the change in the structure of ownership of manufacturing industry was more extensive. Although state ownership was not formally introduced until the Decree of the Council of State of 3 January 1946[20] many large- and medium-scale firms in industry and communications had been taken into public ownership prior to that date. As the Nazi occupiers were driven out and many of the former owners and managerial personnel fled after the Liberation, Polish workers and engineers sympathetic to the Provisional Government endeavoured to bring the surviving plants into operation again, with local and then national government organs taking over guardianship of ownerless property. The strategy of the 1946 Decree was twofold: firstly to legitimate the seizure of mines, transport, banking, insurance and trade that were in the hands of the Nazi Reich and the Free Town of Gdańsk; and secondly to take over, with compensation, mining, industry and other enterprises (with the exception of building and construction enterprises capable of employing more than 50 people per shift), which included transport and communications.[21] Although legal restrictions were placed upon the private sector, there was also legislation enabling the creation of new enterprises and the encouragement of private incentive in industry and trade by extending immunity from expropriation to new enterprises set up after 1946. Consequently, numerous small enterprises appeared, especially in the Western territories.[22] Trade remained outside the scope of the law on nationalisation, being regulated by licences. Thus the structure of ownership in industry was similar to that in a mixed economy and the government gave a significant role to private enterprise.[23]

Just as it would be incorrect to claim that nationalisation of industry and trade was both universal and immediate after 1945, it would also be inaccurate to refer to the instant creation of the machinery of a centrally planned economy. The PPR–PPS coalition was fortunate in having at its disposal many economists (although, initially, most of them were more sympathetic to the PPS) who were involved in constructing plans of a partial sectoral nature between 1936 and 1939. It was these people that formed the nucleus of the Central Planning Office formed in 1945 with the task of setting production targets for the coal industry and later for other branches of industry along with plans for employment, technical development and raw material supplies. In 1946 sector planning was extended to activities outside industrial production (transport, population settlement, agriculture and the reconstruction of the Western territories – the latter being the first venture into regional planning) and a more ambitious venture into national investment planning was introduced for the last three-quarters of 1946.[24] Nonetheless, planning in the post-war period was a very tentative activity: above all, because of the shortage in Poland of trained personnel (particularly economists and accountants) and also because the balance of political power within Poland did not initially rest upon a commitment to the Soviet model of central planning.

Nor did the institutional arrangements for managing the Polish economy resemble anything like the Soviet economy. The economic Committee of the Council of Ministers (KERM) was responsible for the overall management of the national economy. State-owned enterprises were to be run from the Ministry of Industry, and communal enterprises were run by regional self-management unions (*związki samorządu terytorialnego*).[25] Large- and medium-sized state enterprises were grouped in central industrial boards on an industrial branch basis which functioned initially like the Soviet *glavki* (chief departments), but were later transformed, in October 1946, into legally and commercially independent state enterprises[26] supervising factories grouped together along product or regional lines. It was not until 1947 that there was any official move to insist upon uniform business principles for industrial enterprises. The work of these enterprises was then to be administered and supervised by a director and a Council for Social Control (which allowed for a measure of workforce consultation yet placed restrictions upon earlier arrangements for direct worker control that had emerged in some enterprises).

The most striking feature of industrial administration in the late 1940s was the absence of a uniform hierarchy below the level of the ministry. The number of levels in the institutional hierarchy depended very much on the number of enterprises in a branch of industry, but in some cases enterprises which were of key importance to the post-war reconstruction effort would be directly run from the ministry. Until the KERM order of January 1947 industrial enterprises did not conduct business transactions on a uniform basis and it was not until 1950 that this was fully achieved. As the tasks of economic planning grew, so did the size of the administrative structure supervising the economy, and by 1949 the Ministry of Industry had split into six new industrial ministries.[27]

Not all industry was run centrally. At the local level the People's Councils, especially after the local government reform of March 1950, could set up enterprises in their territory after consultation with the appropriate ministry in conjunction with central offices for co-ordinating this small-scale production.

The immediate post-World War II period, then, witnessed neither a rapid nor a wholesale transformation of the Polish economy into a command economy run on the Stalinist model. The legacy of pre-war attempts at planning and state control of industry, despite the intervening effects of war time, facilitated the process of post-war nationalisation and planning,[28] especially the Three-Year Plan of Reconstruction 1947–50 (3YP). This plan coincided with the withdrawal of foreign aid and the initial moves to formalise business operations associated with the hardening of East–West relations and external pressure upon Poland from the USSR. After 1947 laws were passed enforcing the compulsory registration of employers and the imposition of discriminatory turnover taxes, which (along with the compulsory incorporation of private enterprises within state-directed associations) provided increasingly disadvantageous circumstances for the prosperity of the private sector. State control over raw materials, real estate, trade, housing, handicrafts, services and labour, plus the land reform of 1949 (which introduced compulsory deliveries to the state and inaugurated agricultural co-operatives) tended to reinforce this trend. Yet, although the 3YP can be understood to have extended PZPR hegemony over the economy, and to have remedied the ills caused by the serious war-time destruction of capital and by the existence of 'ownerless' factories, it must not be seen as a direct emulation of the Soviet model of planning. Rather, it was the cumulative result of all the aforementioned planning experiments that took place in various sectors of state-owned industry during 1945 and 1946. The 3YP was presented as a set of projects for the construction industry, and as output targets for the basic state-run industries. The global target was to raise gross industrial production above the pre-war level, although gross agricultural production was set a more limited target of between 70% and 80% of pre-1939 output. In industry priority was given to the restoration of the old industrial infrastructure rather than to the development of new technology. The key branches selected for development were coal, iron and steel and electrical power, reflecting the greater emphasis upon heavy manufacturing industry than upon services.[29]

Looking back on the achievements of the 3YP it can certainly be seen to have secured a rapid rise in industrial output in a largely reconstructed pre-war industrial base,[30] and brought a marked increase in employment and an egalitarian redistribution of personal incomes. It was not until after 1950 that the network of a command economy came into existence within the framework of the 6YP.

The 6YP inaugurated a period of forced-pace industrialisation that was again provoked by international political factors. By 1950 the Cold War was at its height and the Korean War meant that the

Soviet Union required an expansion of military capacity to which the countries of Eastern Europe were to make a significant contribution. For Poland, this involved the concentration on armaments production and industries associated with defence. So, the year 1950 is an important watershed marking the transition from largely Keynesian principles of economic management[31] to what has been described as a 'half-war economy'.[32] The latter phrase is understandable in the context of the Korean War and the Western embargo on imports to the Communist bloc. A policy of economic autarky was adopted endorsing priority to producer goods industries (Sector A) at the expense of consumption and services (Sector B). Oscar Lange, the renowned Polish economist applied the label '*sui generis* war economy' to the period up until 1955. He saw that the need to concentrate all resources on certain priority tasks and the shortage and weakness of the industrial workforce made it a 'historical necessity' for such an under-developed country as Poland to choose a highly centralised, administrative planning and management process resting not on economic but 'moral-political' incentives to the workforce.[33] Yet in retrospect Lange was anxious to stress that these centralised administrative methods of planning and management were not characteristic features of socialism, but rather the techniques of a war economy: danger is present precisely when they are equated with socialism. Methods that are necessary and useful in a stage of socialist revolution and intensive industrialisation can be a barrier to further development by wasting resources, by necessitating the construction of a costly bureaucratic apparatus, and by making it difficult to produce for human needs. When a socialist economy begins to outgrow these methods of planning and management, it is necessary to move on to new methods resting on economic laws of activity.[34] Lange did not mention another very important element in the *sui generis* war economy. Besides the high investment outlay and subsequent accumulation of capital, the collectivisation of agriculture and the compulsory delivery of foodstuffs from private farms to the state was necessary to finance this 'primitive socialist accumulation'. Agriculture, however, is the Achilles' heel of the Polish economy, and, as we have already remarked upon above, the political and economic objectives of collectivisation were in conflict. On the one hand collectivisation would enable both political and economic control over a very volatile sector of the economy; on the other hand the regime needed to buy the goodwill and the agricultural produce of the peasantry for the war effort. The failure to resolve this conflict meant that one result of the 6YP was the change in the terms of trade between agriculture and industry. The share of agriculture in national income fell from 40% in 1950 to 28% in 1955 and real agricultural personal income fell, owing to the exigencies of compulsory delivery quotas to the state at fixed prices, reducing any incentive to raise productivity.[35]

As already noted, the relatively miserable life in agriculture encouraged many to leave the villages between 1950 and 1953 for the industrial towns where, as unskilled labour, they would swell the ranks of the working class. Some have referred to this as making the growth of a 'new working class' without any labour traditions,[36] but in a context very different from that in which Mallet uses the term. This flood of rural labour into the towns had a detrimental effect upon the working-class standard of living: the former peasants received real wages that were higher than the income which they had received in agriculture, but, because they were unskilled, they received less than the 'older' working class. The existence of this pool of unskilled labour was claimed to have exerted a depressing effect upon the income of the skilled workforce. While real wages were planned to rise by 40% during the 6YP, the actual real aggregate rise was a mere 4% and this only occurred after 1953.[37]

Yet to discuss the impact of the 6YP without consideration of the developments in planning techniques runs the danger of misinterpreting the causes of low wages, high rates of accumulation and growth in producer goods industries, and the waste and irrationality. Until 1952 the State Commission of Economic Planning (SCEP) had distributed control figures representing the basic proportions of desired macro-economic development to central boards and enterprises. These were then disaggregated and enterprise estimates of their capacity were then passed back to the SCEP. There they were aggregated and the original targets were revised (usually upwards!). In 1952 the planning procedure was changed as ministries and central boards were charged with the task of drafting plans for units under their jurisdiction. These were then passed on to the SCEP which used them to work out the National Economic Plan, and this latter was in turn used by the ministries and boards as the basis for constructing detailed annual and quarterly plans for their enterprises. By 1954 the technical-economic plans received by enterprises had a most detailed and intricate structure. They were very specific in the physical units involved and even went so far as to specify who should be used for sub-contracted work and material and labour inputs. This process of constructing material balances on the basis of extrapolation with imperfect information plus unforeseen circumstances that can cause plans so constructed to go awry, has been lucidly argued elsewhere.[38] However, planning by this process is essentially administrative and not economic in quality, and is conducive to 'plan fetishism' on the part of both central authorities and enterprise management encouraging over-attention to the minutiae of quarterly or even monthly plans.[39]

This planning technique was accompanied by, and even encouraged, a particular type of growth strategy. There was a very high rise in capital/output ratios with the highest growth during those years being found in the construction industry,[40] and capital/labour ratios rose also in the engineering, chemicals, metallurgy, mining and energy industries. However Feiwel argues that plan targets in investment were often considerably under-fulfilled. Many new investment projects were not completed, civilian investment was cut back in favour of defence, investment in the non-socialist sector was drastically reduced due to repressive policies against private industry, and investment in private industry was cut back. In the neglected sectors of the economy, increased output could only be achieved at the cost of employing more labour. In general the rapid rate of capital accumulation took its toll with the failure of the under-capitalised construction and extractive industries to keep pace: the result was waste and a series of bottlenecks throughout the economy.[41]

Thus whatever the economic 'logic' of industrial development in Poland, the policies pursued during the 6YP spilled over into and affected agriculture and had profound consequences for the political climate of support for the PZPR. By late 1953 the PZPR leadership was aware of the hostility engendered by its policy of industrialisation and took measures to attenuate it. At the Second Congress in March 1954 a resolution was passed in favour of halting the drift of the rural population into industry, and of raising the living standard of those already employed in industry. The massive industrial investment programmes were checked and resources were switched to increase the supply of consumer goods and to relax the compulsory deliveries of agricultural products. To complement this the policy of economic autarky ended and trade with Western capitalist countries was revived.[42]

To recapitulate, it is evident that post-war industrial growth strategy and the transition to a planned economy was determined and constrained by political factors both domestic and international. The move to the institutional structure of a command economy after 1948 had been forced as much by the development of the Cold War as by domestic economic needs, and it was events such as the death of Stalin, the uprising in Berlin and its feared repercussions in Poland that inaugurated the changes during 1954–5. Political factors continued to bedevil economic planning in Poland especially after the 1950s, when economic growth became the touchstone of PZPR legitimacy, but the response of the leadership was to begin a whole series of reforms in the economic mechanism.

Economic experimentation and reform, 1956–70

The Polish 'October' of 1956 is often presented as a dramatic surge of revolutionary sentiment that almost succeeded in transforming Poland into a self-managing society, but for the threat of Soviet intervention. This is far too trite an explanation of a movement in which several differing standpoints appeared during 1954 and 1955, and which, despite the restrictions placed upon the activity of Workers' Councils in 1958, did not disappear during the 1960s. Although dogged by a considerable ossification of political structures in the late 1960s and although economists would dispute this categorisation, the period 1956 to 1970 is taken 'in toto'.

The first attempt at economic reform in the mid-1950s, was stimulated by concern about the strategy of economic growth and more obviously by the political repercussions of this. It is impossible to assess economic performance in isolation from the political events and change of leadership of 1956–8 in Poland,[43] and from the change in Soviet policy associated with the Twentieth Party Congress of the CPSU in February 1956 which provided the political climate in which discussion could take place over the desirability of continuing the 'command' economic model. A resolution of the VII Plenum of the PZPR Central Committee in 1956 called for the ending of excessive centralisation in economic planning and management, and for a reduction in the number of central directives binding upon enterprises. Managers of industrial enterprises were to be invested with greater decision-making autonomy and more independence was to be conceded to regional and local authorities. Improvements in supplies of raw materials were promised, and it was proposed that incentive schemes for management should be designed to encourage the elimination of waste, the reduction of costs, and an improvement in the quality of goods produced.[44] The SCEP was reorganised and renamed the Planning Commission (KP), and in late 1956 an order of the Council of Ministers liberated industrial enterprises from excessive numbers of obligatory directive indices: they were given the right to draw up their own technical economic production plans subject to the constraint of only eight directive indices.[45]

To enable these new powers to be fully appreciated, revisions were made in the Five-Year Plan 1956–60 (5YPI), and, to assuage worker discontent, there had to be improvements in living standards. In the year 1956–7 there was an accelerated increase in personal incomes in excess of the rate of growth of output and, in 1957, the total Wages Fund increased faster than even gross industrial output. This had an inflationary effect as the corresponding increase in consumer goods was not so great. International as well as domestic politics had facilitated a change in foreign trade policy and a rapid rise in the import of consumer goods took place during 1956 and 1957. Yet such concessions to personal and social consumption, while politically motivated, were not the major purpose of economic planners. The main goal was to change industrial growth strategy between specific branches of industry. Investment rates declined in metallurgy, engineering and chemicals, while they increased for construction materials, food, electrical power, fuel and light industry. A discriminatory wage policy was used to encourage the relocation of employment away from old heavy industry and the decision to dissolve the collective farms in 1956 helped to improve agricultural productivity. Raw materials, food and fuel exports were to be reduced and replaced by engineering products.

However, neither the adjustments in the 5YPI nor the changes in enterprise powers resulted in a complete departure from the old system of planning and management. Firstly, the planning process did not undergo any remarkable change. The Planning Commission intervened in the following three stages: the drafting of guidelines, the preparation of plan projects, the actual distribution of final plan

targets. By mid-1957 additional directives had been issued especially over employment policy (most enterprises were allowed to decide
upon the size and structure of their employment as long as they did
not exceed the limits on the Wages Fund). Plan fulfilment may not
have been obligatory if the enterprise could demonstrate that there
were insufficient orders for its products, but research revealed that,
for around 80% of enterprise management interviewed, the value of
output continued to be centrally determined.[46] There were many
other areas in which enterprise autonomy was effectively limited by
central control without being subject to directive indices, such as
technological improvements, design and quality control. There was
also a contradiction between the legal powers of the enterprise and
its actual possibilities in the area of investment finance and
payments from the various 'Funds' and over the use and development of its working capital (which was subject to 'guidelines' set by
superior levels in the planning hierarchy). However, experience
meant that by 1957 only 10% of total investment in the socialised
sector was 'non-limited' and by 1958 this was formally labelled
'centralised' and 'decentralised' investment. Without a change in
the financial system that would involve a switch from central
budgetary financing to self-financing, enterprise independence was
meaningless and also had a negative side-effect upon profitability by
encouraging high levels of financial accumulation as insurance
against risk. Furthermore, the incentive to lay aside profits in the
Development Fund and Reserve Fund was low in comparison with
the inducement to direct most of it to the Factory Fund out of which
wages, bonuses and other social amenities were financed. Tinkering
with the enterprise finance system to create a new enterprise
Investment and Repairs Fund in 1958, and finally the recentralisation and control over investment financing during 1959–60 that we
have described above, resulted in the ironical situation whereby
'decentralised' investment was centrally planned.[47] The disequilib-
rium that these financial arrangements provoked might have been
avoided had there been an adjustment in the system of pricing.
While during 1956–8 there was a fall from 1406 to 768 in the
number of centrally planned commodities and the number of
centrally distributed commodities was down to 400 in 1958,[48] the
glaring distortions occasioned by an out-dated producer and
transfer pricing system during the 6YP were not alleviated by any
fundamental price reform. The low price of industrial goods meant

that a large sector of industry produced at a loss, and despite price rises between 1956 and 1961, the result was an odd correspondence between prices and exchange values that the PZPR was reluctant to change by devolving the authority to fix prices to the level of the industrial enterprise.

The reform in 1956 had concentrated on an increase in enterprise autonomy but, by 1960, there was little evidence of any lasting devolution of authority in economic decision-making. Enterprises never acquired powers in price-fixing and, in the sphere of planning for volume of output and nature of product output mixes, the limited autonomy that had existed was swallowed up in the recentralisation that took place in 1959. Hardly a vestige of freedom survived in determining employment, technological change and the purchase of raw materials and supplies. In practice, the number of directive indices passed on to enterprises by industrial ministries and the newly founded industrial associations (which replaced the central boards after 1958) was always greater than officially envisaged. Enterprise control and finance was meaningless without a corresponding increase in the flexibility of management decisions in production and distribution. The important step in the direction of enterprise self-finance (by allowing enterprises to retain for their own use increasing percentages of their profit) was thwarted by the bureaucratic administration of special funds which observed the direct link between making profits and their distribution, and by a pricing system that was irrational. Fundamentally the problem lay in the focus on only one component of the management system (the industrial enterprise) and only after 1957 was attention diverted to other levels in the planning and management hierarchy, albeit in a very *ad hoc* fashion.

Communication within the planning hierarchy was a serious problem. An iterative approach to planning encourages bias on the part of both central planners and enterprise management: on the one hand enterprise targets are subject to continuous upward revision, and on the other hand production potential is understated. Writing in retrospect, Oskar Lange argued that the solution to this problem lay with management at the intermediate level between the enterprise and the central planning authorities. This intermediate unit in the planning hierarchy caused information passed upwards from the enterprise to be 'impoverished' while information passed from the central planners to the enterprise was 'enriched'. Decentralisation of more power to the enterprise was the only sure way of overcoming this problem.[49] Yet, even if enterprise management had wanted to plunge into autonomous decision-making, many enterprises were too small to succeed in this. Thus Lange was really opening up the question of optimal size of economic units for the various tasks of planning and management, as well as communication between central planner and enterprise.

This overdue focus on the enterprise as the basic unit for reform was certainly not accounted for by a paucity of alternative proposals.[50] At the second Congress of the Polish Society of Economists (PTE) in June 1956, it was decided to appoint an Economic Council that would advise the Polish Council of Ministers. This was duly carried out in 1957 and 35 renowned economists, PZPR and government members were nominated. The issues debated by the Council spread far beyond the narrow confines of economics and reflected the political upheavals of the time. In May 1957 the Economic Council produced a report on the question of changes recommended for the system of planning and management. The many proposals upon which consensus was reached were presented as 'Theses' which prescribed changes of a gradual nature based on a democratically determined, although somewhat confused strategy. As a guiding principle, it was proposed that central authorities should take all macro-economic decisions, plus those at the micro-economic level where economic calculation proved difficult, and where long-range forecasting played an important role as, for example, in investment policy. The problem of bringing the requisite amount of decentralisation to provide the opportunity for effective operation and rapid growth of the economy could be facilitated either by the preparation of several alternative plans demonstrating clearly the consequences of macro-economic decisions, or by limitation of the number of macro-economic decisions taken, in order to increase their accuracy, or by a discussion of the implications involved in choices made by planning authorities.[51] Without going into great detail about the Theses, it is fairly accurate to state that they were considered to be a compromise between all the interests involved in their construction. Some of the Theses were predicated upon a fully parametric model where pricing systems and material incentives would stimulate the correct response from individual enterprises, whereas others just involved an extension of existing incentives to plan fulfilment. Contradiction, confusion and uncertainty resulted when some of these proposals were incorporated into the economic reform. As we have seen, the application of economic incentives was underdeveloped and officially regarded as providing very little more than a supplement to the administrative system of directive indices. There was a disincentive to risk-taking and innovation by enterprises for whom the main inducement was to maximise bonuses, and adapt plan strategies to this end.

The economic reform associated with and subsequent to the political upheaval in Poland in 1956 is thus itself tainted with politics. It was observed keenly from Moscow, and therein, perhaps, lies the reason for restraint upon economic decentralisation. That industrial enterprises did not enjoy complete autonomy is as much due to this as to any inherent technical weakness concerning growth of an unfavourable balance of trade, structural unemployment and a sub-optimal investment structure.[52] The reform had been a response to political circumstances but also a serious attempt to provide a blueprint for a new policy of economic growth. The actual rate of economic growth in Poland has been the subject of debate amongst Western economists. It is commonly assumed that for the period 1958–62 (with the exception of 1961) national income grew by less than 6% per annum which marked a drop in comparison with the first half of the 1950s.[53] Yet this has been held to mask the different rates of growth between industry, construction and agriculture and varying capital intensity.[54] The resulting optimism about growth rates in the late 1950s and 1960s has been challenged, and contrarily it is asserted that rates of growth of industrial output have been declining in this period, with high growth of fixed capital stock, moderate increases in employment and a falling labour productivity that is in total all too reminiscent of the Soviet experience.[55] Whichever interpretation of this period is used, both would concur that a strategy of 'extensive' economic growth was being pursued but was inadequate and there needed to be a switch to a more 'intensive' strategy of growth by better use of inputs and technical progress. The difficulty of this being achieved in Poland was even greater than for the Soviet Union.[56] While it is possible to concur with the assertion that a continued strategy of 'extensive' growth has had a deleterious effect on the Polish economy since the late 1950s, it is more important to explore the exact nature of the 'barriers' to growth.

These barriers can be traced in the experience of the 1970s, during the period of the Second and Third Five-Year Plans (5YPII and 5YPIII). In brief, they are a very slow rate of growth of agricultural output: a high rate of capital accumulation, a rapid growth in the industrial workforce, taut planning, foreign trade policy, and domestic and international politics. In both these periods the major objective was to achieve a transition from extensive to intensive growth. (Extensive growth is based upon quantitative increases in factors of production while intensive growth is derived from overall gains in factor productivity.) One economic text on the period 1958–68 argued that the falling rate of growth and increase in capital and input-intensity of industrial production, plus falling social and personal consumption was due to an imbalanced investment cycle. The high industrial investment of the years 1950–5 had come to maturity from 1961–5, but as fewer new enterprises had been set up in the late 1950s, it was not surprising that the effectiveness of investment continued to decline in the late 1960s.[57] Moreover, the structure of investment according to branch of industry was such that it increased in the labour intensive fuels and energy industry at the expense of the more technically advanced chemical and engineering industries with the consequence that much expensive machinery had to be imported. The causes of this were seen to lie in the process of budgetary allocation of investment funds, and the desire of enterprise management to avoid risks by excessive accumulation of reserves, in the structure of industrial administration, which restricted a more efficient allocation of resources, and in the comparatively greater certainty of increasing output (rather than by undertaking more risky technical improvements).[58] The projected 50% increase in gross industrial output for the years 1961–5 to be achieved by focussing simultaneously on high investment in both fuel and consumer goods industries proved unattainable. This variation in success between branches of industry was reflected in above-target growth in chemical engineering and agricultural chemicals; but there was still deficient supply in the construction industry and developments in petrochemicals failed to take off (32% of investment resources had been designated to fuel and energy production).[59]

The next major obstacle to intensive growth was considered by Karpiński to be the structure of employment policy. While the rapid growth of employment in Polish industry in the early 1950s was exceptional throughout the whole of Europe, it has since slowed down and increases have tended to occur in older enterprises in basic heavy and extractive industry with a low level of technological development. Thus, while it was necessary to save investment resources and increase labour productivity, this was being contradicted particularly within the older industries that were least conducive to intensive development.[60] The situation was made more acute by the post-war demographic bulge that released large numbers onto the labour market after 1963: a trend that was accentuated by a declining employment in agriculture. The incremental rise in employment was twice as high as planned, and this had an adverse impact upon the cost of production by increasing the wages bill, and had more profoundly social consequences in the sudden rise in disguised unemployment, particularly among youth and women, and in a high labour turnover.[61] Although planners had argued that the increase in investment resources during 1961–6 could be used to absorb this increased labour supply, they did not make allowance for any acceleration of the pattern of rural migration to the towns. The result was that the increased proportion of national income devoted to raising the number employed in the socialised sector was insufficient to raise average real wages by more than 8%, thereby contributing to the further depression of living standards in Poland. This was reflected in the failure of individual and social consumption to achieve the target of 35% growth during 1961–5. Taken together the increase was only 28% and individual consumption only attained a 25% increase instead of the projected 32.1%.[62] Again, Karpiński blamed the system of planning and management that was in existence during the 1960s, as favouring short-term annual planning of the wage bill, and also the relative ease by which output could be raised by increased employment. The system of fixing wages and incentive levels was in no way conducive to raising labour productivity, given that the goal of plan fulfilment predominated.[63]

Finally, agriculture and foreign trade should be considered together as barriers to growth. Despite the halting of collectivisation in 1956 and the drift of rural population to the towns, labour productivity in agriculture hardly grew, and although the projected increase in output was 22.2%, the final gain was only 14.5% during the 5YPII. To some extent this can be accounted for by poor harvests during 1962 and 1964, and the consequent need to import grain. Agricultural imports had a damaging effect on foreign trade with imports growing faster than exports. The difficulty of acquiring raw materials from CMEA partners meant that Poland became indebted to the West for these, and was obliged to restructure her exports to the West to include machinery and finished products.[64]

By the end of the period 1961–5, the prospect of dismal results stimulated interest in economic reform as the means to enable a faster transition to intensive growth; and yet a 'tautly' planned economy in pursuit of increased growth in both industrial production and national income was maintained, while introducing a multitude of piece-meal reforms. The folly of taut planning as a background to reforms of the managerial structure of the Polish economy has been commented upon by several economists,[65] and illustrates the way in which the political and administrative structures of a command economy are barriers to growth. It was perhaps because there was no change in the political power structure in Poland that the introduction of parametric planning techniques was tolerated by the Soviet Union.

Official legitimation of these techniques was granted with the publication of the article 'The plan, profits and bonuses', by E. Liberman in Pravda in 1962, and their application to the East German economic reform after 1963 and the Soviet economic reform after 1965.[66] This new approach was intended to encourage independent decision-making by enterprise management within the constraint of certain parameters (which can either be centrally regulated, or left in some way to the play of market forces). This does not mean that the enterprise has complete decision-making autonomy, which obviously depends on the type of parameters used (although the extent to which horizontal exchanges prevail over vertical exchanges of information, i.e. between supplier and buyer, as opposed to between ministry, association and enterprise – can be an indication of the extensiveness of autonomy).

Before outlining the elements in the mid-1960 reforms in Poland, it is necessary just to mention briefly the administrative context of planning and management. The Economic Council had initially addressed itself to the enterprise as the basic unit for economic reform, but in its 'Theses' had argued that other levels in the economic administration would also have to be considered. It was for this purpose that the industrial associations replaced the central boards in 1958. While in practice this only involved a minor change, and the Economic Council was disbanded in 1962, in the mid-1960s there was a renewed interest in redefining the relationship between industrial minisiries, associations and enterprises. Prior to this the Fourth Congress of the PZPR in June 1964 announced a new growth strategy that proposed to concentrate on the most advanced sectors of industry with a low material-intensity and a sophisticated production process or on those branches where there were synthetic substitutes for raw material inputs. Such branches of industry as engineering and chemicals were to take a leading role. To achieve this, at the IV Plenum of the Central Committee in July 1965, a series of piece-meal changes were announced that would aim to raise economic efficiency by replacing 'directives' with economic 'instruments', 'incentives' and limits: between July and October 1964 a new bonus scheme was introduced for workers in industrial enterprises and associations; in 1965 a new 'synthetic' index of enterprise output (the index of profitability) replaced value of output as a key success indicator of enterprise performance; interest charges on the value of fixed assets in enterprises, and finally changes in factory prices (that did not come into effect until January 1967) were additional elements in the reform.[67]

To many observers at the time, it was immediately obvious that the reforms did not have the impact intended, and that management of the economy continued to be based upon the use of commands rather than economic stimuli. The discrepancy between the number of directive indices to be officially employed and those that were actually applied was wide. There was also the dilemma of fixing the index of profitability at a level that would be suitable for both enterprises and the superior administration. There were in fact no objective criteria to do this because of the impossibility of foreseeing and assessing all the factors outside the immediate environment of an enterprise. (This was particularly serious for enterprises that were heavily reliant upon sub-contracting arrangements or who were orientated towards a changeable consumer goods market.) The outcome was obvious: enterprises did not have sufficient freedom of action to justify the use of an index of profitability (despite their nominal control over the various Funds) and the index would be frequently revised during the plan year and supplemented by additional tasks. Moreover, enterprise management would seek to revise the index of profitability with a view to securing a more favourable increase in bonus payments for employees rather than achieve real rises in profitability. Although much was expected of the index of profitability for inducing enterprises to operate more 'economically', incentives were still very much tied to specialised funds; financial arrangements remained confined to the short term; and measures to give industrial associations increased financial control over enterprises, and increased powers to co-ordinate branch development, were restrained by central interference. Thus the various elements of the reform counteracted rather than complemented one another, and this was attributed largely to the use of synthetic indicators of performance as well as to 'taut' planning and the retention of a substantial ethos of the command model of planning and management.[68]

The reasons for the eclecticism of the reforms of the mid-1960s are difficult to discern. Perhaps they reflect the staid caution of the administration, or the division amongst economic experts. However, there does tend to be a polite disregard of the more radical 'holistic' approach taking place in Czechoslovakia after 1965. In contrast, the invasion of Czechoslovakia in August 1968 and the disruption of the Reform Programme influenced the policy adopted at the Fifth PZPR Congress in November 1968. There was a return to economic recentralisation: the government abandoned many of the 'financial instruments' adopted during the mid-1960s reform period, and reaffirmed the administrative direction of the economy. The Resolution of the Fifth Congress, and the statement at the ensuing II Plenum of the PZPR Central Committee in 1969 proposed a new strategy of 'intensive selective development' which would take advantage of the 'scientific-technological revolution' by accelerating investment and output in the chemical and engineering industries, and would encourage more exports of these goods.[69] Surprisingly this was accompanied by yet more piece-meal reform measures (new methods for constructing mid-term plans; greater integration of research and development policy into the production process, transfer and retail pricing; incentives; investment and finance)[70] of which the experiment in creating combines through merging enterprises in selected branches of industry was part and will be outlined in Chapter 4.

As in the case of the reforms introduced towards the end of 5YPII likewise in the case of the late 1960s, taut planning counteracted the desired effect. The same goals that were adopted for 5YPII were carried over into the 5YPIII, 1966–70. A slightly more modest rise of national income by 34% was aimed at, and consumption was to increase by 30%.[71] It was hoped that reserves of marketable consumer durables and a judicious regulation of agricultural production would forestall any serious shortages. With respect to trade this meant that the import of foodstuffs would have to decline while import of industrial consumer goods should increase at a slower rate than hitherto. On the export side, the share of foodstuffs relative to machinery and industrial manufactures was to fall. A massive rise in the industrial investment programme of 38% was to be directed to the more advanced sectors of industry and cope with absorbing surplus labour. Unfortunately the initial targets were not achieved, and again the perennial problems besetting the Polish economy seem to be the cause.

Besides taut planning, the most fundamental problem was the declining productivity of agriculture.[72] On three occasions during the 1960s (1962, 1967 and 1969) the rate of growth of agricultural output was below that of the previous year, and in 1967 and 1969 there were exceptionally bad harvests necessitating further food imports. Secondly, in foreign trade, although the global quantity of exports was rising, so was the volume of imports which had to respond to the domestic shortages of raw materials, machinery and consumer goods (especially food). International developments, in particular the formation of the EEC, had created a protectionist barrier against Polish exports. This was particularly so in the case of the Common Agricultural Policy which discriminated heavily against Polish food exports and which probably also was one of the main reasons for the change in export policy.[73] Finally, as to industrial growth, a long investment cycle and the failure to complete projects in progress, produced a widening gap between demand for products and the capacity to supply them – especially in the construction industry. The bottlenecks on the supply side ensured that any expansion of economic growth during these years is attributed largely to increases in numbers employed rather than to increases in labour productivity.[74]

Thus by the late 1960s, there had been no basic change in industrial growth strategy. Massive rates of increase of capital accumulation exceeding that of national income, and the extension of the gestation period for investment projects resulted in pressure on foreign trade and consumer policy. Although it was claimed that real wages and consumption increased up until 1968, thereafter employment, purchasing power and consumption were restrained.

It was this restriction upon employment, social consumption and wages that finally encouraged protest at the economic policies of the Gomułka regime. It was the incentive scheme outlined at the V Plenum of the PZPR Central Committee in May 1970 (and later formulated in greater detail by the Council of Ministers and the General Council of the Trade Unions on 1 July 1970) that contributed to the resentment of the industrial working class against the Gomułka regime. The underlying concept was to ensure that wages and bonuses would be more closely linked to actual real increases in labour productivity rather than just the fulfilment of plan targets. The incentives scheme thus provided an excuse to erode wage increases further and many categories of workers actually experienced a reduction in income: real wage levels fell at a time when nearly 50% of the average working-class family budget was spent on food.[75]

The social consequences of this incentives system finally made themselves felt in December 1970 when the price rises of food products (which was officially presented as an anti-inflationary device) actually threatened an inevitable fall in living standards. The immediate effect of the protest in the Baltic sea ports and other industrial areas was a major upheaval within the ranks of the PZPR, and the suspension of the economic plan for 1971 and a revision of the targets of the Fourth Five-Year Plan (5YPIV) 1971–5. Prices were instantly frozen and the Party–Government leadership of Edward Gierek sought to re-establish a *modus vivendi* with large sections of the Polish working class.

It is easy to see how the centrally directed planning and economic reform strategy had manoeuvred the Polish economy into a tight corner. It is only amazing that the outburst of working-class discontent did not occur earlier in 1970. The origins of the December events can be traced back to 1959 and the ensuing economic growth strategy of the 1960s. A slow rate of growth of labour productivity (accentuated by the problem of agriculture) had been solved by high rates of fixed capital investment, mainly in producer goods industries, but with little incentive to use existing and new capital in an efficient manner. As a result increases in productivity and national income did not rise commensurately with investment – thus reinforcing the vicious spiral. The 1960s were officially labelled as the inauguration of Poland's second wave of industrialisation, but it was difficult to shake off the old strategy:

timid piece-meal solutions were clearly not enough to push Poland into the forefront of industrialised nations. Technical capacity apart it would seem that political concerns were of paramount importance during the period from 1956 to 1970. In 1956 Poland had narrowly missed military invasion by the Soviet Union. The political leadership of Gomułka which began by repudiating the old Stalinist leadership soon reverted to a caution and conservatism that was unwilling to recognise the need for political change to accompany economic reform, and after 1966 became increasingly hostile to dissident intellectuals and used repressive measures to quell student protest in 1968.[76]

Post-1970 prosperity

After some anxious months during which the Gierek leadership stabilised, and directed its efforts towards containing worker discontent, it then embarked on a new economic reform tied in with a radical strategy of import-led growth that was directed towards the import of Western technology. This very ambitious departure was facilitated by international political developments, particularly the climate of East–West *détente* that developed in the 1970s, and more specifically the signing of the 'normalisation' treaty with the Federal Republic of Germany in December 1970. Yet inasmuch as the planned economic growth strategy, reform of the management mechanism and international developments were all interrelated and produced a significant rise in living standards up until 1975, thereafter they conspired to cause imported inflation, a reduction in export potential on account of world recession; massive indebtedness to the West and a decline in living standards. While some of the solutions were new and achieved high rates of economic growth, many of the old problems facing the Polish economy had not disappeared.

As to the economic reform that came into operation in 1973, a detailed description of its mechanics has been outlined elsewhere.[77] Besides redefining the basic unit of the economy as the Large Production Organisation (*Wielka Organizacja Gospodarcza*) which was a conglomerate of enterprises (and which will be examined more closely in following chapters), new synthetic indicators were devised for assessing worker and management performance (value added and net profit) which were then tied to the system of remuneration through the introduction of a coefficient relating changes in value added to changes in the Wages Fund. Other instruments consisted of taxation of material inputs and wages to encourage efficiency, measures to encourage production units to be self-financing (by allowing residual profit to come out of the Development Fund, and by permitting the retention of a proportion of foreign trade earnings) and some changes in pricing. Wanless considers that the various constraints operating at the time when the reform was introduced were sufficient to result in the incomplete implementation of the reform, an inflationary situation, the suspension of the reform in 1976, and modifications to the model in 1977, which thereafter resulted in considerable bureaucratic interference on the part of the industrial ministries.[78] Although the basic aims of the reform were assessed as including a better means for achieving plan targets, the satisfaction of social needs, the achievement of a sustained rate of growth, increased efficiency, expertise and technological progress, bad timing, political weakness (especially after 1976) and inadequate formulation of objectives were seen as the source of failure. Certainly at the commencement of the reform process in 1971 the whole exercise was presented as achieving a clearly integrated (*kompleksowy*) solution to the ills of Polish society. In May 1971 a Party–Government Commission of Experts was appointed with the brief of working out a model of economic change, and was chaired by Jan Szydlak. Another commission on the Polish education system, chaired by Professor Jan Szczepański was also appointed.[79] The Commission on the Economy appointed five sub-committees on wages; industrial organisation; the planning and management mechanism; finance, prices and foreign trade; materials supplies and wholesale and retail trade. Each committee set up teams of experts to investigate particular problems. Although there was much public discussion on the need for reform, there were wide differences of opinion[80] but finally the Commission reported in April 1972.[81]

If the targets of the Fourth Five-Year Plan 1971–5 (5YPIV) are examined in the context of their subsequent achievement, the obstacles to successful economic reform can be located. It has been remarked that the target rates of growth of the principal economic indicators were higher than those achieved in the previous five year period.[82] While industrial manufacturing output was to be raised by 42.5% and agricultural production by between 17.5 and 19.5%, personal consumption was to increase by 35%. Again agriculture proved to be a serious limitation. Political concessions to the peasantry in the form of inclusion within the social welfare system, cheaper credit, and increased freedom to trade privately did not produce the desired effect. The refusal to change procurement prices for agricultural products meant that, in the poorer harvests after 1972, prices of animal feed etc. on the private market shot up, thereby increasing production costs and providing a disincentive to increase supplies to the state, especially of meat. There were serious food shortages particularly of meat by 1975 and 1976.[83]

If agricultural production was below target, growth of net material product and industrial investment was way above target. Average annual growth rates of industrial investment were above 20%, and although the average industrial wage increased in real terms by 41%[84] over the 1970 level and aggregate social consumption rose too, the consumer boom gave way after 1975 to the strains of foreign trade. It had been hoped that an import-led growth strategy would provide for the buoyancy of both industrial and consumer growth rates. Debt-financed transfer of technology from the West[85] plus a reduced reliance upon the import of food products was seen as the prelude to the take-off of exports of technically advanced products to the West that would result in a positive balance of trade. However, bad harvests and poor domestic agricultural performance after 1972 provided the first check to this strategy. Secondly, Western currency was necessary to pay for the initial import of technology and so Poland borrowed funds on the Western currency markets.[86] This policy also had the undesirable side-effect of 'importing' Western inflation.[87] Hence the prices of some consumer durables also increased sharply after 1974 due to the filtering through of Western oil price rises. The increased involvement with Western markets also meant an increased dependence on these markets.[88] The trade recession in the early 1970s in the West reduced the demand for Polish exports of industrial products, as they were still in many cases not competitive with Western equivalents. Thus as well as a balance of payments deficit, there was a negative balance of trade. With the bad harvest of 1974–5, the shortages of foodstuffs, especially meat, were not supplemented by recourse to imports: hence the food price increases of June 1976.[89]

The industrial growth strategy had resulted in pressure on both foreign trade and domestic production. The fears that this would encourage taut planning and destroy the flexibility of the annual plan, either by the issue of too many *ad hoc* indicators by the bureaucracy or by making it impossible to predict capacity because of central intervention over employment and product mix,[90] were eventually proved correct. A review of the most recent Five-Year Plan 1976–80 (5YPV) would reflect that despite very large reductions in planned industrial investment growth, greater incentives to farmers, and slower growth rates for national income and personal incomes, foreign indebtedness to the West has increased, food imports have not fallen significantly, high investment rates continue, and the low relative prices of raw materials and food are seen as encouraging waste, a low labour productivity[91] and an unsustainable standard of living.[92] Measures to grant farmers family ownership rights to their land without loss of pension rights, and the increase of agricultural procurement prices have not raised output[93] or rural living standards commensurately with those in towns. The drift of young people away from the land[94] and to the towns, putting pressure on a very tight housing market,[95] has meant further erosion of the very high increase in living standards of the early 1970s.

Conclusion: economic or socio-political barriers to growth?

It is of course quite accurate to attribute the failure to break through the barrier to 'intensive growth' partly to the planning process. Planning has rarely taken place in an 'ex-ante' fashion and is usually based on an 'ex-post' calculation or 'extrapolation'. This method of plan construction has been conducted in conditions of tautness in supply markets particularly during the 6YP, 5YPI and 5YPIII,[96] and it appears to have re-emerged at the end of 5YPIV and during 5YPV. Where taut planning and the relaxation of central control have alternated, the result has been a lack of consistency in the planning process. Thus it would appear that there is a vicious spiral of plan tautness leading to excessive accumulation, low labour productivity, a low standard of living and finally low economic growth.

Yet, as we have continually stressed in this chapter, it would be incorrect to see this problem as of a purely economic nature: political developments and economic strategy are intricately connected. For example, the persistence of underdevelopment in agriculture in comparison with industry reflects the struggle over collectivisation in the 1950s and the political priorities of a Stalinist economy that have been difficult to shake off. On the other hand the pre-war history of cartelisation and state intervention may have eased the transition to a centrally planned economy, but to label this a system of 'rational redistribution' (Konrad and Szelenyi)[97] is to ignore the considerable irrationality and waste of materials and effort that have persisted long after the official denunciation of Stalinist crimes. In particular, the Soviet Union and developments within the international Communist movement have influenced the choice of economic model and growth strategy. However, therein lie many contradictions: the Soviet Union has endorsed the pursuit of a strategy of intensive growth, but will not countenance the necessary changes in planning and management to achieve this – decentralisation of autonomy to the enterprise and the use of market instruments takes place within circumscribed limits. Even in the heady days of 1956, decentralisation was partial and was revoked because of fears that syndicalism, as expressed through the movement for Workers' Councils, would threaten the whole fabric of a centrally planned economy. The feeble reforms of the 1960s were no more than a distant echo of past hopes for decentralisation. The incorporation of phenomena associated with a freely competitive economy could only be tolerated within the framework of central planning.

Political constraints upon economic growth in Poland should not only be considered in a mechanistic light in terms of Soviet pressure and a conservative elite within Poland. As Rakovski, Konrad and Szelenyi have argued, economic policy is the outcome of a balance of political forces favouring concessions and compromise. It is the technocrats who favour reform, but the workers who oppose it, and consequently worker opposition is bought off by technocratic manipulation encouraging worker demands for greater consumption and participation by incorporating them into consultative bodies. The shifting pressures that result must be taken into account in considering growth strategy.

Returning to the content of reform programmes, one development that, paradoxically, has been encouraged by the Soviet Union, is the concentration of production into even bigger physical and administrative units, that have gradually come to resemble Western business operations. Whether the motivation for this has to be attributed to the inherent logic of a centrally planned economy that has to cope with an ever increasing complexity of the production process and division of labour, cannot be confirmed here; nor can the implications of this for the growth of power over the labour process on the part of an emerging technocratic managerial elite. It is to these issues that we now turn.

3

The emergence of a corporate structure in Polish industry, 1958–68

It is conventional for Western economists to evaluate the success and worth of economic reform in terms of the amount of independence accorded to the industrial enterprise, and to assume a dichotomy of interest between central planners and the enterprise. However, in a complex economy, the interaction of different levels in the planning and management apparatus is considerably more complex. That intermediate levels in the planning and management hierarchy could act to 'enrich' and 'impoverish' the communication between central planning authorities and industrial enterprises had been remarked upon by Oskar Lange,[1] and had also been the consideration of the Economic Council when it recommended the abolition of the central boards and their replacement by industrial associations that would be more sensitive to the needs of the economy. Whereas studies of the operation of bureaucracy in both the public and the private sector in the West have revealed that it is facile to describe it as an impartial executive mechanism implementing policy made at the top of an organisation or by outside policy-makers,[2] Polish sociologists have also acknowledged that intra-organisational conflicts and the socio-cultural and political environment play an important role in defining the cohesion of and goals pursued by an organisation.[3] The pursuit of greater specialisation in the division of labour and a speedier rate of technological innovation has expressed itself in a number of reforms carried out at 'intermediate' levels in the planning and management apparatus which were expressed in the form of various types of merger and concentration of industrial enterprises. As we have noted in the introductory chapter, it is not unreasonable to suppose that the emergence of these corporate structures has implications for management accountability and political control in Poland.[4] A chronicle of this process of enterprise merger and concentration now follows.

The grouping of industrial enterprises in Poland prior to 1958

Some preliminary comment has already been made about the division of responsibility between industrial ministries, central boards and enterprises that evolved during the transition to a centrally planned economy in Poland, and that during 1956 significant changes began to take place.[5] It should also be noted that it was the Soviet experience of industrialisation that provided the model for Eastern Europe after the late 1940s, and that it was the Soviet experience of conducting a war economy simultaneously aiming at rapid economic growth in conditions of autarky that was largely responsible for determining the structure of Soviet industrial administration and the mechanism of planning and management. It can be argued that the die was cast as early as the period of War Communism (1918–21), which witnessed the demise of the syndic-alist ideals upheld by the Workers' Opposition, in favour of the espousal of one-man management and the spawning of a bureaucra-cy around the Supreme Council for the National Economy (VSNKH) and the industrial Commissariats and *glavki*. The foundations of a planned economy had been laid, despite the later relaxation of controls in favour of a mixed economy during the period of the New Economic Policy (NEP).[6] Before considering the developments in Poland after 1956, it is worth noting the differing experiments in grouping of industrial plant in the Soviet Union in the 1920s and 1930s.

During NEP some enterprises were placed together in 'trusts' which had considerable autonomy in conducting their own purchase of supplies and sales, and which could operate according to free market principles of profit maximisation, so much so that the state was no longer able to claim priority in service. The trusts exerted total control over their constituent enterprises which were not full cost accounting units, but in turn the degree of supervision of trusts by VSNKH varied according to whether they belonged to the crucial heavy industrial sector or not, and the ability to forecast in the conditions of an embryonic planning process. However the 'Goods Famine' of 1925–6 and a similar economic crisis during 1927 encouraged stricter central control over production as resource supplies became scarcer, with the result that the contours of a planned economy emerged.[7]

With the introduction of the command model of planning and management after 1928, which pronounced the enterprise, run on the basis of one-man management, as the basic unit of the economy, the trusts gradually lost their powers of control over industrial plant. They were reduced to the level of service agencies concentrating upon 'technical direction, rationalisation and reconstruction', and were to be supplemented by new production associations (*ob'edine-nie*) which replaced the *glavki*. These *ob'edinenie* were obliged to plan and control production, investment, technical policy, supplies and sales, commercial and financial activities, labour training, cadre policy and the appointment and dismissal of managerial staff from the enterprise. Some were set up at an All-Union and some at a Republican level. However, in conditions of growing central powers over planning and management, this resulted in some confusion and the eventual eclipse of these bodies.[8] By 1932 a system of industrial authority consisting of commissariats (ministries after 1946) and *glavki* organised mainly according to particular sectors and branches of industrial production had emerged, in which the 'trusts' and *ob'edinenie* were superfluous. Finally, it should not go unnoted that the command economic model was inherently unsuited to the operation of large production units with freedom to contract supplies, credit and sales. Rather, there was an inbuilt tendency towards the proliferation of a centrally controlled hierarchically organised bureaucracy that extended the 'tentacles of the planning octopus' over the most basic units of the economy: the industrial enterprises.[9]

It was in this mould that Polish industrial organisation was cast. Even after 1956 the reallocation of responsibilities between the new Planning Commission, industrial ministries and central boards was approached in the highly legalistic manner so characteristic of the Stalinist period. It was hoped that, by passing legislation to limit the number of obligatory directive indices to be fulfilled by an enterprise, the operation of enterprise management would change. Obviously the new statutory framework for the operation of enterprises was inadequate if there was no corresponding change in higher levels of administration such as a relaxation of investment controls or freedom to negotiate credit arrangements with the National Bank of Poland (NBP). The central boards which had operated as departments of the industrial ministries were described as being no better than a 'post-box' (*skrzynka pocztowa*) through which central directives could be passed on to the enterprise with scant attention to the method whereby tasks were disaggregated or to the individual needs of enterprises.[10] The 'Thaw' of the years after 1954 had meant that articles appeared in the Press frankly describing the problems faced in industry, and in particular illustrating the friction that existed between management of enterprises and officials of the central boards. The frequency of disputes increased after the legal changes concerning enterprise autonomy and the endorsement of Workers' Councils, particularly as the central boards still retained the power of final confirmation of the annual plan as laid down in the original enterprise law of 1950. The requirements of differing branches of industry in terms of close intervention by the central board went unheeded: both the sugar processing industry and engineering were considered to have the same requirements.[11] As a result, many enterprise directors did not take advantage of their new rights and indeed some did not even see the need for a more innovatory style of management decision-making, feeling it much easier to fulfil orders passed on from above and thereby absolve themselves of responsibility.[12] It was thus appropriate that, in March 1958, the Economic Council held a session that devoted more attention to levels of industrial adminis-tration above the enterprise and drafted legislation to introduce industrial associations (*zjednoczenia przemysłowe*).

The industrial association, 1958–64

The deliberations of the Economic Council prescribed three major tasks for the industrial association: its officials were to occupy themselves chiefly with the development of the whole branch of industry rather than with the current activity of enterprises; the industrial association was to be connected to the enterprise by means of economic 'links' rather than by direct administrative commands; and, finally, some matters hitherto within the compet-ence of the industrial ministry were to be transferred to the industrial association leaving ministerial staff to the task of macro-economic development and perspective planning. It was obvious that this was intended to complement the enterprise reform by moving away from a command model of the economy based on

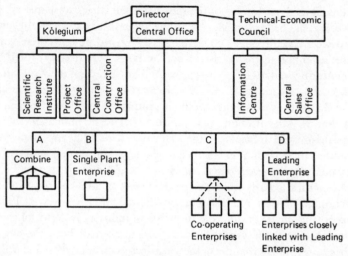

Fig. 1. The internal organisation of an industrial association (branch
model)
Source: M. Doroszewicz 'Zjednoczienie–główne–ogniwo zarządzanie, *ZG*,
44/1965

legalistic change. This is particularly in evidence in the proposals of
the Economic Council for the organisational structure, management
decision-making and technical specialist advice. To consider the
organisational structure first, four models were proposed: the
branch model (as illustrated in Fig. 1), the regional-branch model
where several industrial associations controlled industry in different
areas, the co-operative model and a flexible organisation model. The
latter two involved a very loose framework for industrial association
control over the enterprise, and certain economists such as Bogdań
Gliński had argued against the adoption of a single type of industrial
association, recommending that in certain cases, there was no need
for such an intermediate organisation between large enterprises and
the industrial ministry. Management decision-making was a very
sensitive issue as the 1950 enterprise law had laid down the principle of
one-man management which was later to apply to all economic units.
The Economic Council sessions on the industrial association
proposed the creation of a *kolegium* (a form of consultative committee
of managers) as a means of circumventing the shortcomings of
one-man management (which included the tendency for middle and
lower management to shy away from taking responsibility, as well as

the overload of the chief director of an institution). The kolegium was to be composed of the chief director of the association along with the directors of all the constituent enterprises and auxiliary units, plus the association accountant and chief engineer. However the Economic Council was divided over whether this body should serve in a consultative–advisory function, or should have the right to make decisions collectively concerning the whole industrial association. Some attempt at resolving this was in evidence in the third proposal of a Technical-Economic Council consisting of academics, various specialists actively involved in industry, and representatives of trade unions and *wojewodztwo* (regional) national councils (WRN).[13] Finally, the Economic Council discussed the extent to which the industrial association could redistribute financial resources between enterprises without interference from the ministry. Some felt that this was the most crucial and most sensitive aspect of the reform. Wlodzimierz Brus argued further that without a reform of wholesale and clearing prices, neither the industrial association nor any other element in the reform model would make any sense.[14]

Lack of consensus within the Economic Council and caution on the part of the government was expressed in the industrial association law.[15] Organisational flexibility was rejected by the government in favour of either a branch model, or a regional-branch model; the precise role and powers of both the kolegium and Technical-Economic Council were left vague in the desire to avoid abandoning the principle of one-man management; and financial and price-setting powers did not materialise. The major effect of Decree 128/1958 was to reduce the number of industrial associations relative to the previous number of central boards from 163 to 121.[16] Besides the regrouping of enterprises and reduction in numbers of the industrial associations there was also a cut back in the number of staff working in association offices[17] and the provision for more direct communication with a variety of central economic institutions[18] as outlined in Fig. 2. On the other hand the chief director of the association had a certain amount of discretion in the internal work organisation.[19]

Given the reluctance to abandon one-man management and to experiment with management structure, it is not surprising that the operation of establishing these new industrial associations was tinged with timid caution rather than innovative flair. Instead of the model statute outlined in Decree 128/1958 being adapted to the

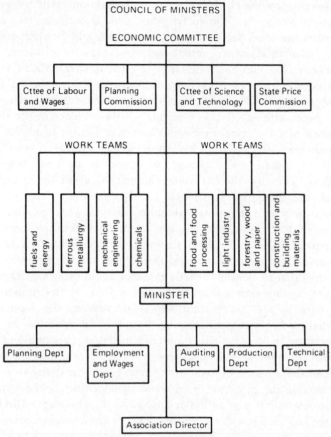

Fig. 2. The relation between central state planning, management institutions and the industrial associations

specific requirements of a branch of industry, the reverse occurred, and the outcome was no more than the administrative juggling of central boards with very little change in management practice. There were other shortcomings such as delays in the approval of the new statutes, in the passage of legislation vital to their operation (such as the procrastination of the Ministry of Finance over the drafting of new financial regulations) and, finally, the tendency for the relationship between the association and its constituent enterprises to be more precisely specified than the mutual responsibilities of the association and the ministry.[20] There was evidence that the industrial ministries took advantage of this to restrict the growth of association autonomy over the control of the enterprises within them. Reform was tolerated as long as it conformed to the opinion from above and did not really disturb the pattern of relations pertaining to the former central boards and ministries.[21]

This initial caution eventually resulted in very little difference in the operation of the industrial associations from the central boards, particularly after 1959 when a recentralisation of power in planning and management took place by means of the industrial associations passing on directive indices set in the ministry, especially after 1962.[22] Some industrial associations with very similar production profiles and yet subordinate to the same ministry, as in the coal industry, were subject to different numbers of directive indices of which they were not informed until very late, often after the beginning of the plan period.[23] These delays were obviously more serious for the industrial enterprises. In one large steel combine (Huty Im. Lenina) the final approval of directive indices for the plan year 1962, took place in December 1962, after protracted bargaining with the iron and steel association, and was quite understandably viewed by members of the workers' self-management bodies to be a challenge to their right to scrutinise the plan before it was adopted.[24]

In such conditions of recentralisation the potential for initiative on the part of the industrial associations and enterprises was paralysed. The problem began at the top of the planning hierarchy and was passed on downwards.[25] Many economists were sceptical of achieving any decentralisation of decision-making to the enterprise as, despite statements to the contrary, ministerial officials would continually intervene, particularly in such matters as investment policy. The contradictions between enterprise initiatives in long-term planning, and the limitations imposed by central institutions upon the annual plan, had meant that the industrial associations were the 'supporters' of their respective ministries, rather than of their enterprises, and had reverted to the practice of the former central boards.[26] They had failed either to lead or to advise enterprises in technical and economic matters. A meeting in November 1959 between the Deputy Premier Jaroszewicz and some chief directors of industrial associations, concluded that the ministries were largely responsible for this. Decree 128/1958 had specified that the association kolegium should have the right to scrutinise and be consulted on a number of matters (the technical-economic plan, product specialisation, materials allocation policy, accounting prices, the distribution of profit, decentralised investment and the redistribution of financial resources). Jaroszewicz pronounced that in fact they met rarely and dealt only with incidental problems rather than the tasks set, thus accusing them of being deaf to the interests of their constituent enterprises and of not progressing beyond the role of a 'post-box' between the ministry and the enterprise.[27] As to the Technical-Economic Councils, one Polish economist noted that, in general, three times as many technical specialists as economists were represented on this, which did not augur well for business decision-making.[28] Yet, it would be incorrect to assume that the industrial ministries were the sole source of interference into the activities of the association. Other sources were the Planning Commission, the Chief Inspectorate of the Ministry of Finance, the central and branch offices of the NBP, the industrial committees of local government councils; and the Central Statistical Office (GUS).[29] Whatever the source of interference, the management of industrial units within the ambit of the industrial association was a highly bureaucratic process.

Thus, while in 1962 an editorial in the Polish business weekly *Życie Gospodarcze* bemoaned the state of the industrial associations (the inadequacy of association control over what was happening in their own scientific research offices, the lack of financial and economic integration with enterprises, cadre/personnel problems, the undemocratic nature of the kolegium and the neglect of the proposals from enterprise self-management bodies),[30] it was not until the Fourth Congress of the PZPR in June 1964 that there was a conscious attempt to review the progress of the industrial association and suggest modifications. It would appear that the legalistic, bureaucratic management style, which had constrained the reform of the enterprise had also limited the ability of the industrial associations to act as independent economic units. The merger of enterprises into industrial associations had remained a purely administrative exercise.

Other measures for grouping enterprises 1958–64

The organisational models for the industrial association had been confined to two basic types on a branch and regional-branch basis. Only in the woollen and coal industries was the latter type used:

there were 2 regional-branch associations in the woollen industry and 7 in the coal industry.[31] At the same time industrial associations for administering local industry were incorporated into local government reform. Already in 1956 local authorities had acquired powers to manage industry located in their territory,[32] but it was not until 1958 with the local government reform that *wojewodztwo* (regional divisions) and *powiat* (district divisions) authorities acquired planning powers and budgetary resources for roads and small local factories. Further legislation in 1959 assigned around 300 industrial enterprises from the centrally planned (key) socialised sector into the control of the national councils (*rady narodowe*). So, the share of locally run enterprises in national output was quite high, especially in the construction industry and services.[33] The associations of local industry were run jointly by the national councils and the industrial ministry concerned (or, as in the case of handicrafts and small-scale industries, by the Committee for Petty-Commodity Production). Some ministries took advantage of this dual control to delegate, whereas others tried to minimise the initiative taken by the national council.[34]

While the local industrial associations were to assume considerable importance in managing local consumer and service industries in the 1970s, at the time of their inception, the industry they controlled was not considered to be a priority sector. It is interesting to reflect on the parallels between them and the creation of the 105 regional economic councils (*sovnarkhozy*) in the Soviet Union, which operated between 1957 and 1965. After the denunciation of Stalinist crimes in the Soviet Union in 1956, the faults of taut planning were attributed to the inadequate central co-ordination between industrial ministries, who indulged in 'empire building'. The abolition of the ministries and their replacement by the *sovnarkhozy*, controlled mainly from the republics, with only Gosplan (State Economic Planning Commission) co-ordinating national economic policy, was not an unqualified success. Excessive competition between regions for supplies and investment resources encouraged greater intervention from Moscow after 1962, but not without confusion and eventual disbandment of the *sovnarkhozy* in 1965.[35] In Poland, although the 'production principle' for planning and management was not wholly rejected in favour of the 'territorial principle', after 1958 there was more attention given to local industry, and regional planning based on the *wojewodztwa* dates from this time.

Besides local industrial associations, other forms of enterprise grouping introduced in 1960 were the patron enterprise (*przedsiębiorstwo patronackie*) and the leading enterprise (*przedsiębiorstwo prowadzący*). The purpose of leading enterprises was to ensure that major management decisions were made as closely as possible to the point of production, and this was achieved by requiring an existing enterprise to perform the tasks of an industrial association for a small group of enterprises involved in a distinctive coherent area of production within a wider branch of industry. The leading enterprise could either be supervised by the industrial association for that branch, or could be run directly from the ministry.[36] Patron enterprises on the other hand were to provide technical economic and organisational advice to smaller enterprises in the branch. Hence only the most advanced enterprises would be singled out for this status, and had no administrative rights over the enterprises which they advised.[37] A fifth type was the leading association (*zjednoczenie wiodące*) which was to be set up in branches of industry where there was a need for co-operation between a variety of very different production units. This was seen as particularly suited to industries where there were many dispersed units or where firms were controlled by different ministries. The director of the leading association would chair a Branch Commission where a system of weighted voting was required for decision-making.[38] By 1964 it was estimated that this structure was quite pervasive, especially in dealing with problems of branch investment with the NBP. However, one economist expressed his scepticism of what he saw to be the temporary and sporadic nature of co-ordination activities: the leading association tended to play a 'fire brigade' role by coping with the various bottlenecks that arose in production rather than drafting long term development plans.[39]

Finally, other institutional forms of branch co-operation were branch agreements drawn up by business institutes (*instytut gestii*), product associations (*zreszenia assortymentowa*) and branch centres (*osrodki branżowe*). The latter two were to be supervised by leading enterprises with the aim of encouraging deeper specialisation and concentration of production, sales exports etc.,[40] but enterprises could be party to several branch agreements which did not necessarily make for better co-ordination in production.[41]

Thus the variety of schemes for improving enterprise co-ordination introduced after the late 1950s represent a greater flexibility of economic organisation than would have been tolerated in the Stalinist period, but, seen as a whole, they are at best an eclectic and *ad hoc* attempt to integrate and concentrate production. They were eclectic as they were not introduced with the purpose of achieving a systematic integration but rather arose in response to different views of how the Polish economy should function: for example branch agreements were originally seen as a means of decentralising decision-making powers, but were later transformed into a means for a leading association to control investment policy on behalf of the ministry. Again it is not unreasonable to suppose that the administrative, legalistic approach to planning and management was an obstacle to economic integration of enterprises into anything remotely resembling a corporate structure.

Industrial associations and economic reform, 1964–6

We have already mentioned the renewed interest in economic reform announced at the Fourth Congress of the PZPR in 1964, and the IV Plenum of the Central Committee in 1965.[42] Although the main elements were: the new bonus scheme; the introduction of a synthetic index to evaluate enterprise performance; and a greater reliance on bank financial control, the focus was not so much on the enterprise as on the respective balance and complementarity between the roles of the enterprise and the industrial association. *Nowe Drogi* published the discussions that took place at a symposium on this topic. There were a variety of conflicting opinions about future policy, but it was agreed that the real problem was the failure to make the industrial association a full cost-accounting unit.[43] It was also noted with alarm that the proliferation of multi-plant enterprises after 1960 made it all the more urgent to improve upon the operation of the industrial association.[44] This growth in size of enterprises was obviously to the administrative convenience of the industrial associations: it was less tiresome to control a few gigantic enterprises than many small ones. Again discussion of the appropriate organisational structure for the industrial association was indecisive.[45] While the Chairman of the NBP proposed four neat variants (based on horizontal integration; multi-plant enterprises; the leading enterprise and the combine), Bogdań Gliński, in stressing the need to make the industrial associations take an innovatory attitude, suggested two additional models: amalgamated plants (*zjednoczone zakłady*) and the association combine (*zjednoczenie kombinat*). Gliński had based his proposals very much on the needs occasioned by specific production processes and the division of labour,[46] but was very much aware that, unless there was a departure from the principle of one-man management, little change could be expected.

The Resolution of the Fourth PZPR Congress endorsed many of the proposals of the above symposium especially greater autonomy from the ministry in employment, investment finance and foreign trade; and also with respect to achieving a more 'consultative' relationship with enterprises in the process of plan construction and amendment with more access for worker self-management represent-atives. To this end, the legal constitution of the industrial association was to vary according to the requirements of the specific sector of industry, and even regional needs. Finally the industrial association was to conduct all its transactions according to the principle of full cost-accounting with the aim of evaluating all its constituent enterprises in terms of a single index of profitability.[47] These were very bold proposals, as although no one dared mention it, the industrial associations were to emerge from their administra-tive niche to behave like fully fledged socialist corporations. Although it was two years before any legal change and experiment-ation took place, much research on Polish industrial structure was conducted during the period 1964–6 that merits more than a cursory glance.

A Government Commission to improve planning and manage-ment was appointed and issued questionnaires to 25 industrial associations in order to ascertain their actual spheres of competence, their relations with the ministry and with the enterprises in their branch. Another questionnaire devised by the Institute of Econo-mics and Industrial Organisation in June and July 1964 attempted to discover whether it was wise to entrust the industrial association with the finance of all branch development for its enterprises.[48] Despite what turned out to be rather inconclusive results, these surveys revealed much interesting information about industrial associations. For example, they were shown to vary enormously in size,[49] the types of service they provided for enterprises within their branch and the number of officials so employed,[50] in the size of the product output mix; and the incorporation of enterprises from outside the branch.[51] If anything, this information about differentiation in size, numbers employed, research, technological development and product mix, could be used to argue that a legalistic approach to enterprise merger and industrial structure would not provide the stimulus for dynamic business activity that would encourage faster growth rates. Yet this was not heeded and the Management Organisation Team from the Council of Ministers echoed the position of the NBP in suggesting only a small number of organisational variants for industrial associations (focusing mainly on the association combine and the leading enterprise model) despite the pleas of Gliński and others that this was too narrow a conception.

These surveys of industrial associations also drew attention to the problem of personnel policy. In order to depart from an administrative process of planning to one governed by economic instruments, it was necessary to have management in the industrial association of adequate calibre. Yet personnel policy and wage incentive schemes provided little inducement for economists and those with business skills to aspire towards employment on the economic staff of an industrial association. It became clear by the mid-1960s that much of the inefficiency of the industrial associations in planning and management could be attributed to the quality of personnel employed. There is evidence that many enterprise directors were better qualified by the early 1960s than those in the industrial associations.[52] While this may have been a reflection upon the relative status of both levels of organisation in the eyes of industrial ministry officials, it was also the consequence of the 'reduction in bureaucracy' that had accompanied the demise of the central boards and their replacement by the industrial associations. Either way, the wage and bonus scheme for association workers resulted in a level of payment lower than that for analogous employees in the enterprise. The bonus system for association staff was very similar to that covering employees in the ministry, and as the association was not awarded a full cost-accounting status by Decree 128/1958, it was unable to accumulate profit in its own right and thus could not distribute funds for housing and other amenities.[53] Bonuses were awarded on a quarterly basis, but amounted to between only 5% and 15% of the Wages Fund, and because their achievement was very much dependent upon the enterprise fulfilment of gross output plans, these payments were not always guaranteed automatically. By 1960, there was a wide discrepancy between wages in enterprises and those in associations.[54] The relative earnings of association staff did increase between 1960 and 1964, mainly with the aid of special *ad hoc* bonus schemes but there was now a substantial variation in the proportions of fixed earnings and bonus. In the association of synthetic chemicals, for example, this bonus varied from 73% of the basic wage of the director, 60% for the chief engineer, to only 5% for the senior economist. In the association of the iron and steel industry, the comparable levels were 47% for the chief engineer, but only 11% for the senior economist.[55] Thus business training was not highly rewarded in Polish industrial associations, and the possibilities for promotion from the post of senior economist to association director were very limited, this latter post being the effective monopoly of those trained as engineers.

If there were problems in personnel policy in association senior management, recruitment and training of middle and lower management was an equally serious one. Highly qualified employees in the industrial association were restricted to a narrow managerial group and many of the rest were people who had left work in industrial enterprises and yet were often incapable or unacquainted with the problems of the industrial enterprises they were dealing with (many such workers were women with only minimal clerical skills). The general quality of administration in the industrial association was thus a source of dissatisfaction to enterprise management, especially when many simple decisions that had to be made by the association or ministry arrived too late for the enterprise to act upon them; or when the industrial associations made decisions independently without consulting the enterprise concerned. The association kolegium would often meet on an *ad hoc* basis and agree to an agenda fixed by association staff without prior discussion.[56]

As we noted in Chapter 2, after July 1964 the wage and bonus system for industrial enterprises underwent change. In the associations all the highly specific bonus systems were swept aside and replaced by an arrangement whereby between 3% and 5% of the Wages Fund would be put aside for financing additional tasks sent to the association in the course of the year. The bonus fund was divided according to the three categories of staff: senior management, technical and economic staff, and clerical-administrative workers with the industrial ministry regulating the relative proportion of funds to be allocated to each group. Hoping that bonus schemes could change personnel and management practice was too optimistic and was not likely to produce immediate change. Not until late 1966 was there any indication that the bonus scheme had contributed to an improvement in the qualifications of association staff, and even then wages continued to remain relatively low.[57]

It must be stressed that, after the Fourth PZPR Congress, it was not intended that economic reform should take place in a piecemeal fashion (although this did in fact occur). The various research groups and the Government Commission did not report until the summer of 1965 by which time there was sufficient agreement on a common policy to announce it at the IV Plenum of the Central Committee.[58] With respect to the status of the industrial association, three aspects were singled out for reform: the financial system; the responsibilities of the ministries *vis à vis* the associations; and the internal organisation and management structure of the associations.

In financial terms, as the industrial association was to become a full cost-accounting unit, its financial basis would extend beyond provisions from budgetary grants and the operation of a depreciation fund to include profits from production trade and bank loans. Thus a number of changes took place between 1965 and 1966 to encourage the industrial association to take a closer financial interest in matters of production. It was to control payments into and out of five basic funds, and enterprise management would similarly have control over five basic funds whose parameters would be set by the association.[59] Other funds for specific purposes would be under the aegis of ministry control. Most industrial associations had been in favour of the removal of directive indices controlling marketing resource allocation, wages, repairs and depreciation; and interviews with senior management had also revealed a preference to have their performance assessed by a single synthetic index: the index of profitability. Although they agreed to limit the total number of directive indices to be achieved by their enterprises to 9, association management expressed a clear desire to stipulate their performance criteria (especially value of sales; the size of the Wages Fund; employment; distribution of profit; payments to the central budget; investment; and the index of costs in the total value of output).[60] After 1 January 1966 both enterprises and associations were evaluated according to an index of net profitability; and most enterprise activity was to be self-financing with association and bank involved in negotiating investment, credit, and depreciation charges.[61] As the association was intended to operate as an economic unit, the acquisition of control over investment policy and the transfer of fixed capital was an important step in this direction.

Yet the decentralisation of financial powers from the industrial ministries was of little use without some reduction in the number of centrally listed commodities. There was some change here with an estimated 30% of products that were previously listed being subject to 'approximate' as opposed to directive indices. However substantial powers of price-fixing were not acquired by the industrial associations and one commentator viewed these changes as no more than a rationalisation of existing difficulties in marketing certain commodities.[62]

Legal clarification of the limits upon the intervention of the ministries in association business was, however, announced. Although this was a reiteration of past policy, it resulted in new statutes being drafted for the industrial ministries. The first, for the chemical industry, came into force in October 1965, and appeared to be sanctioning the installation of new service units to advise on general branch development, inter-branch development, technical development and personnel policy.[63] This legal change was followed one year later by a law on the organisation of industrial associations.[64] It permitted an element of choice according to the type of branch of industry and the number of enterprises. Besides whole-branch associations, regional-branch associations were to be encouraged if there were a large number of enterprises, and, in the case of only a small number of enterprises in a branch, integration into a multi-factory enterprise or amalgamated plants (*zjednoczone zakłady*) was seen as the most suitable solution. The actual structure of each industrial association would be specified in a statute approved by the ministry.

As to the procedure for drafting plans, while the industrial ministry was to devote attention to macro-economic problems, the industrial association was, according to Decree 383/1966, to have the major responsibility for development plans in the branch. Annual plans were to be drawn up allowing for alternative projects and suggestions to be put forward by the enterprises in the association, to be achieved by the formal representation of all enterprises in the association kolegium which was to be a much more dynamic institution than hitherto. In arriving at the final plan project, the industrial association was instructed to consult other institutions with which the industrial association conducted transactions (including other associations with whom it co-operated in production, foreign trade enterprises and local government). The final plan was to be agreed by the industrial association and the ministry with the latter setting no more than five directive indices (including specific production tasks, limits on the maximum use of resources, normative quotas expressing the different requirements of materials in production, and financial quotas) after the association had presented its two-year, five-year and perspective forecasts.[65]

The impression received from these proposals about planning is of a much more corporative process despite no departure from the principle of one-man management. Industrial association management was restricted in the number of directives that it could request enterprises to fulfil, and enterprise management had the right to be consulted regularly in the planning process. However, the right of the industrial association director to decide on planning procedure and the much greater powers at his disposal in the matters of branch development policy, scientific-technical policy, foreign trade transactions and the transfer of fixed capital between enterprises in the association, enhanced the overall position of senior management in the industrial associations. For the first time association directors acquired responsibility for all cadres (personnel) policy within the association, including the appointment of enterprise directors after authorisation from the relevant industrial ministry and after consultation with the representatives of workers' self-management units within the enterprise.[66]

To facilitate the 'rationalisation' of production within industrial associations (especially the 'rationalisation' of cadre policy), Factory Commissions were appointed after the VII Central Committee Plenum in 1966 (November) and continued in existence until mid-1967. These bodies devoted much time to encouraging industrial associations to make production agreements with enterprises outside their branch, and similarly for the purpose of domestic and export marketing.[67]

In summarising the effect of the reform measures on the industrial association between 1964 and 1968, it is important to acknowledge that similar developments were taking place elsewhere in Eastern Europe. Liberman's scheme to incorporate the criterion of profitability into a series of economic parameters and tie this to material incentives was incorporated in the Soviet Economic Reform after 1965, and the East German 'New Economic System' launched at the

Sixth Congress of the Socialist Unity Party (SED) in 1963.
Although, after 1968 and again after 1971, there was some retreat
from the use of indirect parametric techniques back to the utilisation
of 'administrative' measures of planning and management, the
reform that created the New Economic System was hailed as the
most successful implementation of Liberman's ideas.[68]

In the course of the implementation of the New Economic System
in East Germany, substantial changes were made in the organisation of production. Since 1958 industrial enterprises (VEBs) had
been administered by industrial associations (VVBs) in a manner
more or less identical to that in Poland. In 1963 some regrouping
and a general reduction in the number of VVBs took place to enable
them to assume an increasingly important role at the middle level of
planning and management both in co-ordinating the work of VEB
management and in providing such services as advice on technical
matters, research and development and marketing. The financial
full cost-accounting status, and the reform of the pricing mechanism
with a view to providing a complex system of stimuli to ensure
optimal production within the VVBs, encouraged a close identity
between VEB and VVB management (this was especially evident in
their joint responsibility for sales and foreign marketing.[69]

However, there are reports that this newly acquired power of
control over the operational management of the VEBs gave rise to
considerable cause for concern about the future status of the VVBs
by 1967. The manipulation of the financial system, and the ability
for VVBs to negotiate prices in their production contracts, caused
some observers to comment that there was evidence of monopolistic
practice on the part of the VVBs.[70] There was reason to believe that
many VVBs had been acting contrary to the wishes of central
planning institutions, as after 1966 the power of some VVBs to
negotiate prices was curtailed, and the ministry of finance assumed a
more interventionist role in supervising credit arrangements.
Proposals to reform the Law on Enterprises, permitting greater
control over enterprise management by the industrial ministries,
were resisted strongly by the VVB directors.

Some Western social scientists have commented that the creation
of the VVBs provided a springboard for the intrusion of a
managerial technocratic interest within the ranks of the SED. The
Sixth Congress of the SED had recognised the rights of young
technical experts to become Party members, and Ludz[71] argued that

this later led to their penetration of leadership circles, and contributed to the success of the SED elites in conducting a policy of modernisation in East Germany, although the strategic clique of older-style Party members still retained ultimate control. Bayliss[72] challenged this analysis of the recruitment of technical experts into leadership circles, but he does endorse the view that the VVB directors operated from a basis of technocratic power which eventually manifested itself in the changing ideological statements of the SED as it sought to incorporate this group.

While in this chapter it is not proposed to examine the nature of management recruitment into the Polish industrial association, it is necessary to bear in mind the consequences of the East German VVBs in this respect. It could be argued that the pressures of taut planning and growth strategy in Poland in the mid-1960s, plus the impact of the European Economic Community upon Polish trade with the West[73], did not permit the industrial association management such discretion as in East Germany. Only four industrial associations were entrusted with discretionary powers and they were the subject of an experiment under the guidance of the Polish Economics Society (PTE).[74] The industrial associations were in joinery and construction (ZPSB), in pharmaceuticals (ZPF – Polfa), nitrates (ZPA), and shipbuilding (ZPO).

Experiments in four industrial associations, 1966–8: constructing the socialist corporation

While there is evidence that a much more ambitious programme of enterprise integration was under way in the GDR a more restrained attitude prevailed in Poland with experiments into industrial associations confined to only four associations, one of which, in shipbuilding (ZPO), is not well documented. A brief summary of the major innovations in these associations now follows.

The association in the shipbuilding industry was made the subject of an experiment during 1966 and 1967. To achieve a tight degree of integration, the enterprises within the ZPO were to be steered by 6 directive indices,[75] but there was to be no restriction on employment, and the size of the Wages Fund would be regulated by a parameter expressing the labour intensity of production costs. It is impossible to assess the effects of this on the relative powers of the association and enterprise management as there is only reference to the uncontrolled rise in overtime worked in the plant which suggested that the relaxation of employment controls encouraged by the new bonus scheme introduced in 1964 might be increasing the share of labour costs in production.[76] A more scathing judgment on this from a representative of the NBP argued that the industrial association was in possession of the necessary information to calculate accurately the size of the Wages Fund in order to provide the NBP and the ministry with information in advance, but instead management chose not to do so.[77]

Much more information is available about the association of joinery and carpentry which was a leading association in the construction industry involved in 17 branch agreements with a total of over 500 factories.[78] Although there was some delay in approving the statutory basis for the association[79], the emphasis was upon reducing the reliance upon directives limits and norms passed on to the enterprise, increasing the importance of long-term planning and finance, and assessing performance mainly in terms of final value of output. The association was granted considerable freedom in employment and domestic and foreign marketing, but the Wages Fund was regulated by long-term limits. The ZPSB was one of a very few industrial associations in which association officials had been entitled to a share in the distribution from the enterprise Factory Fund, and the close link of the Factory Fund and the Wages Fund to overall association performance tended to be a powerful instrument, encouraging worker interest in the economic experiment (although, as we shall see, this was not without generating problems for industrial relations expressed in a high rate of turnover of the factory workforce and absenteeism).[80] There was much emphasis on encouraging workforce identification: it was the explicit policy of the association kolegium, at least once a year, to open its sessions to include representatives of the Workers' Councils from various enterprises so that they could voice their opinions on both social welfare and technical-economic matters of production within the association. This was the continuation of an earlier policy begun in 1962 when Technical-Economic Commissions were appointed in enterprises in the association in order to work out enterprise plans and agree upon the necessary directive indices with the association, and in which workforce representatives participated.[81]

The remaining two industrial associations were both from the chemical industry from which much was expected in terms of general economic growth and exports. The association of the nitrates industry (ZPA) was relatively new, having been set up in January 1965 to co-ordinate a number of large chemical combines and service units.[82] It was decided that this association should conduct its business in a manner analogous to that of a Western corporation. Decisions on policy were to be made by the 'kolegium' and the chief association director, but the latter was to have complete responsibility for setting enterprise production targets. After 1966 the number of directive indices was to be limited to four main areas supplemented by various 'limits' and 'norms'.[83] The chief director of the association could intervene in the course of the year to change these directive indices and adjust enterprise production targets to national needs. The direct control over internal pricing policy for the association and direct negotiation over wage and employment levels with the chemical workers' trade union signified a high degree of centralised control over enterprise business. The association was also able to conduct directly its own domestic sales and exports policy (with the provision of extra bonuses for high levels of exports), and access to a foreign currency bank account in Warsaw could enable direct purchase of foreign capital goods.

In assessing the experiment in the ZPA, it is clear that decision-making powers were highly centralised in the hands of the chief director, and that the enterprises were not functioning as full cost-accounting units. The chief director's control over the enterprise Wages Fund was an indirect means of controlling personnel policy in the enterprises, but he was more or less autonomous in making new appointments and setting wage rates for ZPA Central Office staff. The statute of the ZPA had specified that the main deliberations in the annual planning process were to take place between May and July, well in advance of the plan year, so that the implications of ministry proposals could be considered fully by the association, enterprise management, workers' self-management representatives and the economic committee of the local national councils, yet the power to change enterprise targets plus association requests for frequent reports from enterprises clearly negated this, having serious implications for the role of the kolegium and Technical-Economic Council. Perhaps it is the recognition that the ZPA could wield considerable influence over enterprise policy that provoked the chemical industry ministry, the NBP and other central institutions to intervene and issue more directives, limits and norms than they were supposed to by law.[84]

The experiment in the association of the pharmaceuticals industry (ZPF – Polfa) was considered to be the most successful of the four in providing rapid economic results. It was a very large grouping of enterprises dating back to 1948, and when it was chosen for the experiment in 1966 it consisted of 11 enterprises but was linked to as many as 46 others through branch agreements. The structure of production is significant: while 96% of its products were pharmaceuticals, because of the nature of health care there were no wild fluctuations in demand. In 1967, 56.7% of its production was directly handed over to the ministry of health and 36.4% was sold abroad. The ZPF thus occupied a near monopoly position in Polish pharmaceuticals.

Considerations of industrial structure become important when examining the high degree of centralised managerial control within Polfa that ensued from the experiment after 1966. The chemicals ministry was to prescribe six directive indices (excluding employment)[85] but the proposed overhaul of internal pricing within the association, and the tying of enterprise funds for development,

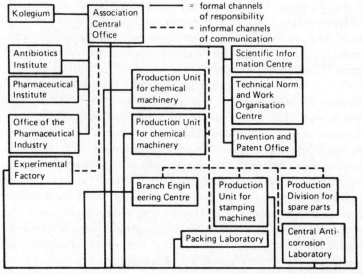

Fig. 3.   The association of the pharmaceutical industry ZPF-Polfa
Source: H. Tarchalska, 'Eksperyment gospoḍarczy zjednoczenia przemystu **farmaceuticznego Polfa**', in 'Konferencja Naukowa n.t. doswiadzcenia zjednoczén eksperymentujacych', PTE papers, Warsaw, 1968

exports and wages to the profit balance of both enterprise and
association as a whole, gave the association management considerable influence over enterprises. The incentive to link industrial
production within its enterprises more directly to foreign trade was
encouraged by the merger of the foreign trade office and the
association. The centralised power to intervene in enterprise
production was too much of a temptation for Polfa management,
made long-term planning difficult,[86] and encouraged the development of a complex bureaucratic structure at the headquarters of the
association as will be evident from Fig. 3.

The four experiments in perspective

Much of the summary in Fig. 3 was gleaned from reports presented
at a conference held in March 1968 by the PTE.[87] A later study
argued that the most distinctive aspect of the experiment was the
greater degree of integration achieved among enterprises, but at the
expense of increased control from the association office. In all the
associations, the director could change directive indices during the
year, and the tighter financial accounting could link all enterprises
together as a whole and be used as the basis for measuring profit and
financial performance. This illustrated a move towards centralisation. More specifically, tying the bonus scheme to aggregate
performance of all enterprises (in ZPSB) the development of a
uniform system of financial accounting for exports (Polfa) and the
use of a common measure of the value of final products (ZPA) all left
less discretionary power in the hands of enterprise management.[88]
There were conflicting opinions on the desirability and extent of
such centralisation. It was generally agreed that the reduction in the
number of directive indices regulating association business and set
by the ministry had allowed them greater flexibility in allocating
resources and implementing plans, and that, in turn, this had a
beneficial effect upon the enterprises who received fewer indices and
were assured of certain services provided by the association that
hitherto had been outside its control and unreliable (research and
development, spare parts etc.). A questionnaire distributed under
the auspices of the business weekly *Życie Gospodarcze* and the Instytut
Planowania asked enterprise management to rank eight aspects of
reform in order of preference. In all cases the reduction of the
number of directive indices was placed either first or second.[89]

Yet enterprise management continued to find particular directive indices very irritating: controls on employment (ZPA), restrictions on investment inputs (ZPA and ZPSB) and limits on the share of costs in total output (ZPA) were mentioned.[90] Opinions on central control of association and enterprise funds were divided. Only the ZPSB found this acceptable (probably because it did not make a break with past experience) and in both the ZPA and Polfa enterprise management and workers' self-management organisations alike were united in finding the degree of enterprise independence to be unsatisfactory.[91] Feelings ran particularly high in the enterprises in these two associations concerning their inability to control the expense arising from the growth of association bureaucracy. These frustrations were expressed in their low opinion of the 'usefulness' of the kolegium actively to influence association policy.[92] Thus in the ZPA and Polfa, decision-making powers had been increasingly centralised in the hands of management, although this was not so pronounced in the ZPSB where there was also some provision for workforce representation in association decision-making.[93]

It would be incorrect to stress the enhanced status of association management without qualification. The industrial ministries were reluctant to relinquish control over the fixing of directives and rendered the application of long-term financial norms impossible by frequently changing them in the course of the year. It is probable that this accounts for the general reluctance to experiment with new forms of management, despite the greater discretionary powers of association management over internal work organisation.[94] Many features of the command model of planning and management were evident in enterprise behaviour, from concealing spare capacity to tying bonus schemes to plan fulfilment, be it wasteful and irrational or not.

To what extent had these experiments encouraged the merger of enterprises into a socialist corporation? Polish economists acknowledged that concentration and specialisation of production drives enterprises into larger economic organisations,[95] and in the case of the three industrial associations the following aspects of concentration and specialisation were given as an example: the uniform nature and interrelatedness of production (Polfa and ZPSB) a high degree of co-operation between enterprises in the association (ZPA); a common basic raw material (ZPSB) or central control over supplies

(Polfa); a single major customer (Polfa and ZPSB) and a large share of production directed at the export market (Polfa and ZPA). It is true that the enterprises were encouraged to act like the divisions of a large Western corporation, but the whole corporate autonomy could only be imperfect in what was still basically a command economy.

This becomes more evident when we turn to an examination of the fate of other industrial associations in the light of the changes that took place within the planning and management mechanism after 1964. Many industrial associations were accused of resigning themselves in advance to a state of impotence when making policy for their branch of industry. A reactive rather than an innovatory strategy was the normal pattern for association management. Brief statistical research rather than thorough evaluation of enterprise performance, bargaining rather than accounting principles were used in allocating resources to enterprises and technical development, while stock requirements and a long-term investment policy were ignored. Even with the transfer from Budget to Bank finance, investment proposals were badly presented, the ministries continued to intervene and specify the size and type of new investment tasks, and association management and Bank officials would collude to restrict finance to enterprises.[96] Management within the industrial associations continued to be a process resting on administration and bargaining. Collective decision-making through association kolegia was a façade for increased powers of association directors.[97] In September 1967 a report was made of an investigation begun in August 1965 by the Institute of Law at the Polish Academy of Sciences in conjunction with the ministries of domestic trade, the chemical industry, heavy industry, and the food processing industry. It concluded that enterprise autonomy suffered significant incursions on the part of the industrial association. This was particularly in evidence in the position of the enterprise director who was insufficiently legally protected for the many responsibilities that were entrusted to him. This encouraged a style of management behaviour displaying either extreme caution or a never-ending cycle of explanations and appeals over decisions.[98]

The VII Plenum of the PZPR Central Committee in 1966 had criticised many of these 'incorrect tendencies and phenomena' in the behaviour of industrial association management. It called for more consultation of the workforce affected by the economic reforms, urging the appointment of factory commissions to 'improve' enterprise organisation and to 'rationalise' cadre (personnel) policy.[99] Yet, as we have stated earlier, much of the responsibility for these 'incorrect tendencies and phenomena' could be laid at the door of the industrial ministries who conducted a fierce policy of interference in association business. This was made the subject of a doctoral thesis that issued a questionnaire to 100 industrial associations. It was concluded that the number of directive indices issued was not so much a problem as the frequent inspections and requests for reports demanded by a number of central economic institutions. The frequency and intensity of these inspections varied: it was most intensive on the part of the industrial ministry, where the various departments of the ministry (production, planning, finance, labour and technical supplies etc.) dealt directly with the association. The inspections by the Planning Commission would be only intermittent, whilst for the ministries, the NBP, GUS and national councils, it was an ongoing process. It was estimated that the inquiries and investigations conducted in some industrial associations could occupy the staff for up to 200 days per annum! Most of these investigations were of an *ad hoc* nature and there was no central co-ordination, and no pooling of information gleaned from the association.[100]

To summarise, we are of the impression that a process of enterprise integration into industrial associations took place, but without ceding complete autonomy to these corporate structures. The increase in the power of industrial associations stimulated a frenzy of bureaucratic interaction with the enterprises coming out worst. The danger that industrial associations might abuse their market position was a major consideration for the industrial ministries. This could only be discouraged by avoiding the location of the majority of branch production in the control of a single association, by encouraging firms to co-operate with units outside of the association, by opening up competition from foreign trade, or by ensuring constant scrutiny.[101] So it would seem that the original conception in 1958 of the industrial association, namely to create an autonomous intermediate link in the planning and management hierarchy, was not realised. The law of 1958 had restricted their independence by denying associations the opportunity of independent accounting status. This had repercussions for staff, because in the majority of cases incentives schemes were not generous, and thus staff were recruited who had qualifications that were inferior to those who worked in industrial enterprise management. Nor was the 1958 reform successful in adapting the structure of industrial associations to the requirements of each branch of industry. The technical needs of integration and specialisation were catered for in an eclectic way, most outstanding amongst which was the construction of a few massive single-site combines and the emergence of multi-factory enterprises. In the course of the reforms that followed the Fourth PZPR Congress in 1964, the industrial associations acquired an independent commercial status (which meant that they were able to offer employees more generous bonuses, and could attract better qualified staff)[102] and their power over resource allocation, supplies, investment, sales and exports meant that they possessed the potential to determine the policy for their branch of industry. Yet this potential was not realised on account of the intervention of the industrial ministries and other central state institutions. This fostered inertia and conservatism at a level of management where an innovatory and risk-taking attitude was required. It was ironical that the very institutions that wished to achieve a greater dynamism in industrial development were at the same time afraid of granting the independence necessary to achieve this.

4

The emergence of a corporate structure in Polish industry, 1968–80

The climate of economic policy in the late 1960s is most important when trying to understand the reforms in industrial structure. The phrase 'scientific-technological revolution' peppered the debate on growth strategy. It was the scientific-technological revolution that would harness the forces of production and enable the Polish economy to travel across the threshold of extensive to intensive development. At the Fifth PZPR Congress in 1968, great emphasis was placed upon raising a flagging growth rate while simultaneously improving individual and social consumption. Annual increases in labour productivity of between 5% and 6% per annum were to be aimed at while simultaneously maintaining conditions of full employment.[1] Two important elements in achieving this would be foreign trade and industrial organisation.

Foreign trade, and more specifically exports, had been a priority ever since the V Plenum of the PZPR Central Committee in 1966. One hundred enterprises all specialising in the production of goods for export (and drawn from 20 industrial associations) were singled out for special treatment, which by 1968 included a much more flexible attitude towards fulfilling plan targets[2] and special arrangements for bonuses and retaining 10% of foreign currency earnings for the purchase of new working capital from abroad. Many of these firms were located in the chemicals and engineering industries where it was felt that an acceleration of investment and output would both encourage exports of these products and reduce the reliance upon imported high technology goods.

Again the assumption was made that large production units and enterprise integration would encourage greater technological innovation. One Western commentator has remarked that Polish industry tends to feature a low level of mass production and long production runs, especially in engineering.[3] It was obvious then that organisational change in Polish industry would be on the agenda. The mediocre results of the industrial associations had encouraged the expression of a variety of views on this subject that can basically be divided into two categories: those who advocated the concentration of all decisions about production at the level of the industrial association (thereby restricting enterprise autonomy), and those who envisaged the association as an agency for co-ordination with limited rights of intervention in the field of enterprise management. Amongst the former, some economists felt that it would be desirable to revert to the structure of industrial management in existence before 1950 when the industrial association conducted business after the fashion of a Western corporation. This had long been the aim of Bogdań Glinski who proposed gathering enterprises into horizontally integrated combines (*koncerny socjalistyczny*) with enterprise management losing many powers of independent decision-making, but gaining a greater degree of integration. The degree of centralisation within the *koncern* would vary according to the requirements of the branch of industry and would be particularly suited to the following conditions: where the branch of industry was not too extensive and was well concentrated; where the process of production was relatively simple and not subject to fluctuations of demand for supplies or sales; and where there already existed an extensive network of co-operative links between enterprises. The benefits of all this would be a greater degree of integration of research and development and economies of scale in management, capital and marketing.[4] The Resolution of the Fifth PZPR Congress reflected this division of opinion by acknowledging the need for several different forms of enterprise integration, many of which we have already touched on in the last chapter.[5] It was against this background that the 'Combine Experiment' was launched during 1969 and 1970.[6]

The Combine Experiment

The combines were set up between 1970 and 1973 and were associated with other reforms in the planning process, investment, prices and of course the notorious move to standardise bonus systems and constrain the growth in wages.[7] The Combine Experiment thus bridged the politically sensitive year of 1970–1. It could be argued that there was nothing innovatory about the combine in a centrally planned economy. They had first been used in the Soviet Union in the 1920s, and again in the 1960s. However, the immediate inspiration for the Polish Combine Experiment came not from the USSR but from the GDR.

In 1967 the GDR government announced that combines consisting of closely integrated enterprises directly accountable to the central government ministries would be set up. Although this was within the terms of reference of the New Economic System (with the emphasis upon long-term planning, optimal use of productive assets, self-financing of investment and a contract-based distribution policy), it was evident that the combines had been designed to overcome the divergence of the VVBs from central policy preferences. As a rule they brought together enterprises within a particular region, either replacing the VVB (as in the textile industry) or drawing together enterprises from different branches of production that were engaged in co-operative activity with the VVB. These combines, however, were equivalent to an enterprise in law, and this meant that the enterprises within them had no autonomy to operate as such any longer. The enterprises were integrated mainly through the use of a synthetic index for evaluating economic performance, and only the combine as a whole operated as a full cost-accounting unit. The enterprises within the combine, while not full cost-accounting units, were expected to cover their own costs of production and to distribute their profits into various funds from which deductions were made towards the upkeep of the combine as a whole. Although the combine was responsible for ensuring that its enterprises kept to the annual production plan and quarterly financial guidelines for the combine as a whole, the enterprise management had a marginal degree of independence in negotiating credit.[8]

Despite the enthusiasm for the East German combines expressed in the pages of *Życie Gospodarcze* in 1968 and 1969 they were not an unqualified success, and the central planners' return to a more administrative-directive style of management after 1971 was prompted partially, if not wholly, by the fear that combine management was too independent. Because of the economies of scale at their disposal, the combines had squeezed many smaller factories out of production, and Western writers noted that there was some evidence to accuse the combines of monopolistic practices.[9] There was a change of attitude in the early 1970s on the part of the Poles who found much to criticise in the confused approach to enterprise integration and specific needs for centralisation in differing industries.[10]

The combines that were created in Poland between 1970 and 1972 were influenced very much by the East German model. It must not go unnoticed, though, that if combines are defined purely as multi-factory enterprises, then these had been in existence in Poland since the late 1950s and early 1960s, especially in the steel, chemicals and copper industries.[11] The essential difference from the 'new' combines was that these traditional combines were administered by a single-management structure and located in a single area.[12] For the new combines set up after 1969 this was not to be the case. Enterprises miles distant from one another and often located in different local government areas were merged to form a single economic unit. The organisational arrangements for the combines were left to the discretion of the appropriate industrial ministries, who were to appoint a Branch Commission and specific work teams (as occurred in the machine tools industry).[13] The combines could be made accountable either to the ministry or to the industrial association (the former was the case in the chemicals industry, while the latter case prevailed in engineering). So initially there were two types of combine: the *kombinat-zjednoczenie* possessing a relatively broad scope of responsibility with its management organisationally separate from that of the enterprises, and the *kombinat-przedsiębiorstwo*, which was supervised directly from the ministry.[14] There were five criteria for combination,[15] most of them conforming to the principle of horizontal integration (i.e. on the basis of a common production process), although vertical integration (i.e. the production process passes through all stages from transformation of raw materials to the final product) was encouraged by Decree 193/1969; but because of the prevalence of an industrial administration that had hitherto encouraged only horizontal integration, it was rarely implemented. The total number of enterprise and other units (including research institutes, sales and trade offices, repair and construction units) could vary according to need.[16]

The management structure of the combines involved the selection of a leading factory (*zakład wiodący*) which would assume the function of general co-ordination and administration. In practice this meant that the duties of the director of the leading factory were duplicated: he was responsible both for the activity of his own factory and for the activity of the combine as a whole. His powers would include the right to centralise all organisational planning, analysis and auditing within the control of the leading factory. The only exception to this arrangement was in the sulphur processing combine for which there was an administrative structure entirely separate from any of the component factories. It must also be noted that this combine was made accountable not to an industrial association, but to the ministry.[17] Consultation with management of the different units within the combine was to be achieved through a kolegium to be attended by the chief combine director and his deputies, the chief accountant and the directors of the factories and other units within the combine.[18] It was possible for the combine director to exercise his discretion and invite representatives from workers' self-management, trade unions and officials from foreign trade offices and the NBP, but they could participate in kolegium meetings in an advisory capacity only.

As to the actual combines that emerged, the initial policy was to confine them to the engineering and chemicals industry. There were 13 combines in the former, encompassing 20% of the total number of enterprises (66 enterprises, 4 construction offices, 3 supply offices and 8 research units in all).[19] In particular, enterprises within the association of the machine tools industry were chosen.[20] By the late 1960s there was excess demand for machine tools and the failure to meet this was attributed to the general stagnation of the industry. Prior to the decision to rearrange production into combines, various other exercises had been attempted.[21] It is thus understandable that this industrial association was designated as a priority case for investment resources after the II Plenum of the PZPR Central Committee in 1969; later the enterprises were rearranged into 8 combines.[22] In addition there were a further 5 combines in the engineering industry that were controlled by different industrial associations.[23] In the chemical industry, the only major venture was to adapt the sulphur processing combine to the new structure.

The majority of these combines began to operate in 1970, but the principles of Decree 193/1969 still continued to be applied to enterprise integration measures well into 1973, long after the announcement that a new comprehensive reform of planning and management was made in May 1972.[24] For example, the organisational advantages of integration were seized upon in the building and construction industry as a means of overcoming the difficulties of co-ordinating numerous small-scale enterprises. Between 1971 and 1974, all the construction industry in Warsaw was reorganised into four combines (three for housing construction and the other for industrial construction).[25] Despite the success claimed for this particular venture, the earlier examples in the combine experiment could not be described as outstanding achievements. In the chemical and engineering industries, which were to be the vanguard of selective and intensive development, there were problems of achieving coherent integration amongst the units combined, and in particular there was confusion about managerial responsibilities. This in turn affected the process of consultation between managerial staff in the kolegium and also with the workforce. Altogether the combines exerted a disturbing effect upon both the planning and the management hierarchy, upon many other central, regional and local organisations such as the NBP, the national councils, and upon PZPR and trade union branches. Whilst many aspects of industrial relations and PZPR control will be examined in Chapters 5 and 6, the author was fortunate in having access to fairly detailed monographs on organisational problems and managerial and workforce attitudes in two industrial combines. These form the basis of the following two case studies.[26]

The combine in the ball bearing industry

This unit (Kombinat Przemysłu Łożysk Tocznych – Prema FLT) was constructed out of a group of enterprises and service organisations that had previously been loosely linked together in the form of a branch union (*zreszenie*) since 1968, because of the similarity of products produced. The four factories in the new combine were geographically dispersed in Kielce, Krasnik, Poznań and Warsaw. (There was also a factory specialising in product experimentation, a marketing office and a central construction office of the combine.) The factory in Kielce, Iskra, was the leading factory, which was probably attributable to its dominant role in production (it produced 50% of the total Polish output of ball bearings) and the whole combine was placed under the supervision of the association of precision engineering (ZPP), which controlled 96.6% of national supplies of ball bearings. A combine kolegium, originally consisting of eleven members, but later expanded to include a further three, was empowered with the legal responsibility for decision-making in the matter of planning common production undertakings, finance activity, development and general welfare policy.[27]

Despite the very specific clarification of the rights and duties of all units in the combine statute, in the course of transition to the new structure several problems arose between plant management and workforce which were not candidly resolved, and which eventually exerted a detrimental effect on the operation of the combine.

The relationship between the leading factory management and that of the other factories was a major source of friction. The chief director of the combine had previously been the secretary of the *zreszenie* and so it was not really surprising that Iskra, the factory situated in Kielce, which he managed, became the leading factory of the combine as it probably already possessed the necessary administrative staff. The precise scope of managerial power of the leading factory was left to negotiations between the ministry, the association and the chief director of the combine. However, the use of Iskra (which was also a major production unit) as a leading factory was found to be unsatisfactory, and in mid-1971 a separate combine administration was set up.[28] One of the reasons for this can be traced to the deterioration in relations between the management of the leading factory and that of the component factories, the latter considering the combine director to be too favourably disposed towards the interests of the leading factory.[29] The primary cause is to be found in the increased powers acquired by the combine director from the industrial association and the ministry during 1970 and 1971. The combine director could assign export tasks, fix financial norms, allocate materials, decide on the introduction of new technology and make investment policy. He could also make changes in the administrative organisation of the factories, negotiate credit agreements with the NBP and the Foreign Trade Bank (with respect to investment credit and the import of capital equipment), decide on the size of the Wages Fund and of bonuses for export activity, 'rationalisation' drives and fix internal transfer prices. Obviously many of these powers implied the right of combine management to interfere in the daily production process of factories rather than just the right to work out the long-term implications for development policy. This could be resented by the management of the plant within the combine (who after all had considerable experience in independent decision-making when their plant had operated as independent enterprises before inclusion in the combine) but it was difficult for them to challenge combine management effectively as the latter had a majority of seats in the kolegium (6 out of 11 in 1970).[30]

Nevertheless, it would be incorrect to assume that a ruthless centralisation of control had taken place. Rather, there was a certain amount of confusion in the planning and management process. For example, the factories in the combine specialised in substantially different areas of production, were geographically distant from one another, and so all tended to organise supplies, construction, personnel policy, credit negotiations and repairs independently. The only effective reason for their integration in the combine was for research and development purposes. Whilst research and development offices had previously been split between enterprises in Warsaw, Krasnik and Kielce, they were centralised at the leading factory headquarters in Kielce after 1972. It was questionable whether this produced economies of scale, as research and development needs varied between factories, who resented the centralisation of this service. Thus it is not surprising that factory management in the combine sought to maintain a wide margin of discretion in decision-making despite the legal powers for integration at the disposal of the combine director.[31] Such a disparate gathering of production units caused one economist to question whether the leading factory undertook any tasks of leadership in the combine at all as the annual combine plan appeared to be little more than the aggregate of all individual factory plans.[32]

The deterioration of inter-factory relations was not to be explained purely by shortcomings on the part of the combine management. Interference in current production on the part of the industrial association, the ministry and the NBP was more frequent and was disliked. Most of the directive indices for production and finance had to be agreed not only with the combine management but also with the industrial association, which, from the viewpoint of the individual factories, made planning a very protracted process. An analysis of the number and nature of regulations received by the combine management in 1971 revealed that the ministry of engineering was most prone to intervention closely followed by the industrial association. While those issued by the ministry reflected a concern with long-term development, the association was more concerned with immediate short-term questions. Perhaps this can be attributed to the shifting balance of power that took place between

combine and association directors during 1970–1. The combine
director had taken over responsibility for several matters that had
hitherto been the preserve of the association (especially marketing
and development policy, although the association still maintained a
strong interest in investment, resource allocation, capital repairs
and pricing policy), so association interference was perhaps
symptomatic of a perceived challenge to its authority from the
combine.[33] An attitudinal survey of the socio-political *aktyw* or
activists (a term referring to all those holding PZPR trade union or
Workers' Council office) in the factory at Poznań revealed that an
overwhelming majority considered the combine management to be a
superfluous level in the industrial administration, and saw the
existence of the combine as facilitating greater ministry and
association control and intervention in everyday management
affairs. While the staff in the non-leading factory in Poznań were
suspicious that the creation of the combine masked a conspiracy
against their independence (in the guise of increasing 'bureaucratisation'), staff in the leading factory in Kielce were more favourably
disposed to the combine.[34] In contrast, it is interesting to observe
that officials in the local *wojewodztwo* committees of the PZPR
(outside Kielce), for whom the creation of the combine had
drastically limited their powers of influence over industrial enterprises, supported the industrial association in making frequent
checks on combine management.[35] From this we can conclude that
the bombardment of the factories in the combine with a multitude of
conflicting directives from the combine management, the ministry
and the industrial association presented an obstacle to the narrowly
conceived objective of rational planning and management,[36] and
shifting coalitions between the PZPR, industrial association, ministry and combine management and workforce emerged illustrating
the arguments of Staniszkis and Narojek[37] that economic reform
produces a 'pathological' response in organisational structure, and
that it has different effects on all the interested parties.

These interests were easily aroused by the arrangements for wages
and bonuses which were manipulated by the combine management
so as to be in favour of the leading factory, Iskra. For example, the
combine could allocate an additional 10% of profit to be distributed
as bonuses in plants specialising in exports, and could also freely
allocate 5% of a reserve bonus fund for special tasks. This tended to
favour the workforce of the leading factory. Moreover, as the general

system of material incentives was such that, for management in each factory, 50% of quarterly bonus payments were dependent upon the results of their factory, and 50% were dependent upon the results of the combine as a whole, it is not surprising that this caused much friction between factory management over the process of allocating supplies adequate to achieving the bonus conditions.[38]

If disputes arose there needed to be some procedure for settling them, but this was conspicuously lacking during the first few years of the existence of the combine. In 1970 there was an attempt to draw up a formal procedure to resolve differences between factory management in the combine, but although proposals were passed on to the ministry and the association, no reply was received,[39] and in general it fell to the combine director (who was also the director of the Kielce plant – Iskra) to settle any disagreement, which must have further soured inter-plant management relations. Yet, it was the failure to take workforce consultation seriously that produced particularly bad industrial relations in the combine. Much of this is attributable to the ambivalent stance taken by the Council of Ministers and the Central Trade Union Council on worker self-management structures for the combine. A joint directive in December 1969 specified that in all units in the combine a conference of workers' self-management should have powers of scrutiny over production in that factory, but that there should be none for the combine as a whole. Rather only an advisory council of self-management representatives for the combine (attended by the Chairman of the Trade Union Council, the Secretary of the PZPR Factory Committee plus the factory director) was proposed.[40] In the ball bearing combine, sessions were presided over by the Chairman of the Workers' Council of the leading factory and were to serve as a means of ventilating matters already raised at the factory level KSR, and of discussing annual and quarterly plans for the whole combine. The combine director had the duty of attending these sessions to explain combine policy and was obliged to implement any recommendations made (although he could veto measures that he considered contrary to the interest of the combine) and could send in his representatives to individual KSR meetings and would invite the chairman of the Workers' Councils to attend occasional sessions of the combine kolegium.[41] Two years later, in December 1971, there was a change in these arrangements to broaden the scope of representation which it was felt at the time had reflected people mainly in management positions rather than in the workforce. In the new Conference of Combine Self-Management Representatives (KPSRK), two of the four delegates would have to be working on the shop floor, and channels were opened so that the youth organisation (ZMS) and professional bodies (NOT and PTE) could be invited to send observers to sessions, which would take place every quarter in each factory in rotation, with a simple majority vote of 2/3 necessary to make or reverse policy decisions. Only after consultation with the industrial association, the ministry and the chief executive of the metalworkers trade union (ZGZZM) could the combine director suspend a resolution of the KPSRK. He was to provide the necessary information and documentation at least 14 days in advance to be distributed by the presidium of the Workers' Council in the leading factory, which made the administrative arrangements for the KPSRK.[42] Even after these changes, worker discontent was not abated, and the Workers' Councils in the factories continued to be the main forum for raising grievances against the management of the leading factory, which included disbanding the combine, placing it under the direct control of the ministry or ending the privileged status of the leading factory.[43]

In conclusion, this case study reveals that an attempt to concentrate the production of ball bearings and associated products by re-grouping enterprises within a new management structure had contributed neither to greater efficiency of production, nor to a more co-ordinated development nor to good industrial relations. The 'organisational pathology' (or organisational survival and control over the environment in a situation of change) had encouraged inter-plant rivalry between management and a concentration of power in the leading factory, but at the same time central planning institutions had reacted by demanding more frequent information reports from the factories and issued more directives to restrict the autonomy of a unit that was supposed to exemplify a corporate unity and independence.

The combine in the sulphur processing industry

As in the case of the ball bearing combine, the purpose of establishing a combine in the sulphur processing industry was to bring the industrial association and other central planning authorities into a much closer relationship of co-ordination with factories in the sulphur industry, thereby fostering the strategy of 'selective and intensive industrial development'. The decision was made in March 1970 to gather together three mines, a processing unit, a marketing office, and to build two new plants – all of which would henceforth function as a combine.[44] What was initially the leading factory was situated in Machów near Tarnobrzeg, which was a poor agricultural region with a surplus of labour, and peasant-workers were typical amongst those employed. The search for sulphur had begun in 1953, and in 1958 a sulphur processing works was constructed in Machów to begin production in December 1960. The works was a large single-site combine (employment was 2,500 in 1959 but rose to 3,500 in 1962). Thus, prior to the rearrangements in 1970, there already existed a considerable degree of integration in the old combine, and the leading factory in Machów contributed 75% of total output.[45]

After July 1970 it was decided that a separate management unit for the whole combine would be located at Machów, which would take over the role of the leading factory.[46] The respective powers of the combine management and director *vis à vis* the other factories were outlined in documents in April and October 1970. The combine was to be run according to the specification of Decree 193/1969, as a full cost-accounting unit on the basis of one-man management. It would be able to set prices for services and by-products (although not for raw sulphur which was a centrally listed commodity), decide on its own cadre (personnel) policy and organise its own purchase of raw materials. The combine administration exercised considerable control over economic policy. It set the directive indices controlling allocations to and distribution from various funds for investment, turnover, technical progress and central administration. As well as fixing the size of employment and wages, it also set the principles of cost-accounting and supervised domestic trade arrangements. Although factory directors within the combine could devise their own plans for resource allocation and development (this meant that they were responsible for the management of fixed capital, for the distribution of profits via the Factory, Wages, and Bonus Funds, and for banking and credit policy), they were also responsible for implementing general combine policy, especially that which was agreed by the kolegium. Their control over wage and bonus payments, and the organisation of production within their factory, was circumscribed by the ruling of the combine director.

The continuing observance of the principle of one-man management within such a highly integrated structure as the sulphur processing combine, gave wide scope to the chief combine director. He was responsible for endorsing the technical-economic and investment plans, setting the directive indices and approving performance of all individual factories and units in the combine. Any reports they might wish to send to the ministry, GUS etc., or any communication with the PZPR and other 'socio-political organisations' (such as local government) and the media, had to receive the authorisation of the combine director. His control over personnel policy extended to approval of all appointments to senior management posts (subject to confirmation from the ministry).

This official centralisation of authority in the hands of the chief director and combine management was a source of disputes as factory management gradually found their initiative circumscribed (especially in the organisation of the labour process and cadre policy). The failure to consult factory directors was frequent. For example, in 1971, what turned out to be impossible targets for labour productivity and employment were set by the combine management after consultation with the ministry, the Planning Commission and the NBP only.[47] Another source of contention was the fixing of wage and bonus levels. If earnings of employees in combine management were compared with those of analogous employees in other factories, then the former certainly appeared to be higher.[48] When the combine began to function in 1970, the high export premium for workers in one of the factories was cut to make it fit in line with the conditions operating in the combine management. The friction generated by such examples rarely erupted into a full-scale dispute resulting in work stoppages, as this would reduce output and result in further loss of earnings.[49]

Thus inter-management relations were such that the official division of responsibility, the principle of one-man management and the system of material incentives, discouraged a collective integrated approach towards policy-making. Theoretically these problems could have been resolved through debate in the combine kolegium, but the chief director's control over senior management appointments tended to produce a very one-sided representation of views in an institution that only met a bare minimum of four times in 1970. Personnel appointments were such that, except for the chief combine director (who had previously been director of the Krasnieński Glass

Works), there was no major change in the composition of senior management, most having held posts of responsibility in enterprises and other units now within the combine. Yet several of the enterprise directors did not receive a post in the combine management, and thus suffered a loss of status, earnings and independence when their plant ceased to be fully independent cost-accounting units on entry into the combine. One study revealed that they expressed their dissatisfaction with combine management by informal appeals for support to the industrial association and also to the local Wojewodztwo Committee of the PZPR.[50]

As to arrangements for central supervision of the combine, after one year's operation in early 1971, the ministry of the chemicals industry took over direct control, but by late 1971 had again entrusted the combine to control by a newly formed industrial association in Kraków for which the combine provided 80% of all output. As well as a near monopoly in the production of sulphur in Poland, the combine thus overshadowed all other production units in the association. The motivation of the ministry in creating this industrial association was construed by one commentator to be a general distaste for the time-consuming activity of directly supervising the combine along with all the other tasks.[51] However, whether this was wise from the point of view of encouraging management co-operation between the association and the combine is another matter. There is reason to believe that the combine was construed as a threat by association management, and the association was seen as an unnecessary source of interference in the eyes of combine management. Attitudinal studies reveal that staff in the plant at Machów were keen to eliminate interference by the industrial association (which was seen as economically unjustifiable), while in the plant at Grzybów staff wanted to disband the combine and return to the former arrangement (*zreszenie*) within which they had greater independence and were free from the prying of combine management. Their grievance was stimulated by the fact that the Grzybów plant was more profitable, and to them it appeared that they were carrying the burden of the Machów plant and combine administration.[52] It is thus not surprising that Grzybów management found sympathy for their plight in the industrial association.

The other dramatis personae were the two *wojewodztwo* councils and PZPR committees in Rzeszów and Kielce. For them the prize for having the combine management headquarters located in their territory was extra revenue from taxation (it must not be forgotten that the combine was a full cost-accounting unit and could only be taxed as a whole). It was not surprising that competition was fierce between these local authorities when the combine was first proposed, and that resentment on the part of the Rzeszów authority that lost out expressed itself in a propensity for intrigue with the Grzybów factory against the Machów plant and combine headquarters.[53]

Finally, industrial relations between workforce and management had deteriorated in the course of setting up the combine, mainly because the four major factories, having lost their status as independent enterprises (the ambiguity of their status was heightened with the splitting of the Machów plant into four separate units), were deprived of the right to hold official meetings of the Conference of Workers' Self-Management. From April to July 1970 there was no official policy on this. Finally, at a meeting in July, it was agreed that there should be a single Workers' Council for the whole combine and hence a single KSR.[54] The first meeting of the new Combine Workers' Council took place in January 1971, and the KSR met seven times during that year, supplemented by monthly production conferences in the factories. That this arrangement made workforce representation any more effective is to be doubted as it was reported that only one KSR resolution in 1971 received official endorsement from the combine director,[55] suggesting that worker self-management was merely a legal formality to be complied with.

So, as with the previous case study, the combine in the sulphur processing industry added an extra layer of management, which had a disturbing effect on the existing institutions involved in the planning and management process. The conflicting interests of management within the combine and workforce and central planning institutions was the 'pathological' response to greater integration and rationalisation of production.

A general evaluation of the Combine Experiment, 1970–2

Both of the above case studies illustrate the difficulty of introducing a new form of industrial organisation into a pre-existing planning and management hierarchy: the original goals of integration (economies of scale resulting from greater specialisation and technological development) become displaced as the particular interests of management, workforce, central and local government etc. become infringed. This suggests that the process of economic reform is highly politicised, but not in the way that is conventionally thought of. That is, it is not just a question of 'progressive' and 'radical' reform proposals facing a hostile conservative establishment. Polish sociologists have chosen to present this as a question of 'organisational pathology'.[56] In particular, four aspects of this bid for organisational survival and control could be seen in the attempt to integrate enterprises into combines. Firstly, there was misspecification of the scope and purpose of management in the combines, which caused confusion with respect to both internal combine organisation and external relations. Secondly, the 'legalism' of the combine experiment caused many conflicts of interest in the course of planning, which were expressed in more frequent intervention and use of directive indices.[57] Thirdly, where the combine was placed under the supervision of an industrial association (which was the usual case), the latter would be induced to interfere frequently, which was symptomatic of fears that the combine would get 'out of control'. If the association tried to overcome this problem by conceding greater independence to the combine, this would inevitably weaken the association's influence over production in its branch of industry. It would be unwise if the combine controlled a large share of branch production, and might also induce the ministry to intervene more frequently. Finally, the very act of creating a combine would disturb the balance of forces within an industry, arousing the different interests of the association, leading factory and former enterprises, provoking shifting alignments[58] and affecting relations with other organisations such as *wojewodztwo* and *powiat* national councils and PZPR organisations, local branches of the NBP and such central organisations as the ministry of finance, NIK and GUS. It was reported that the NBP, GUS and national councils preferred to deal directly with the factories in the combine rather than with combine management: GUS would approach the factories directly for reports; the divisions of the NBP, which had been accustomed to contacting the factories directly on the matter of credit and the distribution of profit from turnover, continued to do so, and the financial departments of the WRNs were not at all interested in the combine administration as a representative of the factories and were more concerned with the broader question of economic development in their region.[59] The result was that the imprecise delineation of tasks of the association and combine had engendered friction within the planning and management hierarchy rather than a more integrated, harmonious and efficient organisation of production.

The source of this can possibly be traced to the simple fact that, as the enterprises joined the combine, so they lost their independent status. The central policy-makers had not reckoned that this could possibly be of interest to the managers of these factories – but it was, especially when they observed that colleagues in other factories were dictating policy to them, receiving higher bonuses, but were no better qualified than them. One writer noted that the experience of the combines in the GDR had demonstrated the impossibility of competent management of the whole of the combine being achieved by the existing combine administration/leading factory alone.[60] The situation was similar in Poland. Only in such combines as that in the ball bearing industry (where the leading factory Iskra had previously been the leading factory in the *zreszenie*) were management and administrative staff suitably qualified and experienced to cope with the new responsibilities in investment policy, the allocation of raw materials, foreign trade, finance and technological innovation. Inexperience and overload on the part of senior factory staff meant that the association had to intervene frequently – much to the resentment of management in the leading factory.[61]

The negative results of the Combine Experiment during the years 1970–2 prompted the dissolution of several combines and their re-incorporation within the industrial associations. In March 1971 the engineering ministry appointed a commission with the brief of simplifying the structure of organisation within that industry by reducing it to two levels: the association and the enterprise. In April 1971 changes in the finance pricing and wages systems of the combines were devised so that they would acquire the status of industrial associations (the ball bearing combine began operating as an association after January 1972). The whole exercise provided an opportunity to reduce the number of administrative staff and it was claimed that 170 clerical and 350 management posts were saved as a result of this exercise in the engineering industry.[62] There were no such systematic rearrangements in the chemical industry, but it could be noted that the tendency towards 'excessive centralisation' in the sulphur industry was the reason given for the eventual break-up of the combine in 1974.[63]

So it is clear that the Combine Experiment was the source of disturbances in the planning and management process in Poland between 1970 and 1972. Although it was still believed that large production units favoured greater technical innovation, specialisation and higher output, with the combines the immediate effect had been a growth in bureaucracy. The reforming Gierek administration endorsed the search for a more flexible form of enterprise integration. The Polish Economics Society held frequent conferences on this subject, attended by lawyers, economists, sociologists and management from enterprises, associations and combines. By early 1971 the business weekly *Życie Gospodarcze* was holding round-table discussions.[64] In one such discussion it was agreed that the major problems to be resolved in industrial structure were information, management organisation, and cadre policy. The concluding editorial remark made the sardonic comment that the whole discussion about industrial management had been conducted in a military jargon, as if it were a campaign of war. This was considered to be regrettably appropriate to a situation in which the development of new structures of planning and management was still constrained by elements left from the command model or semi-war economy of the 1950s.

Enterprise integration after 1970: the WOG

The guidelines for the Sixth PZPR Congress, which were ratified in September 1971 mentioned that a new economic financial system would be introduced and that work was to begin on the transformation of the basic units of industrial production into Large Production Organisations (*Wielka Organizacja Gospodarcza*–WOGs). The endorsement of this policy at the Sixth PZPR Congress in December 1971 and the discussion alluded to earlier raised the issue of the constitution of such WOGs. A leading figure in the debate, Szymon Jakubowicz, observed that, hitherto, Polish industrial organisation had displayed the following features: large units tended to serve a purely administrative purpose, industrial integration tended to be horizontal, the industrial enterprise was always subordinated to the control of some administrative institution, and enterprise management made minimal use of economic techniques. He illustrated his argument with reference to six industrial associations and concluded that, despite the differing technologies and market situations, the same organisational structure prevailed, with only a small variation in the arrangements for raw materials and resource procurement.[65] He drew the conclusion that the existing structure of the industrial associations (despite the innovations introduced as a result of Decree 383/1966) was not likely to encourage a more dynamic economic outlook, especially as organisational matters were conceived of in such a legalistic fashion. As yet there was an element of uncertainty over the future role of the industrial associations: were they to act as a co-ordinating and service unit for independent firms (which Jakubowicz saw to be analogous to the operation of a large Western corporation) or were they to be a very closely integrated grouping of plants? However, Jakubowicz felt that to pose the question in such a manner was to perpetuate the fundamental error of insisting on a rigid uniformity in industrial organisation: the important point was that industrial organisation should adapt to the organisational requirements of Polish industry. He suggested three models that could be the basis for such developments, only one of which was highly integrated.[66]

As it transpired, the industrial association was to be one of the major structures around which WOGs would be formed, but many economists had considerable reservations about this. The differences of opinion were focussed by the reprinting of Oskar Lange's article 'Centralisation and decentralisation in economics'.[67] Lange's central argument that the strength or weakness of the economic mechanism rest on 'intermediate' levels of management was disputed by other economists, who felt that such 'intermediate' levels could only serve an administrative and not an economic role, and that it was also unwise to accept that 'big is beautiful' with respect to Polish industry.[68] Whilst some like M. Rakowski and H. Sadownik considered the industrial association could fulfil a role similar to a capitalist corporation, others like the aging Professor E. Lipiński proposed an extension of enterprise autonomy.[69]

The open parading of such differences subsided with the appointment of a Party–Government Commission for the Modernisation of the Economy and State Organisation in May 1971. This was hailed as a novel departure in providing a forum not only for PZPR and central government functionaries, but also for academics (although it is possible to see a parallel with the earlier Economic Council of 1957–62, and a Reform Commission set up in 1964). It appointed various work teams, one of which was to investigate the organisation and operation of WOGs, aided by a small permanent staff and academic consultants.[70] In May 1972 the Council of Ministers passed a resolution to prepare the way for the introduction of a co-ordinated system of changes in the Polish planning and management mechanism,[71] and by the end of 1972 the Party –Government Commission had proposed six possible models for WOGs, to be mainly vertically integrated (but flexible enough to embrace plants from more than one branch of industry) and 'tailored' to the. organisational requirements of the particular industry.[72] Initially the WOGs were set up in only a few sectors of industry and the experiment was closely monitored. In December 1972 a number of industrial units that were technologically advanced, strong exporters and totalling 20% by value of all industrial production, started to operate as Pilot Units (*Jednostki Inicujące* – JIs). By the end of 1973 there were 24 such Pilot Units in the socialised sector of industry.[73] By early 1976 over two-thirds of industrial production was covered by these units and also a number of industrial associations in the construction industry;[74] and in the following year it was claimed that the WOGs were the basic unit of production in the whole of engineering, chemicals, heavy and light industry and in food processing.[75]

In view of the aforementioned variety of organisational structure, it is difficult to generalise about the Pilot Units. Although only three of the six types of WOG were actually used,[76] not all JIs could be considered to be Large Production Organisations. Even amongst those that were, many economists were reluctant to insist that this necessitated tightly centralised management system: a much looser association of enterprises was required in the consumer goods and retail industries that could bring together small-scale and locally controlled enterprises.[77] Although in branches of industry that were already vertically integrated, such as shipbuilding (which contributed 20% of the value of exports in the engineering industry), where the high degree of centralised managerial control encouraged it to display 'elements of a corporation' in its transactions,[78] some still thought that a highly centralised organisation such as the 'zjednoczenie koncernowe' was highly advantageous. It would combine independent enterprises, with an association central office that would steer the whole operation by means of control over supplies and transfer prices, and co-ordination of marketing, planning and development.[79]

Before passing on to an examination of how some WOGs operated in the new economic and financial system, it is important to sketch in the background as to why this approach was considered acceptable to the PZPR leadership. Again, it is felt that policy developments in Eastern Europe, and in particular in Hungary, and the USSR are relevant here.

While it can be argued that the GDR provided the model for the Polish reform of the industrial association in 1966–8, and the combine experiment of 1969–70, after this many Polish economists turned their attention to the system of enterprise organisation in Hungary as the source of a possible alternative for Poland. In Hungary the process of concentration of enterprises into larger units had begun in 1963, but with the inauguration of the New Economic Mechanism of 1968, such 'trusts' and central boards were replaced gradually by unions of enterprises, not bound by a specific legal structure, and which could be set up on the joint initiative of enterprise management, as well as on the order of central authorities. The union was intended to provide a form of voluntary enterprise co-operation without tendencies to monopoly power in trade, and without a tendency to bureaucracy in its internal transactions. To this end, financial regulations prohibiting practices such as market sharing, price maintenance and barriers to entry were applied.[80]

However, the organisational changes that took place in Hungary in the late 1960s must be seen in the context of the New Economic Mechanism of planning and management. After 1968, the role of the central planning authorities was to be restricted to the approval of Five-Year Plans, whilst the enterprise was to work out the annual plan for itself and to negotiate sales contracts and supplies in advance. Although investment policy was to be supervised by the Central Planning Office, the industrial administration (ministries, trusts, etc.) would have no jurisdiction in this area. The reorganisation of the industrial ministries into three conglomerates (heavy industry, engineering, iron and steel; light industry; and construction and agriculture) also heralded a new role for the ministries in long-term and macro-economic development as opposed to detailed surveillance of the minutiae of day-to-day planning and management. Yet these 'industrial' ministries were to be of secondary importance to the 'functional' ministries (viz. the Planning Office, and the ministries of finance, labour and the State Committee on

Prices and Materials) in directing macro-economic development. Thus, apart from direct control over investment, the New Economic Mechanism permitted central authorities to employ only indirect economic instruments to control prices, wages, taxes, credit and foreign trade.[81]

It must be acknowledged that the New Economic Mechanism was not an unqualified success. The years 1963–73 witnessed a startling rise in the price of raw materials, whose allocation was no longer controlled, and also in the price of consumer goods. The policy of permitting the production unions direct access to foreign trade and the right to conduct their own foreign currency bank accounts was criticised by two Polish economists on the grounds that it weakened central control over investment and technological development by encouraging the purchase of advanced but expensive foreign technology. Incentives to increase the cost-effectiveness of production were thereby weakened and there was little evidence that these unions were any more profitable than small-scale enterprises.[82]

Other measures of enterprise integration elsewhere in Eastern Europe excited little interest in Poland, and not everywhere was it a major element in economic policy. For example, in Czechoslovakia, between 1966 and 1968, the reverse trend was under way: decision-making powers were decentralised to the enterprise, and many large production units were broken up. This was, of course, curtailed after Soviet intervention and the return to a command model of planning and management after 1969.[83] It was the Hungarian model that generated most enthusiasm amongst Polish economists, and in the early stages of the reform after 1971 there were attempts to incorporate some of the elements of the New Economic Mechanism and the production unions, if not to emulate the example completely.

The official sanction for the creation of WOGs, however, was to come from the Soviet Union. At the Twenty-fourth Congress of the CPSU in March 1971, it was announced that highly integrated production associations (combines) should become the basic unit of the Soviet economy within a predominantly two- and three-level administrative structure. This pronouncement was followed in the spring of 1973 by a decision to abolish the rigid division of industry into branches, in order to encourage production associations to form on the basis of horizontal integration drawing in enterprises from different branches. Although the initial experiments for this were confined to the engineering industry, the reform was intended to spread across other branches. These new *ob'edinenie* could be set up by both all-union and republican governments, and so gave rise to further complexity in the industrial management structure which would vary from two or three to four levels of administration. The head offices of the *ob'edinenie* were to be located in the centre of production rather than in government departments in Moscow or in provincial capitals, and were to be autonomous self-financing units assuming responsibility for much detailed planning and supervision of enterprises which would be drawn from a wide geographical area.[84] The merger and re-centralisation of control over industrial enterprises had been particularly marked after 1969 and varied from the highly integrated combine (where enterprises lost their legal and financial autonomy) to a looser grouping in which a central executive enterprise conducted the most important services such as planning, research and development, investment, material–technical supply, marketing, market research and the provision of technical information.[85] It could be traced back to 1961 when, after the first revision in the *sovnarkhozy* venture, 'firms' were set up in Lvov in the Ukraine, and later in Moscow and Leningrad. The purpose was to encourage a higher rate of accumulation and labour productivity. After 1968 'research-production-amalgamations' were formed in order to unite research institutes with project design offices, technological bases and industrial enterprises. By 1969 they totalled 43 (and 48 in 1970) and at that time consisted mainly of groups of between four and eight factories all in a particular locality (differing considerably in size from the VVBs in the GDR which included up to 20 large state enterprises). The basic purpose was to integrate research and development with production, and the benefits anticipated from such a venture seemed to be very similar to the expectations of the combines and WOGs in Poland.[86]

There was some scepticism as to whether the advantages anticipated could be secured, even with the developments after early 1973. Gorlin argues that the partial integration of enterprises in the old 'firms' had negative consequences. The distance between enterprises makes centralisation of supplies impracticable; specialisation and rationalisation of production are only likely to take place near the head enterprise; the possibility of monopoly and its abuses due to autarky within the associations is likely to encourage more central intervention stimulating further bureaucratisation of the administrative structure, the resistance of enterprise management, and the loss of economies of scale.[87] We shall return to these considerations at the end of this chapter, but here shall confine ourselves to the observation that the cue for creating Pilot Units and WOGs was taken from the experience of Hungary and the USSR.

To return to Poland, we have already referred to the new principles of the economic reform relating to the measurement of economic performance, remuneration, use of inputs, disposal of profits and prices.[88] The financial system adopted to accompany this was very important. All Pilot Units were to observe identical financial norms: the index of growth of the Wages Fund, the index regulating fixed and turnover capital, and an index covering bank credit. Annual directive indices issued by the ministry were to be drastically reduced (for the year 1973 these were the scale of export production according to currency area, market supply and a ceiling on investment inputs) and other financial norms would be fixed for three years (including a coefficient correlating the rate of growth of the Wages Fund with the growth of production added, the norm governing payments to the management Premium Fund, and a norm regulating allocations from profits to the Development Fund measured according to the scale of investment projects).[89] There were also major innovations intended for the planning process: as in Hungary, the annual plan was to cease to be a legally binding document and the planning-time horizon was to be extended to focus on five-year programming using 'rolling' plans. The targets of these five year plans, although officially binding for the whole industrial sector and the region, did not need to be wholly consistent, and annual plans were to serve mainly as providers of information to adjust targets.[90] The interventionary powers of the industrial ministries were to be restrained. Unfortunately some of the intended changes in planning and pricing never occurred, and after 1975 the economic–financial system was modified.

On the subject of the organisational structure of WOGs, the chemical industry was still to be at the forefront of the policy of 'selective and intensive development', and so its plants were amongst the first to be adapted to the new system of planning and management. One of the first WOGs was based around Petroche-mia the newly established industrial association in the petrochemic-als industry when crude oil refining, manufacture of petrochemicals, nitrates and artificial materials were merged creating a single unit out of what had hitherto been the nitrates industry and petrochemicals.[91] The nitrates industry contributed about 21% of value of output for the whole chemical industry, disposed of 33% of the fixed capital in that industry, and employed 58,000 people in seven large combines. Hence Petrochemia was to be an important concern. From early 1972 the number of directive indices for the enterprises was reduced to five which were to apply unchanged for a longer time period of five years, and tight restrictions on the Wages Fund and employment were lifted.[92] The merger of nitrates and petrochemicals to form the new industrial association Petrochemia was initially intended to reduce the control of the ministry to the setting of three annual directive indices (the supply of nitrates, and the value in foreign exchange earnings of exports and imports from both socialist and non-socialist states) for the whole of the association, and also to eliminate direct intervention in the production process of the enterprises. The ministry was, however, able to influence enterprise performance indirectly through regulating wages and bonuses for the association as whole, and through discriminatory taxes of excess profits and high cost inputs that would affect payments into the Enterprise Fund (which represented a merger of the pre-existing Factory, Housing and Social Fund). Indirect powers of influence over enterprises were also entrusted to the association by means of control over export orders, internal accounting prices and bonus conditions for management to ensure that all those down to the level of the foreman (*mistrz*) would have an identical incentive to increase productivity.

Other Pilot Units in the chemical industry, despite official emphasis on individual needs, tended to follow the example of Petrochemia. For example, the association for the cosmetics industry Pollena which consisted mainly of medium- and small-scale enterprises with a very low level of organisation of production and technology, and which traded directly on the consumer goods market, employed similar principles to the management of Petrochemia and the pharmaceutical association, Polfa, in fixing the size of the Wages Fund. Although coefficient 'R' (which related the growth of the Wages Fund in comparison with the previous year, to the growth of production added) was fixed for a three-year period in agreement with the ministry at differential rates, the formula was considered adequate to the needs of different market conditions. Moreover, even at the time of establishing Petrochemia and Polfa as

Pilot Units, it was realised that this regulation of the Wages Fund could be used to enforce lower wages or redundancy upon workers, and the fixing of coefficient 'R' was a potential source of dispute in enterprises between trade unions and management.[93]

While there was a similar degree of restraint upon central government intervention in the glass and ceramics industrial association, the ministry could intervene over several matters in the paint and dye industry. In the former, the new industrial association set up in 1972 (when 70 enterprises and service units were merged into 7 combines that were autonomous full cost-accounting units) had the freedom to decide development policy, resource allocation, market research, research and development and employment policy for the combines.[94] The association of the paint and dye industry, Polifarb, differed from those aforementioned as the cost of raw materials took the largest share of total production costs and the uncertainty of supplies tended to encourage the maintenance of high inventories, which the industry was prone to conceal in order to guarantee profitability in the following year. Thus the ministry of the chemical industry set more directive indices and norms (8 in all) and while employment and wages were theoretically free from any restriction, in practice their volume could be indirectly regulated by the NBP through control over credit for the reserve Wages Fund of the association.[95] On the whole, though, there was a remarkable similarity of organisational structure of the Pilot Units/WOGs in the chemical industry, which was viewed as not altogether in keeping with the aims of the reform.[96]

By the close of 1975 the whole of the chemicals industry was reorganised into WOGs, but in other industries such as engineering, food processing and light industry, the transformation had also started. Unlike past reforms, it was not the ministries but the team of experts from the Planning Commission which supervised these preparations. In the high technology association of the aircraft industry Delta, the only central restrictions that could be imposed by the ministry were the volume of sales, and the value of production added,[97] whereas the association of the sugar industry had considerable freedom in marketing (fixing retail prices, wages and foreign currency earnings).[98] Light industry, on the other hand, was not reorganised into WOGs until 1975, and posed a considerable problem. Small technologically outdated factories, which were often run by local authorities, and where wages and raw materials took up a large proportion of production costs, tended to predominate. Large enterprises produced only about 20% of output by value for the whole of light industry and were to be found mainly in cotton textiles. The creation of WOGs was thus difficult and impracticable, and the solution was to entrust certain matters involving enterprise co-ordination to the existing industrial associations (such as control over wholesale prices, market research, research and development and investment planning) while the enterprises were to have a wide margin of independence in current investment, the product assortment, employment, wages policy and the distribution of profit. Even this did not avoid some duplication of responsibility, but was seen as much more suitable than the alternative of complex organisational structure for that industry.[99]

Looking back on the experience of many of the Pilot Units and WOGs since 1972, we can now see that a major preoccupation was the operation of the financial system, and in particular coefficient 'R', and internal accounting prices (*ceny rozliczeniowy*). A discussion amongst Poznań and Warsaw members of the PTE stressed the need to give more attention to these problems in the chemicals industry, especially as the planning-time horizon had in practice shrunk from five to two years, and coefficient 'R' seemed to be unsatisfactory in preventing wages and employment from rising.[100] Above all, it was felt that the tremendous diversity in size of organisation contributed to confusion over the rights of management and workforce representatives. The sensitivity of industrial relations permitted the Pilot Units considerable discretion in regulating wages and employment despite the complex formula governing the size of the Wages Fund. For example, they could introduce special *ad hoc* temporary bonuses.[101] This led many to question the basis for calculation of coefficient 'R': should it be linked to value added or profits; should it take account of investment structure and use of credit facilities?[102] It was also questionable as to whether coefficient 'R' provided a strong enough incentive to motivate the workforce to produce efficiently. For example, in eight Pilot Units the rate of turnover increased more than did sales and so the level of value added was grossly understated, providing a disincentive to raise production. On the other hand, many factories complained about the level at which coefficient 'R' was set, especially those whose performance in the previous year had been good and who received a high target for being frank about their spare capacity.[103] Positions in the debate polarised over the question of whether such synthetic parameters could succeed, particularly in the light of previous experience in the mid-1960s.[104]

In assessing the general performance of the Pilot Units, the initial experience in 1973 and 1974 suggested that they were more profitable than the rest of industry as a whole, and that increases in their raw materials requirements were offset by a greater volume in turnover. However, the high material intensity of production, the rapid increase in employment and wages and investment was problematic and manifested itself in a slower rate of increase of labour productivity.[105] This had two aspects. Firstly, since the early 1970s, immediately after the entry of the post-war 'bulge' of young people onto the labour market, there had been an annual decline in new entrants, yet the wage bill had increased sharply since then, without commensurate increases in output. Secondly, it was argued that investment policy had encouraged the start of many projects which had raised the amount of brand-new capital brought into production but also resulted in a lengthening of the investment cycle due to pressure on resources. As Poland was becoming increasingly dependent upon foreign trade and Western finance, these problems needed resolving.[106] However, the anxiety expressed over these matters at the meeting of the Party–Government Commission on 30 June 1975 was confirmed in the complete overhaul of the parametric system by the ministry of finance in late 1975. Several new parameters were devised, but more importantly more directives were issued by the ministries, who by 1977 re-acquired discretionary powers over day-to-day business in the WOGs.[107]

Industrial concentration and corporate structure in Poland

The above description of the principles behind the creation of WOGs, of the process by which they were set up, and of the economic and financial problems they faced, has so far said nothing about their effect on the concentration of industry and the emergence of corporate power. In this section, the growth of central WOG management will first be examined, followed by an evaluation of the increase in concentration and finally by a consideration of whether the benefits anticipated have been achieved. Firstly, on the subject of WOG management, their powers were certainly increased. Indeed this follows the trend since 1958. Although after 1958 industrial associations were only responsible for appointing

senior enterprise management, by 1966 they were responsible for all
cadre policy within the industrial association and its enterprises
subject to ministerial approval. (This was partly encouraged by the
change in the arrangements for bonus payments.) This trend was
further accentuated in the case of the industrial combines, and the
'Directors' Charter' issued in early 1972 transferred many powers
from the ministry to industrial association management, concerning
the organisation of enterprise production (and in particular the
fixing of internal association transfer prices, the management of the
foreign currency bank account, and the size of the total Wages
Fund). The intention was to amend the law of 1950 to accord
recognition to WOGs, and in particular the industrial association
(with industrial enterprises having varying degrees of autonomy
according to the industry in question) as the basic organisational
unit of Polish industry.[108] Some enterprise directors, sensing that
this decentralisation of authority from the central ministry to the
association had been accompanied by an emasculation of their own
powers, objected to this and there was pressure for revision of such
legislation to incorporate a management council on which all
enterprise directors within the WOG would be able to ensure
representation. However, such proposals foundered on the question
of the right of representation for PZPR, trade union, and the KSR
delegates, and over the nature of the relation between the council
and such organisations as the industrial ministry, local government
and the NBP.[109] This 'Directors' Charter' thus was no more than a
strengthening of the principle of one-man management in the
association. As to whether this was used as a basis for managerial
technocratic power to challenge the PZPR and central planning
institutions will be assessed in the next chapter. Suffice it to say that
in the early 1970s there was an avid interest in Western techniques
of business management from systems analysis to management by
objectives.[110]

One obvious consequence of increasing the powers of WOG
management and making them the basic unit of planning and
management, was to relegate the industrial enterprise to an
ambiguous position. The law of 1950 had not been changed, but in
reality many organisations designated as enterprises varied in their
powers. Gliński, after outlining the shifting interpretations of the
1950 enterprise law, noted that the fundamental criterion of full
cost-accounting and the right to distribute profit was a truly

inadequate definition of the enterprise. Besides full enterprises which were directly concerned with profits and able to negotiate credit, employment etc., there were many units on internal cost-accounting (*rozrachunek wewnętrzny*) that were part of a larger unit which itself had the status of an enterprise and to whose needs profit maximisation was subordinate. There were also factories on full cost-accounting which could belong to either category but which had restricted decision-making powers. Other economic organisations were neither enterprises nor factories; some were not full cost-accounting units (such as road work plants); some were on full cost-accounting (such as scientific-research institutes), and some were public utilities for which the main criterion was providing a social service and not profit and loss.[111] Clearly the combines and WOGs had contributed to this confusion, but Gliński's solution of a behavioural synthetic evaluation of enterprise economic performance has so far not been taken up. The status of the industrial enterprise and the need for its legal redefinition was raised sporadically between 1976 and 1978 but with little enthusiasm, and with no radical concrete changes such as occurred in Hungary at the end of 1977.[112]

As Gliński noted in a later article, organisation was a major weakness of the Polish economy. The absence of a 'socialist' theory of management was reflected in the tremendous variation in the structure of management hierarchies despite the limited legal prescriptions. Rarely was there any periodic review of how this structure related to the expertise required for tasks, and the number of offices tended to grow in order to ensure certain employees promotion into management and access to more privileged wage and bonus conditions.[113] This was echoed in a low evaluation of enterprise merger in terms of managerial efficiency and the tendency for numbers of clerical and lower-management staff to expand.[114] The reflection this cast upon the benefits of industrial merger will be considered below, but first we must pass to a discussion of the degree of concentration in Polish industry.

It is difficult to measure industrial concentration in a state-socialist society, but our aim here is to argue that there has been a significant increase in the size of production units, and that the administrative process of merger by means of the combines and WOGs in particular has conferred considerable market power. Two Polish statisticians argued that there were three fundamental ways in which the concentration of industry in a socialist economy can take place: firstly, by the direct construction of large new enterprises (e.g. Huty im. Lenina, FSO Zerań, Petrochemia in Płock and the Copper Combine in Kielce); secondly, enterprises can become enlarged; and thirdly, smaller enterprises can be linked together. In particular, it was the latter phenomenon that had led to the overall diminution in numbers of enterprises to be observed in Poland since 1960.[115] In the period 1961–71 nearly 25% of the 1960 total had disappeared and this was most pronounced during the years 1963–4 when 602 enterprises disappeared, and again during 1969–70 when 610 disappeared. Although the average number employed per enterprise had increased from 420 in 1960 to 696 in 1970 and 978 in 1975, this could not be construed as indicating an increase in plant size.[116] Rather, the number of multi-factory enterprises had increased as had the number of plants on average per enterprise.[117]

However, to assume a uniform trend towards multi-plant production units throughout Polish industry would be incorrect as the process of production varies between different sectors. For example, the largest reduction in the number of enterprises between 1961 and 1971 occurred in the food processing and light industries,[118] followed by the wood and forestry industry and construction. A glance at the statistical tables would reveal that these are the sectors of industry where there are a large number of enterprises and plants,[119] thus suggesting that there are still large numbers of people employed in small plants where mass production and long runs are not possible. Large-scale production may prevail in energy and fuels, iron and steel, and electrical engineering, but in the rest of the engineering industry small- and medium-sized plant prevail, and (outside textiles) this is also the case in light industry. The two Polish statisticians, Dziewiałtowski and Szeliga, reflected that this persistence of small-scale production could be a barrier to technological innovation, although they conceded that there was evidence that the overall performance of small enterprises is highly competitive with large-scale production. Unfortunately they chose not to pursue this paradox; they seemed content with the proposition that large units set the tone and pace of industrial production, and preferred to look at industrial concentration from the point of view of value of turnover (a bad indicator in a state-socialist economy where value relations tend to reflect government priority in production). However, of the 210 enterprises with a value of turnover of more than 1000 million złoty, these amounted to 92% of all enterprises in iron and steel, 78% in non-ferrous metals, 72% in transport equipment, 61% in energy, 59% in chemicals, 58% in rubber, 41% in fuels and, surprisingly, 41% in the food industry.

In view of the fact that the economic structure of socialist industry has tended to remain the same, concentration must be due mainly to the administrative grouping-together of enterprises. A recent study of mergers among Soviet firms and industrial associations has suggested that taut planning and a sellers' market, which incur uncertain supplies and poor markets for intermediate products, are the main stimuli of this trend.[120] The advantages expected from merger included the extension of co-operation between enterprises by means of increased concentration and specialisation of production, more rational use of material and financial resources, a reduction in enterprise administrative needs, centralisation of planning, research and development, investment allocation, production and sales. In the case of both the combines and the WOGs, Polish economists presented concentration and centralisation of production as the inevitable outcome of the development of the 'forces of production'. It would overcome the excessive 'fragmentation' of industrial enterprises and bring Poland into line with world developments where the producer of final products is integrated with the producer of semi-fabricates.[121] There might be problems in encouraging vertical integration because of the entrenched administrative boundaries between different industries, but the benefits to be achieved would far outweigh the costs. In Poland this trend towards administrative concentration is evident in both the reduction in the total number of enterprises, and in the number of industrial associations.[122] In 1977 the basic production units were WOGs consisting of 105 industrial associations and 33 large multi-plant enterprises or combines. To what extent has this conferred considerable market power upon them?

The assessment of market power in a centrally planned economy is something difficult to assess in behavioural terms. Degrees of competitiveness or restrictive practice cannot be meaningfully recorded within the framework of neo-classical economics. Rather it is only possible to offer the following check list of 'indicators of market autonomy', many of which, unfortunately, are not easily substantiated by the available data.

1. *Type of integration*

Whether vertical or horizontal integration of industrial enterprises and other production units occurs, can confer considerable market power. While vertical integration in its pure form involves taking over the source of supply and sales, horizontal integration occurs at a particular stage in the production process of a commodity and involves the negotiation of supplies and sales externally. Neither pure type exists, and the specific form of integration is usually of a hybrid nature. While it might appear that vertical integration is a source of market power (as in the case of the sulphur processing combine, or the petrochemical association), a large horizontally integrated form such as the Cegielski engineering works can also wield considerable influence over suppliers for whom it is the major customer.

2. *Possession of a product monopoly or domination of a branch of industry*

Here a Large Production Organisation might control the production of a key product either by being the sole producer (again the sulphur combine comes to mind) or by producing an essential intermediate product. Obviously size of unit is irrelevant here.

3. *Centrally listed commodities and price fixing*

For a centrally listed commodity, the exact proportion of desired production is calculated within the annual material balances and its allocation and distribution are centrally controlled. Depending on whether a large organisation is a monopoly/dominant producer of this commodity, it will have the power to bargain with central authorities. Conversely, the reduction in the number of centrally listed commodities and the concession of freedom in wholesale or retail price determination (such as in the case of the cosmetics association Pollena) can also be a source of influence.

4. *Full cost-accounting status*

The ability to conduct business according to the principle of full cost-accounting by ensuring that a production unit operates a profit and loss account, also enables it to engage in transactions in its own right. If a plant does not have this status it must either be a part of another industrial enterprise, or else be an administrative unit financed from the state budget. While full cost-accounting is the basic identity of an industrial enterprise, we have seen that in recent years the situation has become quite confused with many enterprises within WOGs having little business autonomy.

5. The number of directive indices and the time horizon for financial norms

The issuing of a small number of unchanging directive indices well before the start of the plan year enables management of a large organisation to be involved in their early negotiation and consequently to ensure that it has a considerable freedom of manoeuvre. The settling of financial norms for a period longer than a year guarantees a production organisation security in its longer term development. However 'planners' tension' can lead to the issue of more directives, and only those firms able to supply commodities in high demand will be able to resist such central interference. An example of a WOG where central directive indices were minimised was the aircraft industry association Delta, but since 1977 more directives have been issued.

All the following 'indicators of market autonomy' depend very much on the degree of planners' tension.

6. Control over investment policy

A Large Production Organisation will have greater potential market power if it is able to finance some of its investments either out of profit or by negotiating credit freely with branches of the NBP, or to purchase foreign capital. Conversely, if investment is financed solely from central budget grants its independence will be circumscribed. The arrangements for financing investment after 1971 encouraged an explosion of new projects which 'over-heated' the economy and have been difficult to control. It is here that WOGs have considerable hold over their enterprises but have themselves presented problems for central control.

7. Control over foreign marketing

The possibility of negotiating export sales directly, especially with Western firms, and the ability to accumulate the earnings in a

foreign exchange bank account, provides the potential for considerable independence on the part of a Large Production Organisation.
In particular if such earnings can be then devoted to the purchase of
capital equipment and material supplies, such a Large Production
Organisation is able to enjoy some respite from planners' tension. If,
on the other hand, foreign trade has to be conducted through the
offices of the ministry of foreign trade, or if the rate of foreign
currency accumulation is rigidly controlled by directive indices,
then such advantages are lost. Despite the initial proposals in 1972,
the idea of giving the WOGs a share of foreign exchange earnings
was abandoned and their export earnings were closely scrutinised.

8. Control over wages and employment policy

A Large Production Organisation can be more responsive to market
forces if it can decide to increase employment and wages or
introduce special bonus schemes which are not subject to control by
the central planning authorities. Although such discretion was not
permitted to industrial enterprises, between 1971 and 1974 several
WOGs exercised such powers.

Thus these 'indicators' are only a very tentative suggestion of how
market power can be conferred upon industrial associations,
combines and other Large Production Organisations. In particular,
we are able to trace a marked increase in the powers of industrial
association directors over the enterprises within their control after
1966 (especially in such matters as the allocation of fixed capital,
research and development and foreign trade). Yet in the late 1960s,
despite the acquisition of full cost-accounting status and powers over
foreign trade, domestic marketing, research and development, and
wages and employment, the industrial association has remained
organised on essentially horizontal principles of integration subject
to the constraints of annual planning, involving large numbers of
directives and financial norms that could be frequently adjusted
within the course of a year. The reductions in the numbers of
centrally listed commodities were short-lived and conditions of taut
planning prevented industrial associations from having influence
over price fixing. Similar conditions constrained the Combine
Experiment. The major aim had been to foster vertical intergration
and the most successful achievement of this occurred within the
sulphur combine which was accused of restrictive practices and was

broken up in 1974. Management decision-making in this combine had effectively eroded the powers of enterprise management. The only means of enterprise access to central planning institutions and the NBP was through the director himself, and he closely supervised all personnel policy, resource allocation, payments from investment and association fund, and trade, employment and wages policy. The desired degree of centralisation was not completely achieved in the ball bearings combine, where because of administrative barriers the enterprises regarded the combine management as superfluous to their normal transactions with central institutions and the industrial association. With the relative freedom of plant in some combines to conduct their own sales policies, the industrial associations and ministry officials were more prone to intervene. As we have noted above, the WOG management acquired much greater powers over the enterprises, and some economists were worried that the growth in vertical integration (especially in shipbuilding and the chemical and construction industries) might encourage some WOGs to act in an undesirable, monopolistic fashion.[123]

So far we have accepted the proposition that industrial concentration and merger in Poland favoured greater economies of scale, and encouraged innovation and export performance. Confidence in the achievement of these goals however, began to wane after 1976. Whereas in 1974 *Życie Gospodarcze* chose to review Galbraith's *New Industrial State* which had recently been translated into Polish, by 1977 Schumacher's *Small is Beautiful* was receiving attention.[124] One economist felt that the trend towards concentration of plant and enterprises was indiscriminate, bearing no relation to the needs of the branch of industry.[125] We have already alluded to the changes in light industry after 1975 which involved the creation of WOGs out of small technologically backward and distantly located factories. Similarly in food processing large combines were being created to cope with the high number of supplies and sales outlets. The reasons for this were seen to lie in the current trend of investment policy to direct capital to large units in the search for economies of scale and in the pursuit of administrative convenience. The trend in Poland also went against the rest of the world: Italian textiles, the French leather industry, the German clothing industry and Belgian knitwear were all organised in plants employing under 100 employees. In Polish light industry only 16.7% of all enterprises employed under 100 employees and 11% between 100 and 500. In cotton textiles and clothing most enterprises employed between 1000 and 2000 employees.[126] This obviously begged the question of whether large plants (in the latter case) or large administrative groupings of enterprises would be best suited to changes in consumer demand and technological innovation. A review of the relationship between firm size and innovation observed that since the Second World War, many major world innovations have tended to be made by small groups of scientists working in small enterprises, and that small enterprises can achieve a high degree of specialisation with a low level of capital intensity and a high degree of flexibility and customer responsiveness.[127] Thus enthusiasm for large-scale organisation was considerably dampened by 1979.

At present the official government attitude towards the relative merits of small- and large-scale organisation is ambivalent. A leading member of the Politburo writing just before the Eighth PZPR Congress in 1980 pronounced that large-scale organisation has proven to be most effective but warned against the danger of 'gigantism', especially in food processing, shoe making and confectionary.[128] In April 1978 Gierek had met workers in light industry and delivered a speech calling for more attention to the role of small-scale industry in complementing mass production, and a year later the resolution of the XIV Plenum of the PZPR Central Committee announced that raw materials supplies and investment funds would be made more easily available for small firms.[129] Around that time, the pages of *Życie Gospodarcze* were peppered with a series of investigations of enterprises that had either joined WOGs or stayed outside them. These varied from a 6-plant combine employing 3000 staff in the leather industry[130] (where a number of small enterprises had been reluctantly brought together to achieve benefits of scale that had so far eluded them), to the more successful combines in machine tools, and lifts,[131] and to a toy factory that had obstinately refused to join a WOG on the grounds that it would not resolve major problems with suppliers.[132]

In conclusion, we have endeavoured to show that industrial merger has been an important element in economic reform since the 1960s. While it is doubtful whether these industrial associations, combines or WOGs exercise a full corporate autonomy, their very existence points to the need to qualify assessments of economic reform solely in terms of enterprise independence. Moreover, whether they have favoured greater specialisation in the division of labour and speedier technological innovation is highly dubious. Yet, curiously, failures here have awakened interest in Western business management techniques. These techniques and the structure of management required by a large corporation ultimately come up against the barriers of Marxist–Leninist doctrine: 'democratic centralism' and 'one-man management'. As we shall see in the next chapter, the PZPR, although belated in its response, has had to adapt its organisation, behaviour and recruitment to reflect a more 'technicist' approach to its role in industry.

5

The political consequences of industrial integration and concentration: class, Party and management

The main thrust of the argument so far has been to stress the importance of organisational factors in Polish industrial growth strategy. That there tends to be an overemphasis upon the industrial enterprise to the neglect of the role of intermediate levels of economic administration has also been elaborated upon. Yet in tracing the emergence of 'socialist corporations' we have still to assess whether this has been accompanied by the development of technocratic patterns of authority. The problems that these 'socialist corporations' present for the organisation and recruitment into a Marxist–Leninist party such as the PZPR are manifold and extend far beyond the matter of control over the appointment of managerial personnel. It is in the name of working-class interests that economic policy is made in Poland, but, although the PZPR claims a monopoly of legitimate policy-making, the representation of workers' interests is also entrusted to trade unions and the mechanism of workers' self-management. The response of these bodies to workforce interests must be investigated: do they act as an open channel for the articulation of grievances and suggestions, or do they seek to contain and restrain such initiatives, redirecting their force away from wider issues of management to the safer area of material consumption? The manner in which such institutions have responded to the need for economic integration in industry will be left to the next chapter.

The mere observation of institutional change, however, does not provide us with a complete answer to the question of why it occurs in a particular way or whether it reflects a growth in technocratic power. This can only be provided by reference to Polish social structure, and in particular the demographic, social stratification and mobility patterns that have appeared in the course of the history of the People's Republic of Poland. Whether the revolutionary potential of the industrial working class has been displaced by technocratic class interests, whether they combine forces to challenge the legitimacy of Marxism–Leninism, or whether both forces can be easily absorbed into the PZPR can only be determined with reference to social structure. Hence, after due reference to this and recruitment patterns into the PZPR, the process of recruitment into industrial management will be explored.

Class and Party in Poland

The historical origins of the PZPR can be traced back to the political activism of the Polish intelligentsia in the nineteenth century, accompanied by a small industrial workforce in a predominantly agrarian society. Throughout the chequered history of Polish socialism, the main lines of cleavage have centred on the identity of Poland as a nation state. The history of the Luxemburg–Lenin controversy on the nature of the revolutionary party and the factions within Polish socialism are documented elsewhere,[1] along with the misfortunes of the Communist Workers' Party of Poland formed from the Luxemburgist and Left-socialist factions in 1918. We shall not pursue this further, except to note that not the least of the problems facing the Marxist–Leninist groups were illegality, economic crises and the changing relationship with the Soviet Union which culminated in the dissolution of the Communist Party of Poland in 1938 on the orders of Stalin.[2] It was the formation of a new Marxist–Leninist Party out of the Left-Wing resistance during the Second World War, and its eventual 'merger' with the Polish Socialist Party (PPS) in 1948, that created the PZPR.

Although the lessons of the past clearly indicated the folly of a servile adherence to the policies of the Communist Party of the Soviet Union, and of ignoring nationalist and peasant demands in a primarily agrarian country, by 1948 all these issues had reappeared as sensitive items on the political agenda and continued to do so in 1956, 1968, 1970, 1976 and 1980. In particular, the demand for 'National Roads to Socialism' raised by Gomulka in 1948 was closely tied to visions of a self-managing society, which was clearly unacceptable to the CPSU. This important point should not be forgotten in any examination of the fate of industrialisation policy in Poland and of the role assumed by the PZPR in industry.

As stated earlier, Poland underwent the transition from a predominantly agrarian-based economy to industrialisation in just over twenty years. The unique combination of social revolution and industrial revolution is held to have produced three changes in the class structure in Poland: in employment, in the working class and in the peasantry. The structure of employment has changed from the dominance of rural agricultural and handicraft occupations (60% of those employed in 1939) to the dominance of urban industrial occupations (60% of those employed in 1963) (see Table 1). The elimination of concealed employment in agriculture manifested itself in the emergence of hybrid occupational categories such as peasant workers, and a new working class has grown up (only 17% of the total in 1963 had been members of that class before 1939).[3] Thus extensive social and geographical mobility took place in a population that was just 25 million in 1939, and which grew significantly (although the birth-rate fluctuated from a high rate between 1950 and 1955 to a low rate between 1965 and 1970) to reach 32 million in 1973 and 36 million in 1976.[4] So extensive was social mobility that in 1972 it was calculated that 44.3% of the total economically active population belonged to a different socio-economic category from their father.[5]

Table 1 *Economically active population according to occupational category*

Year	Agriculture	Industry*	Services
1931	9.5m	1.8m	2.3m
1946	7.5	1.8	2.4
1950	7.1	2.9	2.4
1960	6.7	4.1	3.2
1970	6.2	5.6	4.6

*Including construction and transport
Source: S. Widerszpil, *Przeobrażenia struktury społecznej* W Polsce, Warsaw, 1973, p. 154.

Two further demographic factors which have a bearing on the class structure of Polish society are urban migration and the predominance of a youthful population. Much of the early industrialisation drive had been accompanied by a massive drift to urban centres (while 30% of the population lived in towns with over 20,000 inhabitants in 1938, by 1970 this had risen to 52.2% and by 1977 to

57.7%[6]) as the attempts at collectivisation of agriculture between 1948 and 1956 weeded out disguised rural unemployment. At the same time it was largely younger people who left the land for the towns and contributed to the 'rejuvenation' of both the industrial manual working class (in 1973 60% were aged under 40 and 50% were under 30) and the white-collar group (in 1973, 36.9% were aged 29 or under and 39.8% aged between 30 and 40!).[7] As a consequence the simple Marxist–Leninist 'two-and-a-half' class formula in no way captures the trend of social class formation over the past thirty years in Poland. A more detailed exposition of the development of contemporary Polish social structure now follows.

To commence with the industrial manual working class, its formation can be traced back to the 1850s, but by 1931 there were only about 1,130,000 people employed in manual jobs in industry and construction. However, after 1945 it underwent a fourfold increase in size by 1970 to reach 4,461,000 industrial and construction workers (plus another million in trade and transport).[8] Hence it is possible to claim that Poland possesses a 'new working class' created under conditions of socialist ownership of the means of production (although consideration of the usage of this term in the manner conceived of by Mallet, Gorz and Touraine will be left aside for the present). Yet caution is called for in assuming a high degree of homogeneity and social cohesion in this group. For example, the work process varies across sectors of industry with a high degree of automation in chemicals, extensive mechanisation in textiles, but with 44.8% manual workers still working directly with their hands in 1965.[9] There is also considerable differentiation according to education, skill levels and wage rates, with higher qualified and better-paid workers found mainly in engineering and chemicals[10] and coal-mining. However, an accurate picture of these differences is difficult to obtain as, for example, workers may be classified as qualified although they have not completed basic education (viz. in the textile industry), and many modern chemical plants employ very low-skilled labour owing to their location in areas where hitherto there was no industry.[11]

The fluid boundary between the working class and the peasantry can be illustrated by the fact that 42% of heads of household living in rural areas earned their living outside agriculture in 1978.[12] This was, of course, subject to regional variations, a particularly high proportion working both inside and outside agriculture in the

Wojewodztwa with the lowest industrial development.[13] While on the one hand this has meant the almost complete eradication of a rural proletariat, culminating in the stabilisation of the drift of peasants into the ranks of the working class by 1964, it has on the other hand contributed to a new social category, the peasant-workers, who constitute a high percentage of the labour force in construction (38.8%), trade and transport, and to whose households an estimated 5 million people belong.[14] There is considerable internal differentiation within this social category depending on whether work outside agriculture is the major source of income, and the number of breadwinners and dwellings per household. Nonetheless, despite the fact that Polish agriculture is predominantly in private ownership (85% agricultural land and 75% farms), an examination of rural social structure reveals that the agrarian economy is by no means isolated from the socialised sector of industry and trade.

Finally, no consideration of Polish social structure would be complete without some reference to developments within the white-collar group, and the boundaries between this and the two other classes. Often this category is referred to as the 'intelligentsia' and the several studies of its origin and 'historic mission' have recently been accused of fabricating an 'intelligentsia myth' which emphasises the manner in which pre-1945 values and culture have been transmitted into and sustained in the state-socialist period.[15] The Polish intelligentsia came into existence in the nineteenth century, attracting members of the small land-holding gentry who were sympathetic to the ideals of Polish national liberation. This group increased in the course of migration to the towns, its members espousing humanistic values with a scorn for a utilitarian approach to life and the world of business. This was reflected in a marked propensity to enter white-collar work, the army and academia.[16] Although it has been argued that this old intelligentsia 'ghetto' began to crumble with the dawn of mass society in Poland after 1945,[17] the character of this class underwent considerable change during the twentieth century with the growth of a new salaried white-collar group in the 1920s and 1930s drawn mainly from people of peasant background. By the post-1945 period, the differentiation between industrial manual working class and the various white-collar groups was not so sharply defined. Having comprised a total of 14% of all workers outside agriculture in 1945, the white-collar group grew to 25% in 1950 and 35% in 1973 of all workers in the socialised sector of the economy,[18] and by 1975 included 3.9 million people.

However, this 'intelligentsia stratum' in post-1945 Poland could include the academically oriented liberal professionals and engineers, but also increasing numbers of those working in industrial administration as accountants, administrators and clerical staff (the majority of whom were female and poorly educated).[19] That persons of peasant family origin were more highly represented in nontechnical posts in the higher-level professions, and in transport and trade in the lower-level white-collar occupations, may have been due to a recruitment policy established during the years 1950–4.[20] However, despite the heterogeneity of the white-collar group, there have been indications that, particularly among the professional intelligentsia, certain sections have become increasingly self-recruiting. As we shall see below, educational pathway has become a significant variable in affecting recruitment into higher- and middle-level professional posts in industry. Beginning in the 1950s (and accelerating in the 1960s) the number of graduates of higher and further education who have followed part-time studies has risen to over one-third of the total, and those of working-class origin seem to be disproportionately represented in this group. The mechanism promoting the entry of working-class and peasant students into full-time higher education has weakened, with considerable impact on recruitment into white-collar managerial occupations in industry.[21]

Thus, to evaluate developments in the white-collar group solely in terms of the decline of the old cultural intelligentsia,[22] or in terms of the displacement of capitalist-inspired positivistic values by a socialist-oriented nationalism,[23] or in terms of a change from the predominance of humanistic to technological cultural values,[24] is to ignore the manner in which social mobility has taken place in Poland since 1945. Developments that have taken place in one class or stratum cannot be seen in isolation from those elsewhere.

Polish sociologists have given much consideration to the development of their class structure. This stands in contrast to official Marxist–Leninist thought, which (sealed with the imprimatur of Moscow) has been at great pains to dissociate developments in the social structure of state-socialist societies from those who would argue for the convergence to a common form of industrial society. That imperatives of technology demand a more highly skilled workforce, and hence signify a numerical decline in the working class and an expansion of a white-collar service/managerial group is resolutely denied, as is the claim that class has been displaced by knowledge as the fundamental social cleavage. Technological determinism and the end of ideology are held up as illusions that obscure real differences arising from the basis of ownership in both state-socialist and capitalist countries. What is conceded, though, is that the passage of state-socialist societies through a phase of 'socialist construction' into that of 'developed socialism' does not signify the end of the historical role of class divisions, although there is some confusion in the literature over what the further overcoming of contradictions between mental and manual labour, the division between town and country, precisely mean.[25] The level of debate in Marxist–Leninist theoretical journals does seem to have been confined to a low level, and Polish sociology has responded at both a theoretical level and an empirical level.

On a theoretical level, the classic work of Stanisław Ossowski[26] begins with an acknowledgment that neither Marx nor Engels provided a framework for the analysis of social structure where the means of production were nationalised. His observation that Marx based his analysis on a synthesis of three already existing models leads him to argue that the choice of a model of class structure applied to a particular instance is symptomatic either of the problems which interest those who apply the model, or of their views on the reality they are describing. Thus, there being no generally agreed concept of class, class must be something that exists at a subjective level – in the social consciousness.[27] Consequently, according to Ossowski, there is as much to be gained by analysing the conceptions of class structure entertained by different social groups as there is by 'objective' analysis. This point is developed by Wesołowski, who notes that the change to socialist relations of production does not mean that all other class characteristics (defined in terms of social position in the production hierarchy) disappear automatically; rather, they continue to characterise the position of a group such as the working class, not in relation to capitalists, but in relation to other groups, classes or strata.[28] The process of 'revolutionary transformation' from capitalism to social-ism leads to a decomposition of old class traits, but in turn leads to a new basis of differentiation more fully related to social positions which are 'cut-off' from the determining influence of the relation to ownership of the means of production, and which retain an 'autonomous' existence. Wesołowski feels that revolutionary change and social disintegration occur both objectively and in the subjective experience of citizens, with the result that there is a dual system of values: those imposed by the regime, and the personal system belonging to a previous era.

This has considerable importance for the relationship between class background, educational opportunity and occupation in Poland. For example, while the 'new' resource of education is officially held to determine the relationship between occupation, income and social prestige, it can also be an important instrument for obtaining other 'older' values. More precisely, educational qualifications have endured as a value of high status, granting low status to the unskilled in an ideological context which attempts to enhance the status of skilled workers. Goldthorpe has argued that members of the new 'service' classes are increasingly selected through educational attainment rather than by means of recruitment from rank-and-file workers in state-socialist societies, and that both groups tend to become increasingly divergent in terms of culture and lifestyles.[29] Ironically, where education is the key determinant of occupational achievement, the opportunities for those who start in a low position are diminished. One consequence of this (as observed by Parkin) was a much more marked social discontinuity between higher and lower white-collar groups under state socialism, than under capitalism, as we shall see. While this may be the 'objective' case, this is not the case in the subjective consciousness of members of these social categories in Poland.[30] In opposition to an ideology that enhances the status of skilled workers, members of the 'new socialist intelligentsia' have asserted that educational qualifications should be the major means of ascribing status, with the result that there has been a greater integration of all intellectual workers (including lower-level clerical grades) into a subjective identification with the intelligentsia, than any *rapprochement* between intelligentsia and working class on the lines envisaged by official doctrine. This is reinforced by empirical investigation into the class structure of Poland which noted that the highest level of acknowledgment that Polish society is divided into classes and strata tends to be found amongst white-collar workers, and the lowest level among manual workers.[31] As Hirszowicz notes, an ideology of professionalism masking a hostility towards egalitarianism, opposition to collective welfare provision and coveting of title, rank and status is the cement that keeps this heterogeneous white-collar group together and is evidence of the importance of subjective experiences in consideration of the relationship between class, education and occupation.

In political terms we are dealing primarily with a complex set of interest groups clustering around institutions, ranks, professional qualities, administrative divisions etc....however, there are some traditions, symbols and cultural traits that cut across institutional and rank boundaries and appeal to that heterogeneous mass of 700,000 members of the educated strata. The intelligentsia exists, in other words, in its self image, in the preservation of status distinctions, even if they have lost their substance long ago, in the sphere of 'symbolic interaction' and 'collective consciousness' based on evaluations inherited from the nineteenth century.[32]

It is these considerations of the complexity of Polish social structure and of the importance of subjective dimensions of social class that are of considerable relevance to our examination of the political consequences of industrial integration and concentration. The question arises as to whether, in order to cope with the needs of industrialisation, the PZPR has become increasingly professionalised, and its internal value system and legitimacy become increasingly tied to technical and administrative competence. Has technological pragmatism provided the basis for consolidating a new class system of power?[33] On the other hand perhaps this new technocratic class, perceiving the maintenance and extension of its privileges as founded on the uninterrupted development of the productive forces, acts as the champion of reform seeking support initially from the traditional working class (by promoting worker participation and greater access to consumption) but later from a new stratum of worker-technicians who are opposed to authoritarian socialism (supported by the more conservative interests of the bureaucracy and the traditional working class).[34] Is the traditional manual working class no longer a force for social change, or are the new technocrats themselves also divided between those interested in reform that maintains privilege, and those who wish to establish a genuinely participatory industrial democracy? Or do shifting alliances take place in response to the maneouvres of a political elite that seeks to frustrate too close a class unity among intellectuals, and to thwart an alliance with the working class by using its power over consumption to broaden its mass base through appeals to egalitarianism?[35]

An attempt to answer these questions will be made by considering the recruitment policy of the PZPR with special reference to industry, the structure of and recruitment to industrial management posts with special reference to the process of industrial concentration, and to the impact of this process upon industrial manual working-class interests.

The recruitment policy of the PZPR

Early studies tended to emphasise that the direction and intensity of PZPR recruitment varies over time in inverse proportion to the already existing percentage of PZPR membership in a given category of personnel, suggesting that the PZPR seeks to be more or less equitably represented in all categories of workers.[36] However, an in-depth survey of PZPR organisations in a number of factories between 1959 and 1960 revealed that males in technical occupations with further or higher education, and who had been employed in their post for over six years, were more highly represented in the Party membership than the rest of the workforce, and although Party activists were fairly evenly dispersed between all occupational groups, and although it was claimed that PZPR membership and militancy did not come into conflict with managerial authority, it was conceded that the various tasks involved in Party work tended to 'attract' different groups.[37] This can be interpreted as a euphemism concealing the tendency for the working-class membership (of both rank and file and officials) to be displaced by a disproportionate representation of white-collar and managerial elites. However, a more systematic analysis of rank-and-file membership is called for.

In aggregate terms, the PZPR membership constitutes around 7% of the total population, and approximately 1 in 10 of all adults over the age of 18, with a steady increase in absolute numbers (apart from a drop in the mid-1950s). However, increases in aggregate numbers alone obscure the fact that in terms of social origin of membership there have been shifting trends. The statistics on occupational background can be misleading due to uncertainty as to whether they refer to social origin or present occupation, and (assuming that upward social mobility is more prevalent than the reverse) the proportion of white-collar membership may be greatly understated (see Table 2).

Table 2 *Social origin of PZPR membership*

Year	Absolute numbers of members and candidates	Workers %	Peasants %	White-collar/ intelligentsia %	Other %
1949	1,368,700	60.0	18.0	17.3	4.7
1954	1,296,900	48.0	13.8	36.2	2.0
1959	1,018,500	40.0	11.5	43.2	5.3
1964	1,640,700	40.2	11.4	43.0	5.4
1968	2,104,300	40.2	11.4	43.0	5.4
1970	2,319,900	40.3	11.5	42.3	5.9
1975	2,359,000	41.8	9.5	41.8	6.9
1980	3,080,000	46.2	9.4	33.0	11.4

Source: Cz. Herod, 'Kształtowanie sie skladu i struktury spoleczno-zawodowej P.Z.P.R.', *ND*, 1/1971, pp. 79–94; 'Sprawożdanie K.C.P.Z.P.R. za okres od VI do VII zjazju', *ND*, 1/1976; Cz. Herod, in A. Dobieszewski (ed.), *Wiedza o Partii: wybrany problemy*, Warsaw, 1972, p. 375; 'Partia', *ZP*, 1/1976, pp. 14–19; L. Bukowski, 'Portret Partii', *ZP*, 12/1975, p. 3; T.K. 'Portret Partii', *ZP*, 2/1980, pp. 12–14.

Table 3 *Social background of new recruits (%)*

Year	Working class	Peasant	White-collar/ intelligentsia	Others
1959	50.5	14.0	34.6	0.9
1960	48.8	14.3	35.1	1.8
1961	46.9	15.6	34.7	2.8
1962	47.6	10.8	38.1	3.5
1963	47.3	12.3	36.5	3.9
1964	48.0	14.4	32.9	4.7
1965	46.7	15.5	32.4	5.4
1966	47.7	16.1	31.8	4.4
1967	49.4	14.7	32.3	3.6
1968	51.3	12.0	33.1	3.6
1969	50.6	13.2	32.9	3.3
1970	51.1	14.1	31.6	3.2
1971	52.0	9.5	not available	
1971–75	67.0	13.4	"	
1976–80	60.0	25.7	"	

Source: Cz. Herod, in A. Dobieszewski (ed.), *Wiedza o Partii: wybrany problemy*, Warsaw, 1972, p. 375. See also citations under Table 2.

The first trend that can be observed is a fall in the proportion of manual workers from above 60% in 1949 to 48% in 1954. (The figures do not acknowledge the fact that the sharpest drop occurred both immediately prior to and after the unification of the Polish Workers' Party and the Polish Socialist Party in 1948.) At the same time, the proportion of peasant members declined more sharply from a high total of 28% in 1945 to around 11% throughout the 1960s, but with a further 2% fall in the 1970s. In contrast, the proportion of white-collar members rose annually (after 1946 from about 10%) to remain at around 43% in the 1960s (during the period 1963–7 the rates of increase in PZPR membership of both white-collar and working-class groups were equal)[38] but to decline by around 20% after 1975.

The fluctuations in social origin of membership do not seem to be reflected in the figures for new recruits (according to social background) at least until after 1970 (see Table 3).

As we shall see below the continuing higher proportion of working-class entrants in the 1960s in comparison to their share in total membership is suggestive of social mobility (either into another social category or out of the Party!). However, the candidate recruitment figures do not reveal the source of fluctuations in absolute members since the early 1950s. In the mid-1950s the PZPR sought to incorporate the new engineering and technical graduates coming onto the labour market in response to the serious skill shortage in Polish industry. While many of these were skilled workers who had been accorded preferential access to higher education because of their political loyalty, and thus were promoted from *within* the Party, by 1958 the pool of engineering graduates suitable for management posts was much larger and they gradually entered management posts, displacing the earlier worker-directors.[39] This lasted until 1963 when the rate of working-class recruitment was more or less identical to the white-collar group. However, after 1970 the balance swung the other way in favour of the manual-worker groups and a consequent sharp decline in recruitment from the white-collar intelligentsia.

The fluctuations in recruitment of Party members from particular social categories are also related to other social factors. The age distribution of members is significant. Firstly, there has been a steady (and not entirely unexpected) decline in those members who joined prior to 'unification' in 1948 from 55.4% of the total membership in 1958 to 33.5% in 1963, 22% in 1967, 18.3% in 1969 and to only 11% in 1980. Secondly, the average age of membership was fairly constant during the 1960s (38.4 years in 1963 and 38.2 years in 1967) and rose only marginally in the 1970s (40.1 years in 1975 and 40.3 years in 1980). This suggests that a regular renewal of Party membership from among young people was taking place (in 1970, 34% candidates and members had joined in the period 1964–8) to enable the PZPR to maintain its youthfulness. However, most striking is the appeal of Party membership to those aged under 25, and increasing prominence of this age-group among new recruits since the late 1960s (see Table 4).

Table 4

Year	Candidate members aged under 25 as a % of total recruits to the PZPR
1959	34.6
1960	35.5
1961	35.7
1962	35.8
1963	35.6
1964	37.0
1965	39.9
1966	42.1
1967	not available
1968	46.8
1969	46.5
1970	48.1

Source: Cz. Herod, in A. Dobieszewski (ed.), *Wiedza o Partii: wybrany problemy*, Warsaw, 1972, pp. 388–9.

There is evidence that in the 1970s the PZPR directed its appeal mainly towards prospective young recruits, 66% of whom between 1971 and 1975, and 70% between 1975 and 1980 were under the age of thirty.[40]

In relating the age distribution of recruits to changes in class origin of recruits over time, it is reasonable to assume that, while in the 1960s a large percentage of young candidates (aged under 25) were from white-collar social background, during the 1970s this was reversed, and a larger percentage were blue-collar workers. As to the types of people entering the PZPR, education is an important variable (see Table 5).

Table 5 *Educational qualifications of members and candidates*

Year	higher education	further education	secondary education	incomplete secondary education
1958	4.6	19.0	44.9	31.5
1971	8.6	27.9	54.9	8.6
1980	12.0	32.0	not available	

Source: Cz. Herod, in A. Dobieszewski (ed.), *Wiedza o Partii: wybrany problemy*, Warsaw, 1972, p.400.

Whilst in all instances this compares very favourably with the population at large (for example, in 1980, of those employed in the socialised sector only 6.9% had higher education and 24.5% further education), of greater interest is the improvement in educational qualifications of members after joining the PZPR. PZPR members in 1968 with educational qualifications obtained since joining were as follows: higher education 43.4%; further education 24.1% (1967); secondary education 5.9%.[41]

It has been estimated that almost 25% of PZPR members had acquired further education and 20% had acquired higher education since joining, thus providing justification for the assertion that the PZPR was 'educating itself'.[42] Bearing in mind that 1 in 6 Party members were experiencing some form of social mobility from worker or peasant background to white-collar jobs, and that part-time education made a significant contribution to this, it is reasonable to assume that the PZPR offered a channel of social advance for the manual working class that would supplement the loss of opportunity in the conventional education system.

However, one further point for consideration is that improvements in educational qualifications of PZPR members in general must also be explained by other factors. It is fair to surmise that, while in the 1960s this can be explained largely by the rapid increase in recruitment from the white-collar technical intelligentsia (especially 1957–63), by the late 1970s such improvements as occurred in the educational qualification of membership must also be due to the recruitment of better-qualified working-class members. Indeed, there is reason to believe that in the 1970s the PZPR was seeking to increase 'Party saturation' among particular categories of employee, and above all amongst the highly skilled working class. The PZPR may well seek to be represented more or less equitably amongst all categories of workers [43] but, during the 1970s, it sought to establish a greater presence amongst the well qualified (especially foremen and brigade leaders where the level could reach 60%)[44] amongst peasant-workers,[45] women[46] and youth and students, and in the most rapidly industrialising areas[47] (although there was nothing new in this geographical bias in recruitment).

To conclude this section on changing trends in PZPR recruitment policy, there is, in the light of the events since the summer of 1980, considerable evidence that the more 'scientific' approach to 'Party saturation' failed. The anxiety over acquiring the requisite balance of membership amongst different occupational categories, tended to over-shadow the purpose of this exercise. The drive to recruit more manual workers, especially amongst young people with only a few years' work experience, encountered two problems: the tendency for workers to be a disproportionately large number (60%) of those dismissed from or who voluntarily left the PZPR in 1976–8, and the tendency for a declining percentage (as low as 40% of young recruits) to have been provided through the Socialist Youth Movement (ZSMP).[48] Younger, more educated working people were being lured into the PZPR in ever greater numbers, but they showed a low inclination either to stay the course or to pass through the conventional 'feeder' organisations. Also, the temptation to enlist people from rural areas who worked in the public sector without consideration of their motivation for joining meant that the PZPR leadership was itself the major instrument in the incorporation of discontent within its ranks. (See postscript.)

Managerial recruitment, the PZPR and industrial concentration

The aforementioned PZPR recruitment strategy only appears to make sense if the changing trends in industrial organisation are considered. In this section we shall argue that the changing direction of PZPR recruitment away from the white-collar technical intelligentsia towards the manual working class indicates that Party saturation amongst certain sectors of white-collar industrial workers was already high, and the expanded powers and privileges of this category consequent upon the process of industrial concentration had to be legitimated. Obviously such a claim involves the necessity of examining the degree of membership of Polish management, its means of access to privilege and its attitudes, but this will be dealt with after a consideration of the nature of the managerial labour process in Polish industry.

Our review of the organisational structure of management within industrial associations, combines and WOGs has revealed a complex hierarchy of posts of responsibility, in both horizontal and vertical terms. Besides the chief directors of these units, the observation of one-man management meant that at all levels there would be a senior line manager (right down to the individual factory), and the highly developed division of labour along functional lines resulted in a high number of other senior management posts at all levels (deputy directors for technical affairs, for economic affairs, for investment, for research and development, for project design, for marketing and chief accountants). This division of labour was of course extended even further at middle- and lower-management level right down to the very bottom rung of the managerial ladder, where the divide between management and workforce found itself in the post of the foreman (see below). Thus Polish industrial management is very diverse, and, as we have already witnessed, the operation of the principle of one-man management makes for an uneven spread of responsibility. Decision-making by one person was obviously an impossibility in industrial management, yet its legal implications were far-reaching: many technical and specialist staff at all levels of management had broad decision-making powers while they could not in practice be held to be formally accountable. The conduciveness of such Marxist–Leninist orthodoxy to management efficiency was not officially questioned. To the contrary it was reaffirmed after 1970.[49]

As a consequence, the role of enterprise directors could be particularly stressful: they could be the subject of contradictory expectations, and demands both from within and outside the enterprise. For example, the greater independence to be enjoyed by enterprise directors with the transition to a parametric system of management was circumscribed by the need to make decisions that conformed to the wishes of superior levels of management; and there was conflict between the dual role of decision-maker and purveyor of information to higher levels.[50] The enterprise director wishes to achieve tasks that will secure him maximum advantage both materially and in terms of prestige. It is the system of bonus payments, on which all other members of staff depend, that induces the director towards suggesting a plan that is both low and easy to implement, towards providing 'inadequate' information of true production capacity. It also encourages him to demand excessive supplies of both material resources and finance in a seller's market in the face of attempts by the Bank to curb these excessive demands for credit (by either withholding it or imposing penalty rates of interest) in order to encourage greater economy in the use of material resources. Thus the enterprise director is under pressure from both within and outside the enterprise and this can render his position stressful, requiring him to adopt tactics to augment his sense of security and to minimise threat.

These pressures were seen to be the cause of high turnover or a *kadre karusel* amongst enterprise directors in the mid-1960s. A sociological inquiry based on a small localised sample (five directors of enterprises in heavy industry in the Warsaw region) provides an illuminating insight into senior management career profiles. They had all begun in middle management in an industrial association followed by employment in the ministry or the Wojewodztwo PZPR apparat and immediately prior to appointment had been senior officials at this level. Yet that three out of the five remarked upon the 'cadre difficulties' that had preceded their appointment is suggestive of stress sufficient to induce resignations from office.[51] They all took a jaundiced view of collective decision-making in their industrial association: rather than the 'kolegium' making policy for the association executive, the reverse was usually the case. The association management neglected to consult enterprise management, was unsympathetic to problems that arose in production, and was most concerned to conduct a multitude of inspections.[52] All this was indicative of a lack of concern with what was really happening in production, or with long-term policy, and provided little incentive for enterprise management to pass on accurate information. Thus it was not surprising that, under pressure from the industrial association and other external Party and government organisations as well as from within the enterprise, enterprise directors resigned their posts and moved to other work. That there was little change in later years was indicated in 1972 when a questionnaire survey of 220 directors in light industry (chiefly textiles) revealed considerable dissatisfaction with powers for independent decision-making. External interference in finance, wages and employment policy was seen as particularly irritating, the greatest culprit being the industrial association.[53]

However stressful the situation of the enterprise director might be, it nonetheless displays a certain ambivalence, in that intervention from above can be allayed by use of informal communication networks, of both the Party and local government. The enterprise director is clearly involved in the process of local community power, where he is under pressure to take account of local interests in manpower, capital resources, social amenities and environmental protection. Close links could be found between staff in local administration and industrial enterprises. Overlap of personnel ensured that many enterprise directors could be councillors in the local political community or could be co-opted onto Council Problem Commissions. In return, representatives of the local PZPR Executive and of local government would often be invited to the enterprise or to a combine kolegium meeting.[54] So, stressful though the situation of the enterprise director might be, it is arguable that ministerial and association management would consider dismissing an enterprise director (despite their legal entitlement to do so), as the network of communication between enterprise and local government and Party organisations would be important in expediting the plan.[55] That the regional dimension of power is of importance to the process of industrial concentration in Poland is already evident from the results of the case studies of the combines. In particular, the problems encountered in plant construction and resource allocation can be attributed to the lack of integration of regional planning and management within the national framework, and revenue considerations could induce local authorities to take a lively interest in industrial location.

However, is senior enterprise management suitably qualified to cope with these pressures in an efficient way? An examination of management education in Poland would indicate that training in business skills has never had a high priority, and few attempts were made to redress this until the late 1960s. In the 1950s higher education in economics was a low status subject, and after 1948 the political sensitivity of theories such as input – output analysis, and linear programming had driven many skilled members of the profession to the West. The main centre of excellence for economics was the School of Planning and Statistics (SGPiS) in Warsaw. Supplemented by small departments of economics at universities and polytechnics, the training that was offered tended to be on a full-time basis, with little opportunity for part-time study. Consequently, economics education was less accessible to students of manual working-class origin, and most economists in the 1950s tended to come from white-collar family background. However, this does not explain why they were not recruited into senior management of industrial enterprises. The reason is to be found in the aforementioned stressful nature of management, and the immediate post-war industrial training policy.

During the period of reconstruction 1945–8, most top management posts in industry were held by pre-war directors and owners. In fact, in Silesia it was proudly boasted that nobody who held the post of enterprise director before the war was prevented from doing so afterwards. Much of this could be attributed to the shortage of skilled personnel: one third of the pre-war total of engineers was lost (the total in 1945 being only 8,000).[56] By late 1945, around 3,000 manual workers had become enterprise directors, although this was usually in response to shortage rather than on account of their ideological reliability.[57] It was the drastic nationalisation and 'Stalinisation' of the late 1940s that resulted in many technically skilled workers leaving their posts to be replaced by promoted workers. The government Decree of 1950 which laid down the principle of one-man management, formally assigned responsibility for technical-economic planning, production, finance and investment in the hands of the enterprise director. The political reliability of the promoted workers had secured them a limited training at technical colleges, and the net result was that, from 1949 to 1952, PZPR membership and class origin determined access to such courses and hence entry into senior enterprise management.[58] Thus began a trend which continued into the 1960s and which left an indelible mark upon the features of Polish management: the tendency for senior posts to be occupied by those with an engineering education, the tendency for the most highly qualified to avoid both the most senior posts and work on the shop-floor, and a relative neglect of economics and business training – even 'on the job'! In conditions of growing complexity in the managerial process consequent upon industrial concentration, it is obvious that at the higher levels of the management hierarchy engineering skills were less relevant and business skills more relevant to the task of management. Also, as we shall see, the demographic surge of highly educated people onto the labour market in the 1960s meant that, paradoxically, at the lower level of management where some posts were of a very routine nature, technically over-qualified staff were to be found.

The claim that professional engineering skills were essential to recruitment into industrial management was gently questioned in research reports that had monitored appointments to senior enterprise management, conducted by a Centre for Management Training (CODKK) whose headquarters were set up in Warsaw in 1961, and which by the early 1970s had branch units located in all industrial ministries.[59] Yet the persistence of such a criterion for appointment was attributed in an intensive study of managerial recruitment in the engineering industry, to the *Taryfikator* (the official job specification outlining the necessary training and experience for posts in the industry). Oddly enough, although it was specified that the post of deputy director for technical affairs and investment receive a higher education and seven years' experience in industry, there was no such job specification for the post of enterprise director. The only other requirement for higher management was that the deputy enterprise director for administration, trade and economic affairs ought to possess a higher degree (although it was perfectly feasible that this could be in engineering or legal studies as well as economics) plus four years' work experience.[60] In a situation where priority in higher education had originally been accorded to engineers, this encouraged their entry into all types of senior management posts irrespective of suitability.[61] Economists would tend to be employed on the planning side of production under the supervision of the deputy director for economic affairs rather than be candidates for senior management positions. During the 1960s the number of enterprise directors with a higher education in economics remained low. By 1965, 56% of enterprise directors had either higher technical or secondary technical education, whilst only 17% had any training in economics. The total number of economists with a degree was estimated to be 9, 129 and these were discovered to be unevenly distributed between occupations.[62]

A study of enterprise directors in five industries in 1970 (heavy, light, food, chemicals, mining and energy industries) revealed that of the posts they occupied prior to their appointment, over 40% had been in middle or senior management in technical affairs or engineering in an enterprise, and only 11% had held the equivalent post in economic affairs.[63]

Thus the logic of advanced industrialisation had not encouraged the promotion of those with formal business skills into senior enterprise management in Poland. In recognition of the urgency for action, the CODKK began courses in 1968 for in-service training not only for the management of industrial enterprises, but also for that of industrial associations and combines. Courses were initially offered to staff from three industries (chemicals, heavy and light industry). However, only two such courses had been held by 1970, attended by 18 and 24 directors respectively. Inasmuch as it is possible to infer anything from their characteristics, all had higher education (81% were engineers) and a large number had only been in post for a short time (out of the first group, 11 out of 18 had only held the job for under two years). Yet despite this, out of the total 42, 24 had already undergone some kind of in-service training (and as many as 20 had attended two or three such courses). On the whole, they tended to be older than average for enterprise directors, 'converted' to the utility of such training for their job (the motivation of 41.7% was considered to be 'task-oriented', as opposed to 22% 'self-oriented' and 25.5% 'people-oriented'.[64] The small number attending denoted lack of importance ascribed to such ventures in the eyes of both government and other eligible managerial candidates.

The decision to form the industrial combines prompted the government to entrust the CODKK with the responsibility of running courses on organisation and management for association and combine directors. Supplementary guidelines issued later in 1970 stressed that at each level in industrial management there should be a 'cadre base' (a reserve list of qualified, politically approved personnel) and that the chief director should undertake responsibility for in-service training of his successors.[65] After March 1970, the CODKK held a number of two-week courses clearly aiming to supply business and management skills. Four such courses had been held by November 1970 (covering such subjects as management of large groups of industrial plant, problems of branch development, cost-accounting, decision-making and information systems, and the individual in the management process). By the time the fifth course was held in February 1971, 95 people had participated (mainly chief directors of associations and combines, plus directors of departments of industrial ministries, foreign trade centres, the National Bank and instructors from the PZPR Central Committee) and by mid-1971 the total reached 136.[66] The people involved in supervising these courses stressed that the increasing complexity of large industrial organisations and the increasing uncertainty in decision-making and pressures upon time required a new type of manager who was not just efficient in carrying out recommendations, but who, above all, was a 'researcher, diagnostician, and innovator'. The majority of directors on these courses had graduated in engineering (of the total 86 who had completed the courses by late 1970, 50 had higher education in engineering and 30 in economics). Their knowledge of management skills was observed to vary enormously and very rarely to have been gained from formal study prior to employment. It was curious, though, that when interviewed regarding their suggestions for further types of management training, many participants on these courses proposed training programmes for the administrative and clerical staff of the industrial association, which indicates, as we shall see below, that weaknesses in management skills were not just confined to senior levels.

Thus it would appear that the CODKK courses touched only the tip of the iceberg and that problems of management skills would require more radical change in educational policy. The vested interests of the engineering profession in industry were adamant that any inadequacies in business skills could best be remedied by supplementary courses in economics rather than by training an economist in technical matters. In 1970 an article in *Nowe Drogi* called for the provision of a post-diploma training in economics for engineers involved in management so that they would acquire specialist knowledge of certain areas of economics such as costing and regional economic development.[67] Joint meetings of the professional organisation of engineers (NOT) and economists (PTE) at regional level took place in the 1970s, but it was not until the late 1970s that a joint programme of co-operation on research and education was considered at a national level, and a joint journal (*Przegląd-techniczne – innowacje*) was launched.[68]

The endeavour for radical change came during 1973–4 when reform of economics education took place. The Directors' Charter of 1972 had been predicated on the assumption that directors of large enterprises and WOGs were skilled in economics and organisation science, and that greater numbers of economists would be employed in senior management.[69] Yet the number of economists amongst higher education graduates employed in different sectors of the economy varied, the proportion of economists among the total number of graduates with higher education was both falling and becoming increasingly feminised, and, despite the growth in the number of posts for which specialist economics training was necessary, there was still much 'substitution' by non-economists.[70] Moreover, where economists were employed in industrial management, they were still being displaced by engineers who earned around 20% more than they did.[71]

To assume that the predominance of engineering graduates in industrial management is indicative of the existence of a cohesive group of technocrats would be false. As Kolankiewicz has noted, engineers are far from being a cohesive political force, and are highly differentiated according to type of training and pay.[72] The development of the post-war engineering profession was made an urgent priority because of the acute shortage of technical personnel in the post-1945 period. It took the form of introducing a two-stage academic career, leading first to the title of 'Engineer' and later 'Master Engineer'. Between 1953 and 1956 a unified curriculum of five years' full-time study was agreed upon, but since 1948 the series of evening classes, correspondence and extra-mural courses provided by the NOT had proliferated at a very rapid rate. This exponential growth of engineering education in the first post-war decade had two unforeseen consequences; firstly, a lowering of standards, which was accompanied by a loss of status for degrees in engineering, and secondly a personnel policy that channelled many people with engineering degrees into middle and lower management posts for which they were unsuited.[73] Again a pattern of managerial recruitment was established that later became difficult to break. Because of the relatively stressful nature of senior management positions in industry, and because of their political reliability (they were workers who had acquired their educational opportunity on account of their partisanship), it was those less-qualified engineers who had undergone part-time study who were recruited into senior enterprise management. Those who had studied full-time preferred to work in the area of research and development.

Yet even within its own terms of reference the policy of recruitment of engineers into management positions in Poland was not rational. By the mid-1970s Poland had a higher proportion of engineers in the industrial workforce than either the USA or West Germany, but paradoxically suffered from a shortage of particular specialists,[74] especially production engineers or supervisors working on the shop floor. Most engineering graduates tended to begin employment in lower management posts and be promoted upwards. Twenty percent of engineers were employed in posts outside the profession, but for as many as 40% their degree was not at all necessary to the work they had to do. For example, in the textile industry, which was technologically backward until 1970 and where very few engineers held senior managerial posts, there was a conscious attempt to recruit more young engineers into management, yet often they ended up doing work for which they were not qualified. In the construction industry, too, the majority of engineering personnel would be employed in project offices and general administration, very few would be working on site, and in the chemicals industry there was evidence of many engineers resigning from work in production to take up research.[75]

Whether this was the fault of personnel policy or of the training curriculum is difficult to disentangle, and the response of the government in the late 1970s was to tackle both. While already in 1965 and 1970 there had been moves to encourage engineers to specialise in the practical application of their knowledge to production, in June 1979 there was a proposal to alter radically the nature of engineering education in Poland. While the two levels of specialisation in engineering studies would be retained, their content would be changed so that the basic level would recruit people directly from the shop floor, and the curriculum would be very much related to their practical work experience. The aim would be to keep these qualified people working in production while the higher level of qualification would be open to those who wished to work in research.[76] The whole issue was highly controversial. In some ways it could be seen as a rationalisation of the effects of demographic change in industry whereby many young highly qualified people are stuck in posts normally occupied by skilled workers or lower management, below the level of their true capabilities. It was also intended to halt the drift into the comfortable world of research and development, and increase the chances of those from working-class backgrounds relative to those of white-collar social origin (see below).

Thus, to recapitulate, Polish industrial managers tended to be trained in engineering, ignorant of formal economics and business training, and the most highly qualified tended to avoid posts both at the most senior level and on the workshop floor. As a group they were divided according to type of educational pathway, and, as we shall see later, were divided also by generational lines and partisanship.

However, so far we have only mentioned senior management posts of which there are about 180,000 in Poland. To convey the impression that management was staffed mainly by higher qualified engineers would be false. There is also a large white-collar group working in industrial administration. Traditionally, very few of these had higher education, many were women, and, as work in industrial administration was of a lower status than that elsewhere (such as in local government), this category tended to be those with the lowest qualifications,[77] and very rule-oriented in their attitude to work. This group grew rapidly in the 1940s as a consequence of the demographic developments, and provided a means for those displaced from agriculture (during the attempt at collectivisation) to earn their living, and later for manual workers to achieve promotion. White-collar work was popular amongst those who had close ties with rural traditions, where peasants and craftsmen were independent property-owners, and this aura of independence (*sobiepaństwo*) could be retained in the new posts, many of which would fall into the management bonus category.

Such work continued to be popular, and the advantageous fringe benefits acted as a lure to recruits. However, the labour intensity of much menial work carried out by such people, and the need for a more modern outlook from those employed in the new combines and WOGs were seen to be a barrier to increased efficiency and labour productivity. Campaigns by the PZPR to eliminate 'excessive bureaucratisation' began in the late 1960s, and in April 1971 there were attempts to restrict the proportion of employees in industrial administration relative to those employed in production (although this proved difficult to achieve with the great variations between branches of industry).[78] There are conflicting reports on the success of this measure. Although the number of administrative staff in government departments (138,000) and industrial associations and co-operatives (50,000) was held to have fallen by 1977 (in comparison with 1972), clerical employment in many WOGs remained high. The looseness of management structure, and the tendency for the numbers and types of departments to grow to ensure that senior management status was guaranteed to an increasing number, meant that, to put it mildly, 'personnel categories were inadequate'.[79] Management organisation was held to be a considerable source of Poland's economic weakness: the failure to adjust structure to meet new tasks, the lack of managerial skills in senior management and absence of basic training at the lowest level were cited.[80]

Yet was this a complete picture of Polish managerial structure? There is still one other group of employees whose role in the labour process has acquired increasing significance to the process of management under conditions of advanced industrialisation and industrial concentration. These are the highly skilled industrial manual working class who occupy the posts of foremen. Historically, their role is derived from that of the master-craftsmen whose skills commanded the whole of the production process. However, after 1945 the foremen's powers were radically circumscribed with the introduction of a planned economy, and as a consequence of the law of 1951 which divided up the work process into functionally specialised activities for the purpose of job evaluation and cost-accounting, foremen became classified as blue-collar workers and were thereby excluded from the management bonus scheme. However, the job specification of the foreman was sufficiently vague as to place him in the invidious position of being a representative both of the workforce and of line management. He would set tasks, decide on the working conditions of staff (the allocation of holidays, time off, etc.) explain management policy and decisions, and would supervise industrial training.[81]

There was a gradual change in the type of people being recruited to these posts as the older foremen who were recruited in the pre-war and immediate post-war period were slowly replaced either by younger working people who had undergone in-service training, or by students from vocational schools who had undergone a fairly technical but theoretical education with little work experience. For some of the latter the post of foreman was an 'initiation rite' to be got over as quickly as possible on the way to promotion into lower and middle management.[82] These 'new-style' foremen had appeared first in the technically advanced sectors of industry such as chemicals and electronics, and hopes were expressed that they would have displaced all the older foremen by 1970 (although this did not happen).[83]

The foremen thus were very important actors in the system of industrial relations in Poland. Although the PZPR trade unions and Workers' Councils formally existed to defend workforce interests, it was the foremen who were often the true representatives of the workforce in terms of wages, overtime, general work conditions and holiday arrangements. Yet, paradoxically, they earned less than many skilled workers and were burdened with responsibility for matters about which they could do very little. The older staff maintained a traditional identification with the working class, but many of the newer foremen had difficulties in getting on with their workmates.[84] In either case, this placed foremen at the centre of industrial unrest; either as the champion of workforce interests or as the butt of worker discontent with management. They were at the forefront of worker protest against the government in 1970,[85] so it was not surprising that the government desired to diffuse their ardour by re-evaluating their role in industry in 1972, and by elevating them and incorporating them into management, thereby extending management wage and bonus schemes to them.[86] In return they were to devote their energy to raising labour productivity by organising 'socialist competition'; by promoting in-service training, and by meeting regularly amongst themselves and with factory Party organisations.[87]

As the structure of Polish industrial management is so complex, and as the nature of the work experience and career path is different between senior, middle and lower management, it is thus difficult to argue that there exists a coherent set of views espoused by these groups that would justify the assertion that there is a cohesive managerial elite running Polish industry. Furthermore, the assertion that the process of industrial concentration has generated an extremely highly qualified elite of directors of socialist corporations who challenge the authority of the PZPR is also questionable.[88] Polish industrial relations were seen to have fostered a convergence of the Party line and management policy in the 1960s, as the pressures for 'intrafactory loyalty' were strong in the context of a hostile and uncertain business environment. Studies of the relationship between the East German Socialist Unity Party (SED) and industrial management have concluded that there are either changes of recruitment policy within the Party as it responds to the technical requirements of advanced industrialisation,[89] or a change in ideology and pedagogical methods takes place to win over the new technical intelligentsia.[90] Certainly by the 1960s most managers in East Germany tended to be members of the SED: the crucial point of dispute is whether their loyalty to the SED rests on differing value systems. In Poland, partisanship amongst senior managers has been high since the 1960s, so reasons for Party membership become an important way of ascribing values in a country where direct attitudinal and opinion survey is under constraint.

From 1949 to 1952, political reliability rather than technical skills had been the main criterion for entry into senior management posts in industrial enterprises. The political and economic insecurity of such work during the delicate period of transition to a command economy made such work unbearable and turnover was high.[91] Consequently, many with a pre-war training in engineering, and many of those who had graduated soon after World War II, expressed a preference for work in the less heated environment of a design office or ministry, rather than in front-line mangement. This group took a back seat in the political arena until after the Second PZPR Congress in 1954, when there was a call to broaden the role of the PZPR in industry and to encourage 'initiative from below' – namely to induce technical specialists to join the Party and thus be eligible to enter senior management posts in industry.[92]

Kolankiewicz, in his study of the Polish technical intelligentsia, notes that the promotion of younger, more qualified people to management positions was perceived as a threat and this was expressed in the hostility of the older worker-managers to democratisation of the enterprise through the creation of Workers' Councils which were in many cases championed by the technically skilled as a means of challenging conventional managerial practice (see Chapter 6). Although the technical intelligentsia were not at the head of political developments in 1956, they found events to be very much in their favour, enabling them to draw attention to the causes of the turnover in management posts and call for 'improved qualifications' through the mouthpiece of their professional organisation NOT.[93]

There was, however, no rapid recruitment of these engineers into the ranks of the PZPR, but the PZPR was well aware of the need to change its management recruitment policy in industry, as the influx of politically reliable but low-skilled managers had meant that many enterprises were being effectively run from the central board or ministry. Thus, by the 1960s there was indeed a rapid increase in the recruitment of engineers into the PZPR. Kolankiewicz sees this as motivated by instrumental reasons such as the need for promotion by those in lower and middle-line management, yet PZPR membership still remained low amongst those working in research and development, design and construction.[94] By 1965 enterprise directors tended, increasingly, to be younger people who, after finishing higher education had worked in industry as engineers or in some managerial post. They could not be described as PZPR activists but a higher proportion were members.[95] Kolankiewicz traces the reason for this phenomenon back to the different social origins of directors, and their career paths. Despite the so-called meritocratic criteria of recruitment into the new socialist intelligentsia, the recruitment of students into full-time higher education did not favour those from manual working-class origin (see above). By 1967 only 40% of the total number of students in full-time higher education were from manual working-class or peasant background, and yet, of those studying part-time, the percentage was as high as 80%. It was this latter group who found that they had limited access to employment in the more prestigious fields of research and development, and who therefore joined the PZPR for instrumental reasons.[96]

So, in the mid-1960s there was a marked difference among enterprise directors in terms of educational achievement, which was strongly related to class background. More working-class directors appeared to have attended a vocational – technical college and to have started work as manual workers, and also to have taken up posts in the PZPR apparat before entering industrial management. By the mid-1960s those who had followed such a 'political career' were less numerous and had been displaced by those pursuing a 'professional career' (having worked only in the technical side of management) and by those who pursued an 'administrative career' (with a predominantly managerial work-experience but of a very broad nature and which could have included work in the offices of an industrial association or bank.[97]

By 1970 a greater proportion of enterprise directors were of white-collar social origin with full-time higher technical education and likely to be PZPR members. Certainly the career path from administrative work in an industrial association, local government,

PZPR or trade union apparat was less frequent. Yet the logic of advanced industrialisation did not automatically lead to the placement of the most technically skilled in the posts carrying the greatest responsibility in Polish industry. Again, the reason for this must be traced back to the *Taryfikator* which specified the necessary length of work-experience or probation *(staż pracy)* for particular posts. This had been drawn up at a time when there was a relative shortage of cadres, but, with increasing numbers of post-war baby-bulge graduates coming into the labour market in the mid-1960s, the wisdom of using such criteria for promotion was doubtful. For example, at higher levels of management in the engineering industry, it was noticeable that those with the longest work-experience were in the most senior posts (77.8% of senior management had been in post for over 10 years in 1968). This correlation of work-experience with age and seniority of post contributed to a 'blockage' in the promotion prospects of the increasingly large numbers of young people with higher education who entered lower management.[98] The most prestigious posts in large and multi-plant enterprises were held by older people with lower qualifications, and the younger, better-qualified staff were more likely to be directors of smaller enterprises or 'frozen' into middle and lower management posts.

This state of affairs continued into the 1970s and, if anything, became more pronounced than attenuated under the Gierek regime. These generational differences in opportunity produced differences in management attitudes, aspirations and morale, and also placed limits upon the extent to which management of the new combines and WOGs was recruited from the most highly qualified and responsive to the PZPR.

To commence with the second point, during the early 1960s, career pathways from employment in middle management in the industrial association to the post of enterprise director were quite frequent and encouraged by a wages policy that made employment in the former less attractive to the well qualified.[99] Moreover, until 1967, directors of multi-factory enterprises in the engineering industry tended to have lower educational qualifications than those who ran smaller enterprises. (A total of 57.11 of directors of leading enterprises in this branch of industry had not yet acquired a Master's Certificate in higher technical education, while around 80% of directors of small enterprises had done so.) There was a lack of correlation between the complexity and responsibility of senior management posts and the qualifications of those occupying them. While by 1970 there seemed to have been some change in senior management recruitment policy to include more highly qualified people (95% of chief directors and deputies of industrial associations had a higher education, and the rest had further technical education) who were nearly all members of the PZPR, a study in 1973 of PZPR organisation within industrial associations by the officials of the Central Warsaw PZPR District (80% of industrial associations had their headquarters here) found that membership levels were low in middle and lower management, and averaged out at around 26%.[100] There was often conflict between association management and Party organisations, not because highly technically qualified managers were challenging the legitimacy of Party control, but because the Party itself was trying to improve the efficiency of management procedure and management qualifications (in some industrial associations only half the middle management had further education or above).[101] As many industrial associations acquired the status of WOG, the new managerial bonus scheme provided little incentive to achieve a complete overhaul of all these administrative staff: a streamlined technically expert managerial structure did not accompany the process of industrial concentration.

On the other matter of management attitudes, aspirations and morale, many young graduates of higher education who were looking for posts in industry in the 1970s were faced with a choice between bitter resentment of their lot or a cynical attitude towards appointments policies in industry. In 1977 it was noted that Poland's population of graduates had attained 700,000 but, of these, 50% had acquired their education since 1971.[102] The Gierek government had reformed higher education in the early 1970s and there had been a rapid response to the improved access to places as aspirations were raised. However, as one social statistician acidly remarked, such a policy 'stems not only from the need to produce a qualified labour force...it very often creates manpower qualifications over-reaching the level of economic development, which in turn exerts pressure for the accelerated development of the economy and its structural transformation to a full use of manpower resources'.[103] The consequence was that, to many young graduates, relations with one's peer group, superiors, and membership of 'informal groups' were the determining criteria for promotion rather than one's professional qualification.[104] Thus it was not surprising that the PZPR faced problems with 'young political professionals' joining the Party's student organisation at university (ZSMP after 1973) in order to obtain a post in the *wojewodztwo* Party apparat when they left, as this was construed as improving career chances to a greater extent[105] than would a job practising their skill in a lower management post such as that of a foreman.[106] Unfortunately, the response of the Gierek government to the demand that it had created was to justify cuts in full-time student places in higher education from 71,500 in 1979 to 60,000 in 1980 (16%), and part-time places from 42,000 to 30,000 (28%). To those whose taste for social advance had been encouraged (particularly those of working-class origin who were the major beneficiaries of part-time education, and whose chances of entry into management ranks in the 1970s were becoming fewer), such policies presented a considerable threat.

There is some evidence that by the early 1970s senior management was becoming increasingly recruited from people who had begun their career in lower management, rather than in manual work, who were more likely to come from white-collar or peasant families, who were also highly likely to have been active in the PZPR, trade union or youth movements at the start of their career, and who enjoyed a more privileged standard of living.[107] In 1977 it was estimated that there were about 180,000 people fulfilling the post of industrial enterprise director in Poland, and a further 20,000 who held such senior posts in industrial ministries and 'corporations' (associations, combines and WOGs). A survey of 270 directors in Warsaw in late 1972 (including senior industrial association, ministry and local government officials as well as those in enterprises and factories employing over 500 people) revealed that, in comparison with the white-collar group in general or with the rest of Warsaw citizens, directors were more likely to come from white-collar, professionally educated smaller families, living in rural areas and small and medium-sized towns, and to have experienced a longer period in education.[108] The political activism of this group was high and, while this tended to wane after the commencement of a 'professional-technical' career, for those who entered political careers (work in the PZPR apparat) before their appointment to the post of director, political activism continued to be high.[109] While in the past it would have been the sons of manual workers who were most likely to adopt a 'political' career and undergo in-service higher education, by the early 1970s those directors from peasant families were more prevalent in this category. In short, access to senior management positions in Polish industry was becoming sealed off from those of working-class social origin and opportunities for the promotion of manual workers were becoming limited. Senior industrial management was becoming more highly educated, and pay levels increased at the same time (bonuses sometimes exceeded the basic rate of pay).[110] To a younger generation with **higher** and further education, whose career prospects were 'frozen' often in posts below their level of competence, such privilege seemed both irrational and unjust. Some turned their back on the Party and sought refuge in increased professional identification: others, often holding the post of foreman, took advantage of PZPR overtures and were recruited in large numbers. Some of the latter were moved by motives of cynical instrumentalism: Party activism was a means to promotion. Others were spurred on by a belief that things could be changed by 'entrism'. Nonetheless, a generational division within the framework of Polish industrial management structure was acquiring increasing political significance.

Conclusion

It is impossible to argue that the political consequence of industrial integration and concentration has been the unambiguous growth of a new class of technocrats challenging the legitimacy of the PZPR. To refer to a cohesive managerial interest in Polish industry is to ignore the diverse outcomes of policies made in the 1950s (the principle of one-man management, the high status of engineering education, partisanship as a criterion for appointment to senior positions, the reward of privileged access to the means of social consumption) and to ignore the impact of demographic trends upon manpower policy. The logic of advanced industrialisation has not encouraged the promotion of the most qualified or those with business skills into senior industrial management. At the same time, the career prospects of a highly educated generation, who find themselves in lower management or skilled manual work are blocked by the presence of less qualified middle management and clerical staff.

Moreover, our study of socio-structural change has pointed to the inaccuracy of assuming that boundaries between social classes are clear and immutable. There is now a new working class in Poland, new in terms of both its age and its qualifications. Yet it also shares many common experiences with groups such as worker-peasants and technicians. These common experiences can both reinforce solidarity and highlight conflicting interests, thus emphasising the importance of subjective as well as objective aspects of class position. Denied privileged access to the means of social consumption, many technicians can find themselves identifying with manual workers, and many white-collar workers will hide behind a cloak of 'professionalism' to ward off incursions into their independence.

Although attitudinal change is difficult to measure in a country like Poland, it is not possible to say that a transformation in the values of senior industrial management has occurred from 'politically minded, traditional and past-oriented people to rational and achievement-oriented men'.[111] This is evident in the reasons for joining the PZPR which can vary according to social origin, current occupation, generation and educational experience. Instrumental reasons can prevail amongst those senior recruits from intelligentsia origin who need to use the PZPR to attenuate the stress of senior management positions, and similarly for graduates who are aware that the fastest route to promotion is through work in the PZPR apparat. On the other hand, a more affective orientation towards the PZPR is often displayed by those of working-class origin for whom the Party has hitherto been a means of acquiring in-service education and an alternative channel of social mobility. However, these opportunities in recent years have become increasingly limited as access to both full-time and part-time education has been restricted, and degree qualifications have been overhauled and devalued, by a government that was pledged after 1970 to increase opportunity but has discovered that its economic strategy will not permit this. It is at this juncture that several interests across class boundaries can meet (the young worker-technicians, worker-peasants, the aristocracy of labour, graduate foremen etc.). However, whether they are challenging a cohesive technocratic class is another matter. Nor can they accuse the authorities of not attempting to change the political process. As we shall see in the following chapter, the PZPR after 1971 was fully cognisant of the need to reform socio-political institutions (not least of all itself) to cope with concentration and integration of industrial enterprises. It was rather the manner in which such change was envisaged to take place that belied the 'technocratism' of the grand design, and as such raises doubts about the ability of a Marxist–Leninist party to cope with the process of advanced industrialisation.

6

The political consequences of industrial integration and concentration: the 'leading role' of the PZPR, workforce participation and socio-political reform

A complete understanding of the problems of Party control over a changing industrial structure cannot be acquired simply by reference to social structure and recruitment policies. The manner in which the PZPR chooses to organise and operate is of equal importance. In common with other Marxist–Leninist political parties this conforms to the principles of democratic centralism and of the vanguard-cadre party (the 'leading role' of the Party). If, as we have seen, the process of industrial concentration generates complexity in managerial practices and the accompanying strategy of economic growth generates social demands, can a Marxist–Leninist party change its mode of organisation and institutionalise political conflict? This involves a consideration of whether the principles underlying the PZPR are based on a 'limited theory of organisational contradiction'[1] as suggested by E. Olin Wright. In comparing and contrasting the writings of Lenin and Max Weber about bureaucracy, he concludes that both suffer from 'theoretical underdevelopment'. Lenin, in particular, fails to develop a notion of how the role and mechanism of the vanguard party can keep it responsive to the working class; he envisages the exercise of mass control and accountability to be inherently simple, and he assumes that experts do not pose a threat of bureaucratic usurpation. Theoretical weaknesses of Marxism–Leninism have also been central to Tellenback's analysis of the role of the PZPR in industrialising the economy: while its industrialisation policy has generated conflict within civil society, the PZPR has been unable to provide a mechanism for gradual and piecemeal solution to this. Our analysis in Chapter 5 would tend towards rejecting his arguments about value change (that the PZPR has compensated by increasingly recruiting professional/technical personnel, the effect of which

153

is to encourage a pragmatism on the part of the policy makers and a homogenisation of value systems within civil society towards apolitical privatised petty-bourgeois ideals), but Tellenback's other major point, that the PZPR will increasingly base its legitimacy on technical and administrative competence (rather than ideological commitment) and back this up by social welfare policy, is more acceptable. In this chapter we shall endeavour to demonstrate that the structure and operation of the PZPR has responded (albeit belatedly) to the development of combines, multi-factory enterprises and WOGs. Furthermore, at the height of the process of industrial concentration in the mid-1970s, this was accompanied by extensive reform of the constitution, local government and industrial relations in order to incorporate better the demands of wider civil society. Finally, we point to the increasingly important role assumed by social welfare in securing regime legitimacy while its susceptibility to unequal social distribution has served to exacerbate divisions in wider civil society rather than to attenuate them.

The 'leading role' of the Party and industrial concentration

Any consideration of this must commence by considering the formal organisational structure of the PZPR, stretching from the supreme body of Congress right down to the Basic Party Organisation (POP).

The PZPR statutes specify that Basic Party Organisations can be set up in all places of work according to the production principle. In some urban areas and parts of the countryside, a branch POP can be set up for enterprises and institutions engaged in a similar form of productive activity; POPs can also be organised on the 'territorial principle' if there are no large factories or places of work. A POP can be formed where there is a minimum of 3 (5 after 1971) members, but as soon as the total number of members and candidates in a workplace exceed 100, Sectional Party Organisations (OOP) can be set up Fig. 4 shows these organisational structures. Report-back/ Electoral Conferences should be held every two years and interim Party business at that level should be dealt with by an elected executive (or, in very large factories, a committee) which should report to a monthly general meeting of the POP.[2]

The work of a POP can be seen as providing a forum for the exchange of ideas, as a basis for transmitting Party ideas to the

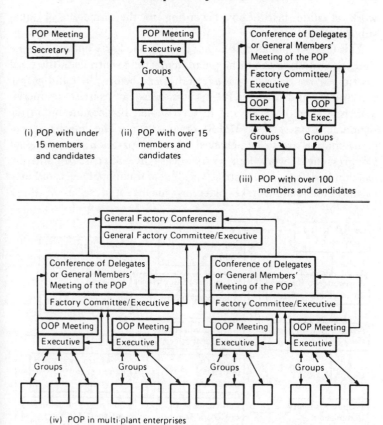

Fig. 4. The organisational structure of a Basic Party Organisation (POP)
Source: A. Dobieszewski *Wiedza o Partii: wybrany problemy*, Warsaw, 1972,
p. 370

masses, and as a means of harmonising the different interests of groups and individuals. Membership requirements are nomination by either two existing Party members of at least two years' standing, or members from affiliated organisations such as the Socialist Youth (ZMS before 1973 and ZSMP afterwards), and willingness to assume an activist and exemplary role in educational and ideological activity in the workplace. Those whose behaviour falls below a certain standard could be struck off the list, but not without due warning and discussion at a full POP meeting. One particular aspect of its leading role is the supervision and evaluation of the work of state institutions according to the principle of 'dual subordination'.

This task is replicated at higher levels in the Party but at the same time, according to the principle of democratic centralism, the rural district, urban district (*gromada* and *powiat* before 1973 and *gminna* afterwards) and town PZPR organisations can exercise a supervisory role over the POP and in turn should be accountable to the regional (*wojewodztwo*) PZPR organisation. The mechanics of co-ordination are to be achieved in the preparation for a national Congress held every four years (every five after 1976) and the election of delegates to district, regional and national levels of Party organisation should take place by means of a series of Party

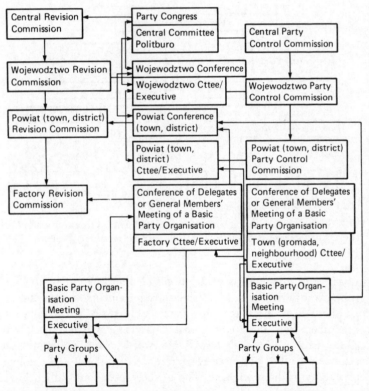

Fig. 5.   The organisational structure of the PZPR
Source: A. Dobieszewski *Wiedza o Partii: wybrany problemy*, Warsaw, 1972, p. 312

conferences prior to the Congress. All executive posts (secretaries etc.) should be elected at all levels, with, at the national level, a Central Committee normally consisting of 65–80 members, which should meet in plenary session every three or four months. At the summit of the Basic Party Organisation are the Politburo aided by a secretariat, a Central Party Control Commission (attending to membership enrolment and discipline) and a Central Revision Commission (to look after the operation of the PZPR apparat and its finances), should synthesise views at all levels of the Party and formulate policy[3] (see Fig. 5).

So, PZPR committees and executive bodies at all levels exist to direct the work of their respective organisations, and amongst their responsibilities are included the implementation of the Party line (the leading role), the placement and training of cadres, and the education of workers in the basic principles of Marxism–Leninism.[4] It is a commonplace for social scientists to argue that democratic centralism 'does not work', but whether or not this is by design or the 'theoretical underdevelopment' of Leninism already alluded to is rarely explored. Yet it must be if we are to understand the relationship between changes in economic organisation and political unrest. After both of the two major political upheavals in Poland in 1956 and 1970, the new first secretaries of the Party referred to mistakes in Party policy and behaviour and a degree of unresponsiveness to the masses. In both cases this was followed by a turnover of membership at the central level, and of middle-level elites, and later by a more thorough evaluation of mass membership through the 'exchange of Party cards'.[5] Yet, even after 1970, an analysis of the major speeches delivered by Edward Gierek between 1971 and 1977 implied that the role of the PZPR had not really changed. Rather it represented a continuation of past experiences and the enhancement of several elements that together would act to reinforce the 'organisational–inspirational' role of the Party.[6] While one very pessimistic evaluation describes a society geared towards the 'self-reproduction of artificial reality', where the lack of political alternatives and the ideological legitimation of argument is a trap for the ruling group,[7] there is substantial evidence that political leadership in Poland was aware of the need for changes in PZPR organisation to correspond to changes in industrial structure, even if it did respond slowly.

A review of trends in PZPR organisation during the 1960s

revealed that there had been considerable increases in the size of POPs. In late 1969, while the total number of POPs was 72,269, there were 603 operating in large industrial plants where the total number of members and candidates was over 400, and where the aggregate PZPR membership amounted to 22.5% of the national total. By 1971, the number of POPs had risen to 73,000 and there were 648 with over 400 members.[8] The creation of multi-factory enterprises and combines aggravated the problem of communication between different levels of Party organisation (POP and OOP), the activists and non-Party workforce in industry. Although the self-criticism of the PZPR following the December 1970 disturbances stressed the breakdown of 'democratic modes' of Party work, it was quite clear that the content of PZPR activity was constrained by the official structure of the Party. For example, the decision to set up OOPs in industry rested in the hands of the appropriate *wojewodztwo* committee of the PZPR, and the lower-level *powiat* committee was empowered to extend the decision-making powers of an OOP in a large enterprise situated in its territory. However, this meant that the executive of a POP could be quite remote from the influence of the workforce, and in some cases, such as the single-site combine Huty im.Lenina, the POP had decision-making powers identical to those of the local *powiat* Party organisation which caused problems in relations between large industrial plants and local administration.[9] Nor had the structure of POPs been adapted to conform to the requirements of the new combines set up after 1969. Decree 193/1969 made no mention of this, and the structure of 'dual subordination' was disrupted as Party organisations in the constituent enterprises remained in an ambiguous position *vis à vis* the Party organisation in the leading factory of the combine.[10]

Furthermore, at higher levels, the network of Party controls operating upon the work of industrial associations and ministries was much weaker than those affecting the industrial enterprise. While the enterprise Party organisations could exert a measure of political control over enterprise management by reporting on their militancy to higher levels, POPs in ministries and industrial associations did not have the right to supervise managerial policy and practice, but could only report the failings of individual Party members.[11] These formal arrangements were very important and were reflected in the different roles assumed by enterprise and association directors in the early 1960s. While association directors were held to perform a 'purely economic role', the enterprise directors were seen to be constrained by 'socio-political requirements'. Their policy was under the close scrutiny of the enterprise PZPR committee, but there was no such interference in the work of senior management of the industrial association, who were accountable only to the industrial ministry and other central state institutions (such as the NBP, the ministry of finance, Committee on Labour and Wages etc.).[12] Hence, there were considerable fears that the proposals to make the industrial association a more economically independent organisation after 1965 might result in weakening the powers of scrutiny exerted by local Party organisations. Awareness of these dangers prompted the IV Central Committee Plenum in 1965 to call upon PZPR organisations in industrial associations to assume a greater involvement in administration.

However, the major instrument at the disposal of the PZPR to maintain its leading role is its control over senior appointments: the *nomenklatura*. Until the issuing of Decree 383/1966 on the industrial association, all leading industrial management appointments (down to the level of industrial association and enterprise directors and their deputies) could only be made by the ministry. After this date the association directors were permitted to make senior enterprise management appointments in the name of the minister[13] (subject to subsequent ratification). All these appointments at enterprise level, though, had to be cleared by the cadre department of the *wojewodztwo* PZPR committee on whose territory the enterprise was situated, irrespective of whether the enterprise belonged to centrally or locally controlled industry. The enterprise director and POP executive dealt with all appointments to middle- and lower-level management within the enterprise. In theory, the PZPR could maintain its leading role over appointments at all levels, but in practice this was far from attainable. To be effective, cadre policy had to be based on past records of managerial candidates, and information gleaned in the course of continuous inspection activities was vital to this. With the increased powers of industrial associations and the emergence of multi-site combines in the late 1960s, the possibility for *wojewodztwo* cadre departments to fulfil this activity at all, let alone rationally, was diminished.

Thus the process of industrial concentration was presenting considerable problems for the PZPR. Size of economic unit affected possibilities for effective communication and democratic control; the

structure of local government and local PZPR units precluded
effective control over the activities of multi-factory enterprises and
combines, and rendered this impossible in the case of industrial
associations and WOGs; and centralisation of economic decision-
making without corresponding developments in cadre policy
weakened the effectiveness of the *nomenklatura*. All these matters
were addressed by the PZPR in the 1970s during the period of the
Gierek leadership.

Party communication and democratic control in large industrial plants

One particular grievance voiced during the industrial unrest of
1970–1 concerned the degeneration of PZPR production meetings
between enterprise management and workers into a mere formality:
the enterprise director would report to the factory PZPR committee
or Production Conference (*Narad Wytwórczy*) often without any
further discussion taking place. At first the change in the PZPR
Statutes at the Sixth Congress endeavoured to counteract this by
specifying that POP meetings could only be quorate if at least 50%
of all members attended and that the number of manual workers
represented in the Executive of the POP should be proportionate to
their share in the total membership of the POP.[14] The Secretariat
also issued new guidelines for the enrolment of members, and
recommended in June 1971 that a series of courses for activists in
large plants should be provided through the newly opened Higher
School of Social Sciences (WSNS); and eventually it was announced
by the Politburo that 164 large industrial plants had been selected
for observation and experiment, the results of which were to be
reported at the Seventh PZPR Congress.[15] All of these proposals
were individual elements in a much more fundamental solution,
which was made the subject of discussion at a National Conference
of PZPR Activists (in itself an innovatory departure) held in
January 1973.[16]

The experiments in the 164 large industrial plants are of
particular interest. They accounted for about 27% of the total
output of Polish industry and employed 25% of the Polish industrial
workforce. In terms of Party membership, at the beginning of the
experiment the total number of PZPR members and candidates was
215,000 (over 8% of the total PZPR membership and about 14% of

all working-class members) organised into 852 POPs, 4,100 OOPs and 16,000 groups.[17] Of the industrial plants that took part in this exercise, the most frequently reported were the Cegielski engineering works in Poznań, the Ursus tractor factory in Radom, the Gdańsk shipyards, the nitrates factory in Tarnów and the steel works in Stalowa Wola.[18] During the course of the experiments representatives of the PZPR Central Committee, and of the Central Trade Union Council (CRZZ) attended both the meetings of the Party and the Conferences of Workers' Self-Management. In February 1974, the Politburo established an Institute of Basic Problems of Marxism–Leninism, staffed with social scientists and other academics on secondment. The system of industrial relations including wage, social welfare and personnel policy was studied and the Institute supervised the collection of masses of data on such subjects. Work groups were also appointed to investigate such matters as new modes of interpreting the leading role of the Party in matters such as technical innovation, its relations with various groups and institutions, and the changing composition of PZPR membership.[19] Conferences were held at the WSNS in December 1973 and at the Cegielski engineering works (the results of the latter were published).[20]

Gradually, there emerged a model of how a Marxist–Leninist party should operate during the 1970s to interpret Gierek's famous phrase uttered at the VIII Plenum in 1970 that 'the Party should lead but should not govern'. The emphasis was upon organisation, co-ordination and participation. On the first subject it is interesting to note the change in emphasis upon organisational levels in the PZPR: while there had been a tendency for the overall number of POPs and OOPs to increase after 1976, there was a decline in the number of POPs, but a marked increase in the number of basic-level Party groups.[21] The Party group assumed great importance in all areas of life. In industry it was intended that, through group meetings, problems and strategy could be solved in a plant workshop and moreover that the group would attract non-Party *aktyw* (activists) thereby overcoming barriers to democracy and communication, and providing a clear channel for information to be passed up to the executive of the OOP and POP in big plants.[22]

With respect to the purpose of co-ordination, the PZPR organisations within industrial plants were to work more closely with the trade union, workers' self-management, youth and professional organisations (NOT and PTE) and to liaise more closely with local authorities outside (especially over the provision of social amenities such as day nurseries, housing, shopping facilities etc.). The formal mechanisation by means of which this was to be achieved involved extending the scope of the leading role of the Party to include sending delegates to local government meetings and, eventually (as will be demonstrated below), multiple office-holding of senior Party, trade union and workers' self-management posts in the plant.

A variety of methods was also tried with a view to enhancing the potential for all Party members to participate. These included the convening of frequent meetings of the POP executive with OOP secretaries and individual Party groups, joint executive meetings of the plant POP and OOPs, the opening up of plenary sessions of the Conference of Workers' Self-Management (KSR) and Trade Union Factory Council (RZ) to include representatives from the Party groups and OOP secretaries, and even the opening up of some plenary sessions to participation by non-Party activists.[23] There were considerable innovations in the propaganda and educational role of the PZPR in industry. Regional branches of the Party School were re-opened and made responsible for the provision of a vast amount of in-service training and, although the call for measures to improve contact between apparat and membership was not new, the form that it assumed was, drawing as it did upon Western techniques of personnel and business management. The whole exercise was dressed up as a public relations venture and hailed to benefit both Party members and non-Party activists alike with possibilities for orchestrated mass affirmation to take place at all levels from National Party Conferences summoned between congresses, down to days of voluntary service (*dni czynny*).[24]

Party control over state and economic administration

The concern with the weakness of PZPR control over managerial activity in industrial associations and ministries is reflected in amendments to Clause 51 of the PZPR Statute accepted at the Sixth Congress in 1971. PZPR organisations at this level were now entrusted with the responsibility of directly intervening in the management/administrative process.[25] These changes were seen as essential to the improvement of cadre policy at this level, whose effectiveness was hampered by large numbers of low-skilled employees. Personnel matters were seen as very important in improving the standard of administrative activity in the ministries and industrial associations which appeared to have varying levels of Party membership and educational attainment among their staff.[26] While it was hoped that many of the low-skilled staff could be dismissed and the system of appointment and promotion could be made more rational,[27] this solution could not be adopted in scientific research institutes and laboratories. Here an official investigation by *wojewodztwo* and Central Committee Party research departments attributed the poor co-ordination of research and development, construction and project design to the fact that the professionalisation and apathy of university-trained engineers rendered Party organisation there dormant.[28]

By May 1974 the Central Committee Secretariat of the PZPR had reported on the manner in which the revisions to Clause 51 of the Party Statute should be interpreted for the purpose of making ministerial work more efficient. As 80% of industrial association offices and 80,000 government ministry personnel were located and worked in the Central Warsaw Party District, it fell to this branch of the PZPR to initiate the changes.[29] A certain amount of flexibility was permitted in the interpretation of the new powers of PZPR organisations in the ministries and industrial associations. In the engineering industry, where the Party organisations had not been adapted to the combines after 1970, fourteen 'party-professional' groups were set up to liaise with key plants, and the Party executive committee in the ministry could intervene more in personnel evaluation, and making the internal organisation of work more efficient. Periodic meetings of association directors, Party secretaries in the association and Party representatives from the ministry were to be held.[30] Yet despite reports of exemplary communication occurring in one association in the electrical industry (Elektromontaz), elsewhere the strengthening of ministry and association Party organisations was resisted, especially when activities aimed at rationalisation and improvement of organisational efficiency culminated in the reduction of staff employment, or a loss of status due to amalgamation of posts,[31] and as communication between the ministries, associations and large plants remained weak.[32]

Further revisions to the PZPR Statute were made after the Seventh Congress which took place in December 1975. Clauses 48 and 55 relating to the procedure for establishing POPs and OOPs in industry were revised to enable the Central Committee, either on the recommendation of a particular *wojewodztwo* authority or on its own initiative, to specify directly the sort of Party organisation structure desirable in combines and multi-factory enterprises and to transfer powers of scrutiny from the now defunct *powiat* level of local government to the *wojewodztwo*.[33] On one level this could be seen as an attempt to 'tidy up' Party organisation in the wake of extensive reform of local government, but these changes in regional and local government structure, which took place between 1973 and 1975, were designed to increase central control, especially over the *nomenklatura*. To appreciate this, some comment on relations between industry and local government is necessary.

Regional and local administration could be both a source of pressure upon industrial management and a means whereby, through involvement in the local political process, enterprise directors could enlist support against central planning institutions (see Chapter 5). Moreover, the overlap of PZPR and local government structures in many *wojewodztwa* provided a regional power base for many PZPR secretaries to become local 'barons' or to act as 'brokers' between central government and local interests over the disposal of considerable resources.

To illustrate this, it is necessary to understand that the three-tier system of local authorities which came into existence in 1950 was entrusted with considerable powers over expenditure after 1956. Initially, the levy of a turnover tax on industry located on their territory, and later the creation of regional industrial associations, ensured local control over around 13.5% of output in the socialised sector of industry between 1958 and 1970.[34] Despite the powers at the disposal of local authorities to control and inspect all enterprises located in their area, the centrally planned sector of industry retained a measure of autonomy from their control, as central industrial ministries would not tolerate any interference. The result was that the local authority officials felt themselves to be inadequately informed on such subjects as manpower policy, the capacity of local construction enterprises and the long-term spatial plan.[35]

The dynamic of local politics encouraged the emergence of a 'power elite': studies of council recruitment and decision-making revealed a complex political interaction that was consensual rather than conflictory in nature, and which could be used to explain the strong local loyalties of Party organisations in the area.[36] Because the PZPR 'shadowed' local government structure and took a hegemonic role in local politics (which is often the main forum for the representation of other political parties), there was often dual office-holding of council and Party posts. Naturally the degree of PZPR penetration varied according to the level of the national council concerned.[37] Dual office-holding provided the means for the PZPR officials to exert its leading role, especially in the Presidium, where Party group meetings would often take place in *wojewodztwo* and town authorities. However, there is reason to believe that, by the early 1970s, the frequency of these 'caucus' meetings fell.[38]

Functional though this overlap of personnel in Party, local authority and industrial management might be to the expediting of industrial management tasks, it could present a considerable obstacle to the policy prescriptions of central PZPR organisations. After the disturbances of December 1970 there was much criticism of this arrangement and the immediate result was the replacement of many provincial Party officials. Yet personnel changes were insufficient to break the pattern of local control over industry. The resolution of the Sixth PZPR Congress had pledged that the tasks of the PZPR and the state apparat were to be kept separate, but, paradoxically, between 1973 and 1975, a series of local government reforms took place which were to bring the PZPR into even closer relations with local authorities.

In the name of decentralising control over local revenue and encouraging local participation, the 4313 *gromada* authorities then the *powiata* were the first to be affected and ceased to function as of 1 January 1973. They were replaced by some 2366 *gminna* (communes) of which 318 incorporated small towns. This was followed later in 1973 by a reform of electoral law, which was heralded to bring greater democracy into local government, and by a PZPR directive calling for the merger of the post of PZPR first secretary and local council chairman at all levels, and for the appointment of a politically approved chief executive to run local administration.[39] The official justification of these changes with respect to the *wojewodztwo* authorities was that councils and their committees could no longer be over-burdened with administrative work, would be free to devote themselves to the task of popular representation, and that PZPR scrutiny would be made easier.[40]

What purported to be an exercise in democracy was in fact a disguised form of recentralisation aimed at tidying up local administration. This became increasingly evident during 1973–4, when central control over local finance was tightened.[41] However, the most drastic change took place in 1975, when eight new planning regions were formed, to be run by experts employed in Regional Planning Commissions, who would be supervised by Regional Development Committees on which local interests would be represented. This 'rationalisation' of the pre-existing regional planning system into eight units that were larger than the original 17 *wojewodztwa*, also involved the replacement of the latter by 49 new *wojewodztwa* varying greatly in population size from 3.4 million in Katowice to 224,000 in Chelm.[42] While there is reason to believe that this aimed to make the regional co-ordination of production much easier, the 1975 Reform symbolised a reaffirmation of PZPR control and centralisation of powers in relation to local authorities in Poland. The reforms of 1973–5 were intended to counteract the departmental empires in local government, to break the power base of Regional Party Secretaries and to enable central authorities to intervene more directly, particularly in cadre policy. It is to this latter issue that we now turn.

The Party and cadre policy

There are several aspects to cadre policy. In a narrow sense it covers the *nomenklatura* (around 200,000 posts of responsibility for which local and national Party organisations are obliged to nominate politically reliable candidates). After 1970 the issue came to be perceived more broadly than mere political reliability and the possession of adequate educational qualifications. For a start, the process of recruitment into administration and industry was now to be treated in a more dynamic manner and as bearing a strong relationship to mode of formal education, work experience and post-entry training and promotion. It was not merely enough that the 'right person be found for the right job', but there should also be a pool of people eligible to replace them, and procedures for assessing whether the job was adequately carried out.

So, gradually during the 1970s, the 'lid' was taken off cadre policy. It was frankly admitted that after the Second World War there had been a skill shortage which encouraged the use of political criteria as the basis for appointment and promotion, but by the late 1960s the passport to entry into a managerial post had become the possession of a master's degree. Yet this latter period was also the time when the post-war 'baby-bulge' left school and flooded the labour market.[43] While there was no increase in the number of places in higher education, the numbers embarking on vocational education rose dramatically. The lack of policy initiatives to cope with this had several unforeseen consequences. For example, certain sectors of economic activity seemed more attractive to higher education graduates than others. Light industry, non-ferrous metallurgy, clothing and textiles recruited more graduates than did the shipbuilding industry or public administration and services. Unfortunately this did not always correspond to official require-ments. Secondly, for many employees the educational qualifications that they possessed were above that required by the job specifica-tion, again suggesting a mis-match between training and the labour market[44] and a source of frustrated aspiration (see Chapter 5). Thirdly, a more serious indictment of vocational education and placement policy was the rising proportion of employees for whom the job they carried out did not correspond to the trade they had learned.[45] The problems first encountered in the sphere of vocation-al education spread with the expansion of access to higher education. As was shown in Chapter 5, graduates possessing a university diploma were in greater supply than the number of white-collar management posts,[46] and disillusionment with the absence of rational criteria and selection mechanisms for appoint-ment and promotion of management was widespread.

Thus, in the broad sense of cadre policy, the problems facing the Gierek government were considerable in 1971. It responded firstly by paying attention to leading cadres (people under the Central Committee *nomenklatura*) for whom an extensive system of in-service training was to be provided. The general principles of this policy were outlined at the Sixth PZPR Congress in December 1971 (elaborated in the section of the report entitled: 'Problemy kadr kierowniczy'). Further refinements were added in a Politburo resolution of October 1972, and ratified at the IX Central Committee Plenum in June 1973, which called upon all levels of the Party organisation to adopt Leninist principles of 'choice, rational-isation, development and improvement of cadres' and to draw up a reserve list for leading posts.[47]

In terms of policy implementation, this involved building upon the work begun by the Centre for Management Training (CODKK) set up in 1961. It was the inadequacy of business skills on the part of Polish management that had prompted the CODKK to begin training courses in 1968 for both industrial enterprise and association management, and for the Central Statistical Office to commence monitoring senior appointments in its 'spis kadrowy' (or list of managerial appointments). Courses were initially provided for management in the chemicals, heavy industry and light industry sectors. By the early 1970s CODKK branch offices were set up in all industrial ministries.[48] After 1973 a Centre for Cadre Training was attached to the Central Committee to be responsible to the Party apparat. It was claimed that between 1972 and 1975, 80% of all cadres under the Central Committee *nomenklatura* were sent on courses, and 60% of those were on courses lasting a month (the duration varying according to seniority of position). However, the effectiveness of these courses is impossible to ascertain, and a glance at the content of some gives little ground for presuming that they provided a comprehensive management or business administration training.[49] In particular, the use of Western business management techniques was considered to be indispensable to the work of the PZPR in cadre placement. Management by Objectives (MBO) involving a synthesis of decisions on the choice, education, further training, evaluation and rotation of leading cadres was first applied in the Paris Commune shipyards in Szczecin and in the Bydgoszcz cable factory, and later in local government.[50]

The new Central Committee Centre for Cadre Training supervised the conduct of interviews of all Party members in senior management ('leading') posts in the economy and state administration[51] and used this as the basis for in-service training and dismissal. By June 1978 it was claimed that officials in the regional and local PZPR apparat were better qualified and that plans were under way to commence in-service training at the lowest level of the apparat.[52]

In terms of cadre policy in the wider sense of the state and economic administration, an institutional reshuffle transformed the CODKK in 1973 into the Institute for Training Management Cadres of the State Administration, part of whose brief was to provide in-service training for middle management in the WOGs and ministries, and for lower management working in local government or WOGs. At the same time, in conjunction with the Society for Scientific Organisation and Management (TNOiK), one major task was to set up a 'cadre reserve' to provide a pool of young suitably qualified people in order that the principle of seniority could be departed from in promotion policy.[53] A survey of POPs in industrial associations and local government had shown many to be particularly lethargic in evaluating the effectiveness of their cadre policy, with the result that it appeared to be the outcome of interest pressures and accident. Senior posts were held by people who had acquired their qualifications between 15 and 20 years previously, and there was a high turnover in employment amongst those aged under 30 (where it could be as high as 60% per annum!).[54]

The creation of a cadre reserve proved to be a very difficult objective to achieve. It involved more than just drawing up a list of names: rather it was to be based on a precise review of a particular candidate's qualifications with respect to the job specification, which should have been reviewed in advance by the ministry or the industrial association. Evidence of success was scanty. One report quoted a study of 214 factories in 20 industrial associations where, of all the promotions monitored over an 18-month period, 48% of promotions amongst industrial association staff and 34% of promotions amongst plant staff had been drawn from the cadre reserve. Lower and middle management candidates (from foreman to section manager) in the reserve tended to be better qualified than those in appointment (43.6% of the former had higher education compared with 27.9% of the latter), and of those who were promoted only 14% had received adequate management training beforehand.[55] It was felt that the major obstacle was the condition of one-man management, which ensured that the decision to place people on the reserve list depended very much on the director of the industrial association or enterprise.[56]

Thus, in its cadre policy as well as in its role of supervision of the state and economic administration and its 'inspirational–organisational' role in the workplace, the PZPR after 1970 demonstrated a concern to adapt itself to the new stage of intensive economic growth and consequent concentration of industry. Although response to this was belated (considering that the trend towards concentration was already far gone in the late 1960s), it was nonetheless a conscious response. Yet this new interpretation of the leading role of the PZPR did not succeed in overcoming some basic contradictions. For example, the attempt to evade bureaucratisation

by restricting the size of the PZPR apparat[57] meant that this had to be
supplemented by a new form of linkage between Party organisation,
mass membership and non-members. Yet try as it may to encourage
the formation of activist groups and open up its meetings to a wider
audience, there is no escaping the fact that this institutionalisation of
political conflict was a form of participation sanctioned from above
rather than below. Secondly, the mechanism of communication
between central Party organisations and the grass roots was
hampered, as before, by weaknesses at the middle levels. Town and
regional Party organisations would resist efforts to create combines
and WOGs which would place large economic units on their
territory outside their control, particularly with respect to cadre
policy and administration. Party organisations within the constituent enterprises would resist concentration if it meant loss of
status.[58] In both these respects Leninist principles of the leading role
of the Party did suffer from 'theoretical underdevelopment' and
caused even more problems for the legitimacy of other structures of
workforce participation.

Industrial concentration and workforce participation

Although a strict interpretation of the 'leading role of the Party'
implies, amongst other things, that the PZPR embodies the best
interests of the workforce, each industrial enterprise also has a
Trade Union Factory Council (RZ) whose 'representative' role has
been subject to varying interpretations during the course of Polish
history since 1944 (many of which are coloured by the fate of trade
unions in the USSR).[59] Contrary to popular assumptions, trade
unions in state-socialist societies do not simply act as a distorted
one-way communication network to enforce labour discipline. Trade
union factory committees in the Soviet Union have been shown to
take an important role in negotiating conditions of work and service
with ultimate recourse to industrial action,[60] and besides their
important role in negotiating wage rates and productivity deals for
their industry, the 23 branch unions in Poland also provide other
facilities through the workplace (including canteens, housing,
hospitals and medical programmes, supplementary pensions, vaca-
tion centres and sports facilities).[61] So, inasmuch as a Factory Trade
Union Council is important in mobilising the workforce, it also has

considerable powers over determining access to many items of collective consumption. These powers had been augmented in the late 1950s as a consequence of the emergence of a new structure of workforce participation during 1956–8: the Workers' Council (RR).[62]

What began in the troubled summer of 1956 as a spontaneous movement protesting against the under-representation of the manual working class in both the trade union and Party apparat, soon became an arena of debate over the question of democratic participation and technical advice, in which many different interests participated.[63] The institutionalisation of this debate took place with the passage of the Workers' Council Law of 19 November 1956. This stipulated that at least two-thirds of the candidates to be elected should be of manual working-class background, and that the powers of the Workers' Council should include the right to scrutinise and to comment on the annual plan, profits and performance, to agree to any changes in the internal organisational structure and production process of the enterprise, to approve the distribution of profits between wages and bonuses and the newly created Factory Fund, and to approve the appointment of the enterprise director.[64] The assignment of such considerable powers to an organisation that was not formally dominated by the PZPR, was soon viewed by the latter as constituting a pluralistic threat. Thereafter, a gradual process of colonisation of the Workers' Councils by PZPR and trade union functionaries was legitimised in the law of 20 December 1958, establishing that enterprises should be co-managed through Conferences of Workers' Self-Management (KSR) consisting of representatives from the Workers' Council (RR), the Enterprise PZPR Committee (KZ) and the Trade Union Factory Council (RZ), plus the chief director of the enterprise. The KSR would be convened once every quarter, supplemented by periodic production conferences to be held in various sections of the enterprise, and the RZ was to act as its secretariat. The competence of the KSR was seen to fall into three main areas:

(i) the direction and co-ordination of other 'institutions of self-management' (the Workers' Council and departmental Workers' Councils);
(ii) the determination of the major functions of enterprise activity (ratification of the plan document, approval of investment

decisions, labour regulations, and the principles governing the distribution of the Factory Fund);

(iii)   control and supervision of the activities of the whole enterprise.[65]

In practice, the presidium of the KSR was dominated by management and those functionaries of the trade unions and Party apparat most sensitive to managerial interests: the *Wielka Czwórka* ('Big Four': Enterprise Director, PZPR secretary and chairmen of the RZ and RR).

Thus there are several arenas of workforce participation in the industrial enterprise. While the trade union structure has traditionally exercised the right of guardian of workforce interests in the production process, the Workers' Councils have constituted a challenge to this authority. The precarious status of the RR was resolved by its incorporation into the much more manageable unit of the KSR. It is to this organisation alone that enterprise management is accountable. Yet the *Wielka Czwórka* would use the KSR as a screen from behind which they could challenge (in the name of the workforce) organisations outside the enterprise over sensitive matters of planning and production. Moreover, despite frequent calls for more worker participation in the plenary sessions and presidium meetings of the KSR, the mass of manual workers have appeared to be singularly disinterested, and it has been those in lower management, particularly the foremen and non-line management technical experts who have been the most vociferous and active at meetings. Two further aspects of workforce participation in Poland are that there has been a slowness (and in some cases failure) on the part of organisations representing workforce interests to adjust to an industrial structure which is no longer dominated by the single-plant enterprise; and that in the face of greater complexity and scale of management, the workforce has sought to extend its control over material conditions in the workplace and to exploit the benefits of large-sized production units in the provision of specialist services and benefits. While it has been argued elsewhere that dual standards operate in the evaluation of mechanisms for participation in capitalist and state-socialist societies, and that a literal interpretation of Marx's texts will always render the final assessment of existing schemes of worker participation disappointing and academically unfruitful,[66] these points must be taken into consideration when evaluating the effectiveness of workforce participation under conditions of industrial concentration.

To commence with the issue of formal organisations for workforce participation, with the creation of industrial associations in 1958 there was no channel whereby an enterprise Workers' Council would challenge the decision of the association director, who was not obliged to take account of resolutions passed by an enterprise KSR. It was clear that a 'ladder' of self-management institutions stretching upwards from the industrial enterprise was not officially contemplated and formal organisational links between enterprise, Party and trade union organisations and the association via regional Party and trade union offices did not exist. Consequently, despite recommendations to the contrary voiced at the Fourth Trade Union Congress in 1957, the only formal channel of contact available to the KSR was through the person of the enterprise director.[67] The sole concession was the extension of a two-tier system of Conferences of Workers' Self-Management to multi-factory units where the plants were full cost-accounting units.

Any problems that arose between enterprises and industrial associations were seen to be matters requiring arbitration rather than participation. In 1957 Arbitration Commissions (*Komisje Rozjemcze*) were appointed by each of the industrial ministries to resolve disputes between the enterprise KSR and any higher level state economic institution with which it was in dispute. This proved to be more of a formality than a substantive concession. Although a Workers' Council had the power to summon an Arbitration Commission in all situations where they considered their rights to have been infringed, and in cases of dispute over resource allocation and directive indices, the procedure for nomination of workforce representatives onto the Arbitration Commission ensured that, although half were to be nominated by the enterprise Trade Union Council, those eventually appointed were ultimately dependent on managerial approval. By 1960 even these limited rights of redress were further restricted when disputes concerning the directive indices were excluded from the jurisdiction of the Arbitration Commissions and could only be resolved upon appeal by the enterprise KSR to the ministry and trade union headquarters.[68] It was not until after December 1970 that efforts were made to make the system of arbitration more responsive to enterprise workforce pressure, and trade unions were called upon to eliminate 'bureaucratic practices' by abandoning their divisional offices (and thereby permitting unimpeded access of the enterprise Trade Union Factory Council to the ministry) and by conducting more open elections to Arbitration Commissions. Much of this was formalised in the 1974 Labour Code (see below, p. 181).

In turning to a consideration of the actual character and causes of disputes between the Workers' Council, the KSR and the industrial association, it can be seen that they usually arose over drawing up the enterprise plans, particularly over the fixing of directive indices (those for employment, the size of the Wages Fund, the rate of accumulation, and investment limits were prominent) for which Workers' Council and KSR had no immediate access to appeal. Disputes arose as much from the manner of fixing plan indices as from their content. Frequent delay meant that for large enterprises it was often impossible for divisional/sectional Workers' Councils, their problem commissions and the workforce, to meet to give full consideration to association management proposals prior to the full session of the KSR which was to endorse them. In such cases the KSR representatives were forced to rely upon the analysis of association proposals prepared by enterprise management; yet in others the enterprise management would use the KSR protest as a 'screen' to conceal their own vested interests. Whatever the motive, rarely would the association modify its final directive indices, even after KSR representation.[69] Although the literature does cite isolated cases where association management was in daily contact with Workers' Council representatives, and their chairmen might be invited frequently to meetings of the association kolegium,[70] at a time when the industrial associations acquired greater powers over enterprise co-ordination in the mid-1960s, the only arena of workforce consultation and participation remained confined to the enterprise.

The vagueness of Decree 383/1966 in specifying the need for frequent consultation of enterprise workforce by association management (despite proposals made at the XIV Plenum of the Central Trade Union Council) meant that the most that was achieved was the presence of a trade union official as an observer at the association kolegium meetings. Only when certain items were on the agenda: the general association plan, proposals for joint enterprise financing of projects, and the construction and use of social welfare and recreational facilities, could KSR representatives be invited to present their views, with no guarantee that their opinions would be implemented. Yet in matters of primary concern to the workforce such as wages and employment policy, there was no provision for KSR representation. Where experiments were carried out in certain industrial associations during the period 1966–8, it was rarely with the full notification and approval of enterprise KSR bodies, and KSR objections to penalty taxation rates applied to the growth of the Wages Fund or to the linking of bonuses to special export tasks went unheeded.[71] Many KSR organisations would relegate the issues of wages and employment policy to a subordinate position and accept the indices of the technical-economic plan rather than halt production (such was the experience of the pharmaceuticals plant in Jelenia Góra which was run by the association Polfa). The precise nature of the workforce interests represented surfaced over the matter of distribution of special bonuses that were not available at the same rate to white-collar and blue-collar workers. This caused further rifts to manifest themselves between the various interests represented in the Workers' Council (mainly manual workers) and the KSR (mainly white-collar managerial staff). Similarly, changes in the planning process such as the method of 'two-stage planning' obliged ministry and association officials to provide a two-year forecast every spring to allow KSR officials time for analysis and comment. While this was considered to have been successful in the chemical and metallurgical industries, in mining, light industry, construction and food processing there were delays in issuing plan indices to enterprises which meant that management and the KSR often had less than three days for discussion.[72] Not until 1969 was any official procedure devised that specified the rights of an enterprise KSR to be consulted by central economic administration (including the industrial association) on key issues,[73] and even two years later it was reported that there was little evidence that this was frequently observed.[74]

The unsatisfactory outcome for workforce representation at the level of the industrial association could be attributed partially to the legal status of the latter as an economic-administrative unit rather than a production unit. Of all the many types of production unit, only industrial enterprises could elect Workers' Councils and convene Conferences of Workers' Self-Management.[75] With the industrial combines created after 1969, such legal obstacles could, theoretically, be overcome. Yet the legislation ushering in the

Combine Experiment in 1969 made scant reference to any procedure for conducting workforce participation. A separate resolution of the Council of Ministers and the CRZZ in December 1969 did, however, deal with this matter, proposing that existing KSR bodies in the enterprises that were to be integrated should continue to function and to make decisions in matters pertaining exclusively to their plant. In addition, a council of KSR representatives from all of the enterprises in the combine was to be created with members drawn from enterprise Party committees, Workers' Councils and Trade Union Councils. The responsibility for convening these sessions was to lie with the management of the leading factory of the combine, which could also invite representatives of individual enterprise KSRs as witnesses or observers to combine kolegium sessions. Such arrangements, alas, did not escape confusion surrounding the uncertain legal status of the constituent enterprises that were no longer full cost-accounting units (but whose performance was internally balanced within the combine). As under Polish industrial law, only full cost-accounting units could convene a KSR, the position held by the latter in the constituent enterprises of a combine was precarious. Those Workers' Councils and KSRs that continued to meet were without the authority to make individual decisions, and, at the most, their representatives would be invited to attend kolegium sessions in an advisory capacity only. This situation persisted until 1973 and the dismissive attitude of combine management made enterprise workforce frequently anxious to exclude any management and administrative staff. This occurred in one of the combines in the machine tools industry.[76]

In general, this legal ambiguity was felt to be the root cause of bad industrial relations within many combines. Evidence of satisfactory arrangements was reported,[77] but either a complex and cumbersome multi-level structure of workforce representation was created (as was the case in one steel mill, and which created as many problems as it resolved)[78] or a highly centralised management structure disregarded the plea of Workers' Councils in constituent enterprises to be considered as an equal partner in discussion. This was the situation in the sulphur processing combine where the smouldering industrial relations were reported in the press and made the subject of a sociological enquiry.[79] Because the combine was without a leading factory (rather it had a separate combine administration) and because there were changes in the central supervision of the combine, management was able to argue that proposals for an all-combine Conference of Workers' Self-Management were out of order. Yet the high degree of centralisation of management decision-making within the combine (from cadre policy to technological development, raw materials supplies, investment programming, finance, wages and employment policy) made it all the more imperative to have an institution of workers' self-management for the whole combine. Much haggling took place over the exact interpretation of the combine statute between management and enterprise Workers' Councils. Management tried to brush the issue aside by claiming that they had attended KSR sessions in factories and consulted staff, but in July 1970 the chemical workers' trade union reached an agreement to create a Workers' Council for the whole combine. The first session took place in January 1971 with seven meetings of the KSR supplemented by monthly production conferences in factories.[80] Still, the settlement of disputes between combine management and enterprise workforce tended to be conducted on an *ad hoc* basis (rather than through the Arbitration Commission network) with officials of the PZPR, trade union, Workers' Council and management being the main source of appointment to the new combine KSR.

It is impossible to generalise about arrangements for workers' self-management in the combines. For example, in the ball bearing combine, a Council of Workers' Self-Management representatives was proposed in early 1970[81] but by December 1971, as it was judged to be more representative of management than of workforce from the constituent plants in the combine, it was replaced by a Conference of Combine Self-Management Representatives (KPSRK), to which each plant would send four delegates, at least two of which were to be working on the shop floor.[82] Elsewhere, in the combine Polam in the electrical industry, representation in the combine KSR was proportional to the size of the workforce in each factory and there was a conscious attempt to include manual workers who were not in formal positions of authority or in the *Wielka Czwórka*.[83] What is common though, is the increasingly cumbersome and legalistic procedures for workforce participation, and the tendency for decision-making to be forced 'upwards' so that many crucial decisions on social welfare, wages and employment policy were beyond the control of the workforce of individual factories. It is not surprising that a new bonus system announced in

May 1970, which would have meant effective wage cuts for some workers, plus the December 1970 price rises, drew attention to the unsatisfactory channels for participation.

At the commencement of Edward Gierek's period of office the need to overhaul the system of workers' self-management generally, and particularly the arrangements operating in combines, was acknowledged. A large-scale project was commenced by industrial sociologists and a round-table discussion organised by the journal *Samorząd Robotniczy* and the Warsaw committee of the metal workers' trade union,[84] attended by Workers' Council and trade union activists from several combines and multi-factory enterprises. However, decisions were deferred until the new financial economic reform and the attendant creation of WOGs was completed, and until after reforms in the PZPR trade union and local government structure.

It is true that many combines and industrial associations became WOGs after May 1972, but the problems confronting effective worker self-management were made more acute. Firstly, the Directors' Charter of 1972 conferred upon association management considerable powers of intervention in enterprises (such as the setting of growth rates, employment and wages) many of which had not been included in the 1958 Workers' Self-Management Law, and hence over which there was no legal right of workforce representation. Secondly, when a two-tier structure of workforce representation had not proved successful in the combines, the requirement of a three-tier structure for many WOGs (at the division, enterprise and association level) did not augur well. The alternative of a single unit of workforce representation for the whole of the WOG would be too remote from the workforce, and would be impolitic when complaints of under-representation of worker interest had been prominent in the protest of 1970–1. Thirdly, the complexity of management processes required that workforce representatives possessed a minimum level of managerial competence, which would involve the unskilled receiving less representation.[85] The question of the competence of manual workers to enable them to participate effectively masked the *de facto* situation whereby representation in both plant and combine KSR had been drawn heavily from officials of the Party, trade union, youth and professional organisations. A 'high socio-political consciousness', long service and acquaintance with managerial practices were all seen to be desirable qualities for such representatives.[86] Such criteria were bound to favour the recruitment of technically trained white-collar employees and those highly skilled manual workers who had entered these 'sociopolitical' organisations. This was not universally accepted as a legitimate criterion for workforce representation, but the corollary to this was that even when provision was made for manual workforce participation this did not occur to the extent anticipated.[87]

Yet to what extent was white-collar involvement in workers' self-management unavoidable? It could be argued that the subjects on the agenda of KSR meetings (the plan, development strategy, investment policy, disputes with the industrial association) are of more interest to the technically trained and those in management than to shop floor workers for whom the issues of most immediate relevance were wages, bonuses, work organisation and access to social welfare services provided at the places of work.

Unfortunately, with the new WOGs, the level at which decisions were taken on these matters was pushed upwards beyond the level of the individual plant. At best this induced cynicism and apathy on the part of manual workers towards institutions in their plant that no longer had adequate decision-making authority; at worst it encouraged the more qualified and educated workers to come forward to use the sessions of enterprise and WOG Workers' Council and Conference of Workers' Self-Management to point out management failings and the need for reform.[88] Add to this considerations of socio-occupational mobility and it is possible to see a variety of motives on the part of highly qualified workers and the technically skilled for becoming involved (see Chapter 5).

Unfortunately, this particular problem was never wholly confronted. Instead, in the early 1970s proposals were floated, variously advocating a single-, dual-, or triple-tier structure for workforce representation according to the structure and location of firms and according to the degree of vertical or horizontal integration undertaken by the WOG.[89] Again, in the absence of an agreed policy, arrangements tended to be of an *ad hoc* semi-formal nature: in the machine tools combine in the engineering industry, the KSR was drawn from the leadership of the 'socio-political' organisations in the plants (and very often only those in the leading factory would be consulted by management);[90] in the Cegielski engineering works in Poznań there were 75 sectional Workers' Councils and a KSR for the whole plant (which created considerable headaches over communication)[91] and in the new combine Stalowa Wola founded in October 1972 a hybrid arrangement of 43 Workers' Councils was proposed, many of which were excluded from representation on the presidium of the combine KSR.[92] An impression of sheer gigantism of arrangements can be gleaned from the example of the shipbuilding association (ZPO), which employed 65,500 people in five shipyards, 25 enterprises and five service units. Each of the enterprises and shipyards could convene sectional and full KSRs and would send delegates to a Council of Representatives for the whole association.[93] The quality of representation that could be achieved in these structures was rarely reflected upon, and as late as 1979 there seemed to be little official awareness that effective workforce consultation and supervisory powers were blocked by anything more than the law on one-man management and the status of the enterprise.[94]

Although there was no modification to the 1958 law on workers' self-management until May 1978, the changes that eventually took place then were very much affected by changes in the structure of trade unions. In the name of increasing trade union activism at the plant level, in April 1973 and at the V Plenum of the CRZZ it was decided to eliminate the district and regional trade union offices (at *powiat* and *wojewodztwo* level) to permit unimpeded contact between officials at trade union headquarters and the plant Trade Union Councils.[95] At the same time, it was decided that quarterly production conferences, preceded by trade union group meetings and organised by the plant Trade Union Council at sectional level should be the basic forum for staff participation in management. Here, representatives of the Trade Union Council, Workers' Council and management would meet to report to the workforce. Only then, it was held, would workers be adequately prepared to be effective participants in workers' self-management.[96] Changes took place first in the mining, textiles, construction and transport industries. The arrangements in the mining industry provided for a corporate system of representation at the level of industrial associations in a collective Trade Union Group (*Zespoly Wspoldzialania Zwiazkowego*) to be attended by representatives from all enterprise Trade Union Councils plus central trade union officials and association management on a bi-monthly basis.[97] A further addition in October 1975 was the creation of New Trade Union Councils (*Zwiazkowy Rady*) to act as a means of communicating staff opinions to superior levels of state economic administration.[98] These institutional changes in the structure of Polish trade unions indicated that, in the early years of the Gierek regime, Trade Union Factory Councils and other consultative trade union bodies were to be the main means of satisfying demands for worker participation, rather than a revitalisation of Workers' Councils and Conferences of Workers' Self-Management.

At the same time there was a genuine attempt to rationalise the structure of industrial relations. The notorious Labour Code promulgated in July 1974 came into operation in January 1975 to incorporate the three principles of 'unity, universality and systematisation' into what had become a jungle of labour legislation.[99] This did not just cover work conditions but health, holiday and maternity leave schemes. While many of the latter schemes had been negotiated at plant level and jealously guarded over by the plant Trade Union Councils, they now became largely freed from responsibilities here. The procedures for arbitration were also clarified, but in practice this piece of labour legislation became associated with a tightening up of labour discipline, so that persistent absenteeism, alcoholism and other misdemeanours were no longer regarded so benevolently.

Finally, to ensure that the new trade union structure would employ its new communications network and labour legislation in the interests of raising productivity, at the V Central Committee Plenum in April 1977 Gierek announced that the PZPR was to strengthen its leading role in trade unions and KSRs. It is ironical that this coincided with the holding of the first National Conference of Workers' Self-Management delegates in 1977, which inaugurated the policy to modify the 1958 Law. One year later, in July 1978, workers and Party activists met again, to ratify the Politburo guidelines on workers' self-management issued on 22 May 1978. The major principles of the new policy were that all enterprises and factories should now be included (especially factories in WOGs, multi-factory enterprises and combines); that there should be a multi-level structure stretching from production conferences in the various sections of an enterprise (and even sectional conferences of Workers' Self-Management in very large enterprises) to an annual meeting of KSR delegates with association management; and finally, enterprise and WOG PZPR organisations were to have a greater role in co-ordinating all the sessions and implementing decisions (responsibilities that were hitherto exclusively in the hands of the Presidium of the Workers' Council and management respectively).[100] While there was very little change in the process of election (one-third of KSR members should be manual workers elected annually at the Production Conference, the rest would be supplied by the Party Committee, the Trade Union Council, the youth, technicians and economists organisations), two new responsibilities had been added to the competence of the KSR: rationalisation of resource use and labour discipline; but above all there was no mention of Workers' Councils. As a separate channel of workforce representation alongside the trade unions, Workers' Councils had been eclipsed. The posts of Chairman of the KSR and First Secretary, of the Plant Committee of the PZPR had been merged and the Party was firmly in command.

However, were the control mechanisms of the PZPR that effective? Doubtless it had been very skilful in rearranging the structure of workforce participation so that, behind a façade of many more levels of involvement and greater regularity of communication and consultation, it now possessed an instrument highly functional to the mobilisation of labour. It was true that, in many enterprises, Workers' Councils had ceased to function, but the new production conferences did not always receive lively support.[101] Trade Union and workforce acquiescence had to be bought in return for support for institutional reform. This was achieved by augmenting the goods and services that could be collectively distributed in enterprises. Yet the distribution of the means of social consumption was later to be the same issue on which support was withdrawn from the PZPR.

The role of Trade Union Factory Councils in distributing social services can be traced back to the mid-1950s when after the 1956 Law reforming the principles of enterprise operation, a Factory Fund (and later in 1958 a Social Fund and a Housing Fund) was introduced to provide a means of financing house construction and other recreational and welfare services at the place of work. Unfortunately, the plant Housing and Social Funds were forced to compete with the Wages Fund and they ended up being traded against one another in the bargaining process. However, as increasing amounts of workforce income were paid out in bonuses according to measured labour productivity, total disposable income could vary between people in equivalent posts but in different factories, and so could the payments into the Factory Fund. It was partly in order to redress inequalities between industries and firms, but more importantly to win support for its reforms in general and of trade union structure and workers' self-management in particular, that prompted the PZPR to change these arrangements.

In June 1973 three new funds were announced to commence operation in 1974: a Bonus Fund (8.5% of the Wages Fund) and a separate Social Fund (2% of the Wages Fund) and a Housing Fund (1% of the Wages Fund). All these were to be administered and distributed by the plant Trade Union Council subject to general decisions of principle agreed upon at the KSR.[102] It was also possible for a large firm to sell such services to others to overcome unnecessary duplication of capital purchase and labour time.[103] Between 1971 and 1975 real wages in Poland rose by some 40%.[104] It was a period of consumer boom as the Gierek regime opened up the Polish economy to penetration by Western imports, and the new arrangements for the Factory, Housing and Social Funds served to increase expenditure on crèches, kindergartens, health services, holiday homes, recreation centres and, above all, housing. However, the downswing in the economy after 1976 placed considerable pressure on social expenditure at the place of work, especially as it appeared that employee contribution rates were falling.[105] In particular, expenditure on holiday homes increased, and at a greater rate than the number of places provided.[106] Demographic conditions aggravated this as large numbers of people went into retirement, pushing up pension payments by 21% between 1976 and 1978,[107] and as the age of marriage came down, accentuating the 'bulge' of young people on the waiting list for a home.[108] As larger or more profitable enterprises could afford to spend proportionately more than smaller or less profitable enterprises, the level of provision and access to social welfare facilities and housing became a major concern for the workforce and influenced decisions in searching for jobs. It was the enterprise Trade Union Councils which decided upon staff entitlement to these services, but the attempts to 'rationalise' the duplication of services between enterprises and local authorities during 1978 and 1979[109] drew attention to the privileged access of functionaries in the 'socio-political' organisations to the rewards of social consumption.[110]

The Polish United Workers' Party had paid a high price for its reform of industrial relations. It had attempted to expand the channels of communication between central management of WOGs and the workforce, but by adopting a very emphatic interpretation of its leading role. The major participants thus turned out to be officials of the Party, youth and trade union organisations. The PZPR had consciously intended to be strongly represented in trade unions and production conferences, but could not conceive of this beyond the terms of cadre policy, control of the agenda, and access to all records and documentation. Its attempts to incorporate the living forces within Polish industrial relations eventually backfired. Foremen had been heavily cajoled into joining the PZPR and being active in the KSRs, and production conferences in WOGs were often the most vociferous critics of the industrial relations structure in general,[111] as it was they who had to explain to a workforce they felt to be already over-stretched that management was cutting wages and benefits. The older peasant-workers found it difficult to adjust to the tightening up of labour discipline and responded with increased absenteeism and alcoholism and labour turnover. Younger worker-peasants found that the exigencies of running their small-holding made it very difficult to acquire a good work attendance record, and hence they found themselves at the end of the queue for housing and welfare benefits provided in industry.[112]

Despite warnings against the dangers of 'formalism' in constructing a system of workers' self-management adapted to the needs of industrial concentration, the reforms that took place between 1973 and 1978 were exceedingly mechanical in conception. In full sessions of the KSR, the majority of discussions would focus on the plan, exports, supply situation, disputes with the industrial associations/WOG headquarters, etc., and the anxieties of the workforce over poor work conditions, the lack of a free Saturday, poor promotion prospects for the young, and labour shortage, received short shrift.[113] By 1980 there was an awareness that the tendency increasingly to concentrate managerial decision-making powers had prescribed very narrow limits within which worker participation should function, and needed reconsideration.[114] This instrumental and manipulative approach to workers' self-management heralded danger. If the mechanism of plant democracy did not fulfil the expectations of the workforce, then there was a growing likelihood that they would seek other means of so doing.

To conclude, the experience of the 1960s and 1970s gives little ground for optimism over the ability of a Marxist–Leninist party such as the PZPR to change its mode of organisation and institutionalise political conflict. An aggressive and clumsy interpretation of its 'leading role' was the end product of what was initially a genuine concern to open up channels of communication and encourage greater accountability in Polish political life. Unfortunately, insufficient attention to the scope and purpose of participatory activity in an economy run by corporate structures resulted in the naive belief that participation could be orchestrated from above and legitimated by higher living standards. Such was the nature of the 'technocratism' in Party values and, as the events of 1976 and 1980 testify, it rested on frail foundations.

7

Summary and conclusion

This work began with a concern to examine the political consequences of and barriers to economic growth and technical innovation in a state-socialist society, and now concludes with the observation that in the Polish context, particularly since 1970, the PZPR has displayed an awareness of the need for change in its organisational structure, its methods of operation and its recruitment strategy, but that these changes misfired. The background against which this was demonstrated was a policy of industrial integration and concentration begun in the late 1950s and which by the 1970s had assumed the force of a dominant trend in the economy.

The political economy of state-socialist societies tends to focus conventionally upon the role of the industrial enterprise as the basic unit of economic activity. To do so, however, is to ignore developments since the late 1950s that have tended towards the integration of plant into ever bigger production units whose form can vary, but which can be said to possess a closer resemblance to Western corporate structures than to the ideal-typical industrial enterprise prescribed by Polish economic law. This development is by no means unique to the Polish experience. Just as the transformation of industrial structure in Poland after 1945 drew heavily upon the forms that emerged in the Soviet Union during the 1920s and 1930s, the process of industrial integration and concentration that took place in Poland during the 1960s and the 1970s was largely inspired by changes that had taken place elsewhere in Eastern Europe. The creation of industrial combines in the GDR in 1967 provided a model for a similar experiment in Poland a couple of years later, and the new Pilot Units and WOGs introduced after 1973 originally emulated the production unions created in Hungary after 1968. However, the almost simultaneous launching of the

186

ob'edinenie in the Soviet Union in 1974 acted as a constraint upon the full implementation of the Hungarian model in Poland.

The significance of the organisational structure of industrial production is only apparent when placed in the much wider context of economic growth strategy. The legitimation of the command model of economic planning and management has rested on the ability to achieve higher rates of economic growth. However, the slow-down in economic growth in the Soviet Union during the period 1959–63,[1] the growing inefficiency of investment programmes, very slow rates of technical innovation and growth of labour productivity all prompted a concern to reform economic mechanisms. The conception of reform varied from the incorporation of notions of profitability (Libermanism) to the use of market clearing mechanisms of a simulated or natural type and to changes in the structure of economic units such as are considered here in this work. Wherever enterprise integration and concentration was proposed it was seen as integral to a particular strategy of economic growth. For example, the original creation of industrial associations in Poland in 1958 was envisaged as functional to a strategy of decentralised investment, while the increase in their powers in the mid-1960s was considered necessary for a more aggressive export strategy. The industrial combines were presented as part of the unfolding logic of the 'scientific-technological revolution' whereby certain advanced branches of industry (notably chemicals and engineering in the Polish case) would be isolated for the purpose of 'selective and intensive development'. To a certain extent this theme was continued with the WOG experiment of the 1970s, but the 'integrated' (*kompleksowy*) nature of the reform was now held to be functional to Gierek's strategy of import-led growth.

However, in Chapter 2 it was pointed out that there were certain obstacles to the achievement of Polish economic growth strategies that were not of a purely economic nature, nor did they pertain solely to the industrial sector. Institutional factors such as the pre-war system of property ownership and industrial structure affected, in particular, relations between town and country and industry and agriculture, and demographic factors constrained labour market strategy. The problem was that the obstacles to economic growth lay in an imbalanced investment cycle, a demographic surge onto the labour market in the mid-1960s, low labour productivity and under-capitalisation in agriculture, and a changing position in world trade. These matters revived interest in economic reform in the mid-1960s in Poland, but at the same time placed limits upon its success. It was no accident that economic reform was introduced at times of considerable strain in the economy. Tautness in the planning process placed considerable pressure upon intermediate levels in the economic mechanism and directed attention to their role in planning and management. Yet considerations of a purely economic nature are not adequate in explaining the barriers to economic growth that exist in Poland. Political factors are also important. The timid piece-meal nature of Polish economic reform in the 1960s can be explained by external relations with the USSR and by the domestic dynamics of agricultural and local interests. No reform of the economic mechanism in industry, be it organisational or purely in the nature of the instruments used, could avoid being influenced by such processes.

Hence one major underlying theme of this work has been that the process of economic reform is both highly politicised, and also political in its consequences. Yet, a suitable framework of analysis to cope with this is difficult to obtain. While the relations between large business corporations and the state has become a legitimate subject for political analysis in the West, there is considerable difficulty in transposing this to the context of merger of industrial enterprises in state-socialist society. Conventional social science analysis that falls into the category of theories of convergence or of the common problems facing industrial society was also rejected in favour of a synthesis of concepts drawn from New Left and East European writings. These works focus attention on four major areas. The first is the nature in which the changing system of control and ownership has affected the division of labour and the labour process, and the extent to which elements persisting from a pre-socialist phase affect this. The second concern is the nature of class relations and the basis of political power. The extent to which a cohesive class of technocrats has emerged, displacing the power base of earlier revolutionary activists or *apparatchiki* and which maintains its power and extends its privilege by adapting market phenomena to the economic mechanism, or by acting as the 'rational redistributors' of the means of consumption, is a question of fundamental importance. The relations between the highly skilled and the industrial manual working class in whose name social transformation had taken place was also felt to be a legitimate subject of analysis. Changes in the division of labour and the labour process were held to leave their mark on class composition. Whether this resulted in the displacement of the old industrial manual working class to a marginal position or whether certain sectors of this group proved to be particularly open to the effects of technical change with the subsequent emergence of a new working class is a crucial point here. This question of the nature of class power and the fluidity of boundaries between classes raises a third issue: the nature of the values upheld by particular groups and the extent of change in this sphere. Is the consciousness of the working class now raised only over matters of consumption and the control over distribution? Are the technical intelligentsia now the repository of concern about the extent of democratic control over the production process and about the nature of the planning process? Above all, has value change taken place away from 'expressive' and 'affective' values to a more instrumental outlook on life? The fourth area is that the methods of recruitment and operation of a Marxist–Leninist party like the PZPR have to be considered in the light of the aforementioned changes in the division of labour and the labour process, the structure of class power and the values and attitudes held. The ability of the PZPR to adjust to changes in all those areas was crucial, and so each was considered in turn.

The chronicle of the process of industrial concentration and integration in Poland related in Chapters 3 and 4, while reluctant to enter into a precise evaluation of the market power of new 'corporate' structures, did indicate that certain trends were under way. The growth in the size of production units, though mainly attributable to the emergence of multi-plant enterprises and combines, also seemed to be accompanied by a growing centralisation of managerial control in these units, and also in industrial associations. Firstly, at the level of investment policy, research and development and, at a later date, exports, employment and wages policy, many decisions came to be taken (especially after the 1972 Directors' Charter) on a more 'corporate' basis away from the control of constituent plant management and workforce. Secondly, the nature of business law derived from the orthodox Marxist – Leninist principle of one-man management encouraged autocratic decision-making while at the same time making its implementation ineffective. By pushing responsibility upwards, it made accountability in the management process difficult to achieve and was accompanied by an expansion of bureaucratic posts in an endeavour to counteract this. The orthodoxy of the legal statutes prescribing the mode of organisation and operation of industrial associations and combines in particular meant that the new corporate structures were often totally unresponsive to the division of labour and particular needs of an industry. This inflexibility and the principle of one-man management constrained attempts to move towards a corporate management strategy. It is certainly correct that a process of integration and concentration took place in Polish industry, but without ceding full corporate autonomy. On this, central government ministries remained ambivalent: integration and concentration definitely facilitated control over the increasingly complex industrial structure, but the greater possibility for ministerial intervention meant that this corporate autonomy would be imperfect, it induced caution on the part of the ministry and behaviour such as would maximise the scope of decision-making on the part of the managers of production units. Even though economists and other planning experts, rather than the vested interests of ministerial officials, were the architects of the WOG reforms in the early 1970s, the constraints remained. Industrial merger has been important in Polish economic policy since the late 1950s, but it is doubtful whether the goals that it was supposed to achieve have been met. Increasingly, the process seems to have been confronted with the barriers of Marxist–Leninist doctrine.

In terms of class relations, the process of industrial concentration and integration has not contributed to the unambiguous emergence of a class of technocrats. There has been extensive social mobility in Poland since 1945, and the consequences of this have been that, both inter- and intra-generationally, the boundaries between social classes have been fairly fluid. At the same time, this implies that social classes cannot be seen as isolated entities unaffected by what happens in other classes, and that there is as much social differentiation within classes as between them. Similarly, the inter-relation between class background and occupation holds a further degree of complexity. As a consequence, it is not possible to identify clearly objective characteristics of technocrats as distinct from ideologues and 'apparatchiki'. The process of recruitment into industrial management has tended towards the predominance of graduate engineers, but this is not to imply that the most highly skilled or those most acquainted with business management or the most antipathetic to the PZPR now occupy senior managerial positions in the new corporate management structures. Although there has been a tendency since the late 1960s for a limitation upon the chances of working-class entry into both higher education and senior industrial management relative to those of the peasantry and white-collar groups, personnel policy has tended to ensure that the most prestigious posts go to those with the longest work experience rather than those who are most qualified. The ability of senior management to exercise technocratic power in decision-making is as much circumscribed by the inferior skills of middle and lower management (and, as a corollary of one-man management, by the tendency to push decision-making responsibility upwards), as it is by the mechanisms of Party control. The function of management is performed by a wide variety of people in industry from the chief director down to the foreman, and hence it is often difficult to isolate discrete groups.

Although the study of attitudes in state-socialist societies is fraught with difficulties, it is possible to evaluate them by imputation. While it is not possible logically to separate Party membership from management, it is possible to discern a variety of reasons for partisanship on the part of people in the workplace. Different opportunities for access to higher education and for promotion into industrial management between people from different social classes and generations produce differences in attitudes, aspiration and morale between senior and lower management. Depending on social background, membership of the PZPR can be variously regarded as the instrument of rapid social advance, as a useful mechanism for expediting plan tasks, as a source of social identity and as the main arena for political debate. The first two can be considered technocratic orientations, but this is not the case for the latter two.

In a system which claims to uphold the primacy of the working class as the most progressive social force, meritocratic principles of educational opportunity and career advance and a minimum level of egalitarian distribution of material necessities, these legitimacy formulae have come to appear singularly hollow in the late 1970s. At this time channels of inter-class social mobility became frozen, and working-class, and to a lesser extent peasant, chances of entry into higher education and career promotion became restricted. The distribution of the means of both individual and collective consumption tended to reinforce rather than counteract the cleavage between blue-collar and white-collar workers, at a time when there was a call for restriction in the social wage. In the late 1970s there was much talk of the imminence of a national morale crisis.[2] While the interests of the different social classes had not always been identical during the three periods of Poland's history since 1945 (Popular Revolution, Construction of Socialism, Construction of a Developed Socialist Society), these interests and differences have not remained fixed. It was argued that, whilst in the first place there was some conflict of interests between peasantry and intelligentsia on the one hand and the working class on the other, during the second phase these conflicts between the peasantry and the working class became accentuated as the 'socio-cultural' needs of the peasantry were neglected, as contradictions between working-class and peasant interests appeared in the consumer goods market, and as differences within the peasantry manifested themselves. However, in the most recent phase, while it was felt that there was an increasing *rapprochement* between working-class and intelligentsia interests, and despite government efforts to improve the terms of trade between industry and agriculture, a widening earnings differential combined with problems of distribution and supply had encouraged the development of negative attitudes towards the regime on the part of the peasantry, with manifested itself in the growth of a whole series of private sector activities.

While it could be argued with equal force that the working class suffered an even greater restriction upon its opportunities and powers of consumption in the late 1970s and had even fewer sources of redress than the peasantry (it could not turn so easily to private entrepreneurial activity and the 'black economy'), Party theoreticians argued that channels for improved mediation and arbitration of group interests needed to be opened up and 'socio-political institutions' (and in particular the PZPR)[3] should play a greater role in raising morale. This was considered to be crucial in order to redress the imbalance between the forces for integration and disintegration in the workplace.[4] The prevalence of autocratic styles of management could be a dangerous barrier to the integration of the working class and the technical intelligentsia in the management process. The experience of collective agreement upon the division of labour both in the workshop and in the work brigade and the influence of workers' self-management upon the economic and social policy of the industrial enterprise were particularly important to counteract the consequences of increasing power and specialisation of management (manifesting itself in the operation of the principle of one-man management, a higher degree of Party involvement in the managerial process, the excessive specialisation of research and development and its isolation from the work process, and the differences in lifestyle between management and workforce).

Thus, at a time when over 75% of Polish industry had been merged into 'corporate' structures with all the attendant problems of remoteness of increasingly centralised management decision-making, and when a heightened sense of social injustice was contributing to a general turmoil in social values, how did the PZPR respond to avoid social disintegration? Hindsight, in the light of the events in Poland since the summer of 1980 might tell us that the PZPR quite simply failed to respond. However, as was argued in Chapters 5 and 6, although slow in reacting, after 1971 there were dramatic changes in PZPR recruitment strategy to incorporate more working-class members, and a general re-interpretation of its leading role in industry in terms of new ways of communicating between apparat, rank-and-file membership and non-Party activists in terms of its supervision of management in the state and economic administration, and finally in terms of cadre policy. It is an inescapable fact that the PZPR was aware of the need for change and did respond. However, the form of its response belied a basically technocratic approach to the need to articulate and mediate social demands. Nowhere is this more evident than in the neglect of provisions for workers' self-management. Here, there was no change in the 1958 Law until 1978 to take account of the increasing integration and concentration of industry and, even then, the solution permitted greater PZPR control over personnel and agenda in a structure which granted no place to Workers' Councils. These measures, designed to incorporate shop-floor worker interests, were rejected by various sections of the Polish workforce around whom alternative forms of representation have developed: unofficial shop-floor committees where the interests of certain sectors of the working class and the technically skilled have met.[5]

Unfortunately, the PZPR interpretation of its leading role was aggressive and clumsy, and the provisions that it made for mass control and accountability were naive. This applied equally to the reforms of the trade union structure and local government and to the structure of workers' self-management. An institutionalisation of conflict had taken place, not so as to mediate demands into the policy process speedily, but rather to contain and control worker interests.[6] This meant that complaints about work organisation, rationalisation and supplies on the one hand, and lengthening waiting lists for housing, cars, places in the factory holiday home, queues for basic foodstuffs (which certain people, particularly those in management posts, could 'jump'), and inflationary pricing policies on the other hand, all made the claims of the PZPR to be 'building a second Poland' pathetically transparent. The result has been a crisis of legitimacy whose solution will require more than the reorganisation of industry into corporate structures and the efficiency of Party representation can provide.

Postscript: the events of 1980

It might well appear that the events of 1980 in Poland have very little to do with the process of industrial integration and concentration begun in 1958. The immediate cause of the strikes that spread like a tidal wave from the west of Warsaw to Lublin, the Baltic Sea ports and from thence to Lower and Upper Silesia[1] might ostensibly lie in the announcement on 1 July 1980 of increases of 30–90% in the price of meat products sold in commercial shops, but in reality the underlying economic forces involved broader issues of individual and collective consumption, civil rights and democracy in industrial relations. We will consider these in the context of the events that brought about the downfall of the government of Edward Gierek at the IV Central Committee Plenum of 24 August 1980 and his replacement by Stanisław Kania,[2] and developments that have taken place up until the end of 1980.

The most outstanding result of this protest was Solidarność, the independent self-governing trade union born in October 1980, and finally registered as such on 10 November 1980.[3] Unlike the established trade unions it was formed from the grass-roots upwards, being a federation of local committees to which branches formed at particular places of work could affiliate. Its effect upon the conventional trade union structure since August 1980 has been devastating and there are reports of several trade unions leaving the official Central Council for Trade Unions by the end of October 1980,[4] forcing the government to appoint a working group[5] to draft a new Trade Union Law to cope with both this and the breakdown of the system of workers' self-management.

Obviously, that such an autonomous form of workforce representation can exist independently of the leading role of the PZPR has proved a shock to both the Soviet Union and Western international relations experts alike. However, before speculating upon the possibility of Warsaw Pact military intervention, it is important to consider the origins of the nucleus of 'Solidarność'.

Commentators on social movements in Eastern Europe have dwelt extensively upon the obstacles to the long-awaited union of the working class and white-collar intelligentsia which is held to be the pre-requisite of the overthrow of Marxism–Leninism.[6] As we have stated elsewhere,[7] it is incorrect to pronounce this developing bond between intellectuals and the working class to be the fruit of the 'historic mission' of the Polish intelligentsia. We have seen in Chapter 5 that the educated elite in contemporary Poland is drawn from various cultural and social backgrounds, and that the traditions of the older intelligentsia are more prevalent in some occupations than in others. Two groups in particular were behind the formation of the Inter-Factory Strike Committee (MKS) that eventually was transformed into Solidarność: worker-technicians and a group of intellectuals who were gathered together around the Committee for Social Self-Defence and Workers' Defence (KSS–KOR), formed originally in 1976.

Highly educated worker-technicians, often holding the post of foreman, had become increasingly frustrated by their lack of promotion prospects, by the unresponsiveness of management to their suggestions for reform of the work process, for improved work and pay conditions, and by their indifference to the workforce. The major organisers of the strike committees set up in the Baltic shipyards and elsewhere were drawn from this category during 1970–1, and again in 1976. Once more, in 1978, their anger was aroused, but this time by the new arrangements for workers' self-management, which deprived them of a forum for genuine debate on living standards which were under attack by cuts of both individual wages and other social consumption services in the workplace. It was not surprising that many echoed the demand originally made in Gdańsk in 1970 for independent trade unions. Aided by the Committee for Workers' Defence (KOR) set up to aid and defend those arrested in the disturbances of June 1976, and invoking International Labour Organisation (ILO) Convention Numbers 87 and 98 (which had been ratified by the Polish government in 1966) in the course of the recent events of the summer of 1980, industrial workers across Poland demanded free trade unions and the right to strike. This is illustrated by the first Protocol of Agreement (*Protokoł Porozumienia*) signed on 31 August by members of the Government Commission who visited Gdańsk and members of MKS.[8] It was the spread of this demand to the aristocracy of labour, the Silesian coal miners who were angered by the introduction in January 1978, against their wishes, of the exhausting 'Four Brigade' shift system,[9] that provided the PZPR with the signal that technocratism in the workplace would not be tolerated.

It has been argued that in the past there was a wide gulf between the workers and cultural intelligentsia (evident in the failure of both groups to revolt simultaneously in 1968 and 1970) but that this is now seen to have narrowed.[10] The protest of June 1976 occurred because workers at the Ursus tractor factory in Radom were distressed by food price increases, yet many intellectuals were also upset by earlier proposals to reform the Constitution, which were construed as a restriction upon civil rights. It was not surprising that fourteen intellectuals rallied to the workers' cause first by sending an 'open letter' to the Polish parliament, and later by an appeal to the Italian Communist Party for international support, and eventually by forming the Workers' Defence Committee (KOR). KOR, however, remained an organisation that existed to defend workers' interests, rather than a joint organisation of workers and intellectuals, receiving tacit (if not overt) support from the Roman Catholic Church.[11] One year later, by October 1977, the ranks of KOR had expanded to include more traditionalist elements concerned to defend civil rights, and it changed its title to the Committee for Social Self-Defence and Workers' Defence (KSS–KOR). It began publication of an underground newpaper *Robotnik*, from which arose demands for greater control over factory conditions, housing and worker representation at the workplace.

Thus, the composition of the protest movement that began in the summer of 1980 is very diverse. The intellectuals gathered around KSS–KOR were but one group in this, and their demands for free trade unions and civil liberties have as much to do with immediate conditions as with traditional values and beliefs. The dissident movement in Poland displays considerable realism as much as it does idealism. Mindful of the danger of the USSR and anxious to avoid military intervention (which in any case would be undertaken with considerable reluctance in the present configuration of world politics), their demands display an only too acute awareness of *realpolitik*.

Nonetheless, the rule of thumb in this *realpolitik* is to avoid any direct challenge to the legitimacy of Marxism–Leninism, and in particular to the leading role of the Party and democratic centralism. This is often very difficult to achieve and in this respect Solidarność often treads a tightrope. Problems arise because of considerable disillusionment, not only with the PZPR, but also from *within* its own ranks. We have already mentioned the worker-technicians who hold the posts of foremen in industry amongst whom Party membership was an average 42% (but could be over 60%) at the time of the Eighth PZPR Congress,[12] and the PZPR recruitment strategy during the 1970s focussed very heavily upon the working class. However, between 1976 and 1978, nearly 60% of those dismissed from the PZPR were working-class members[13] disillusioned with the privileged access to control over the distribution of social welfare and the unresponsiveness of Party organisations in plants where 1 in 4 manual workers were members. Similarly, the PZPR faced problems with its youth members in that a genuine grass-roots youth organisation did not exist at a time when good relations between the Party and young people were very important. The problem lay in the fact that young graduates would join the youth movement in order to get a post in the Party apparat to avoid taking a lower management position in industry and thus to further their career prospects.[14] The heavy-handed interpretation of its leading role in trade unions, workers' self-management and local government meant that the expansion of democratic centralism in these areas encouraged empire-building and the fostering of privilege, which acted against a rational and just system of resource allocation.[15]

There had been warnings from within the PZPR that the continuation of these practices would result in a crisis of legitimacy.[16] In particular the provincial governor, J. Kołodziejski, and the First Secretary of the Wojewodztwo Party Committee, T. Fiszbach, in Gdańsk, had warned on several occasions of the dangers facing the Party if it abused popular trust.[17] Problems of consumer supplies, housing, transport, bottlenecks in production due to lack of raw materials etc. were not just of economic portent, but also had a profoundly political significance.

Indeed, the policy of the PZPR in Gdańsk and Gdynia makes an interesting case study of how hopeless was the situation facing even an innovative and dedicated local Party leadership. Wacławek's study of industrial relations in the late 1960s, had remarked upon the importance of small informal groups to communication between Party and workforce in the Paris Commune shipyards in Gdynia.[18] The encouragement of this was especially important amongst a young workforce, the majority of whom were under the age of 40, and where labour turnover could average out around 25% per annum. Yet neglect of this meant that many of these informal groups provided the nuclei for the strike committees that sprang up in Gdańsk and Gdynia in December 1970, and so it was decided by the local Party organisation that thenceforth they should be turned to good use[19] and integrated into the formal Party structure. By the late 1970s, the town PZPR. Committee in Gdynia was well satisfied with its activity in visiting large plants in the area and meeting worker delegates, and by the fact that the level of education of Party activists seemed to have improved dramatically,[20] but at the same time the chief director of the Lenin shipyards in nearby Gdańsk was less sanguine about developments.[21] Despite a slight improvement in early 1978, problems with supplies, the implementation of new technology and the definition of profitability criteria, were producing frequent hold-ups in production, underfulfilment of plan targets and hence reduced bonus payments for the workforce. In a town where the waiting list for housing was one of the largest in the country, there were particular problems with not only the distribution of houses built and funded out of the plant Social Welfare Fund, but also with the funding of housing co-operatives. The organisation of the labour process also appeared to be chaotic.[22] Hence the PZPR organisations in the Baltic Sea ports had little ground for complacency. Even though Party groups were very active in the Lenin shipyards in Gdańsk (where there were over 300), and in the Paris Commune shipyards in Gdynia (where there were 200), there needed to be more effort directed towards convincing both young PZPR members and non-Party activists alike that the PZPR was making a genuine attempt to solve problems both of production and of consumption.[23] The cut in central government grants to Gdańsk *wojewodztwo* and frequent central interference[24] can have done little to encourage this.

The specific problems of the Gdańsk and Gdynia shipyards and those of the national economy met over the issue of new measures for job enlargement and payment by group results introduced in November 1979. The effect of the harsh winter of 1979–80, and the distortion of the relation between individual work effort and wages, meant that some employees did not receive their bonuses for the year 1980 and others achieved only 70% of their former earnings level.[25] These changes were part of a drive to raise labour productivity. This became a major concern after 1978 as the very high capital intensity of industrial production due to the massive capital formation of the years 1976–9 and a prolonged investment cycle, expressed itself in falling rates of growth of labour productivity.[26] This was accentuated by the state of foreign trade and agriculture. The costs of many imported raw materials (especially fuel oil) had risen, and this affected the balance of trade as exports failed to keep pace with imports, especially since the mid-1970s, when imports from non-socialist countries reached astronomical proportions. Considerable effort was made after 1977 to redress this imbalance, and for the first half of 1980, in volume terms, exports were higher than imports, although in value terms the reverse was the case.[27]

The situation in agriculture had repercussions both for labour productivity in industry and for foreign trade. During the period 1970–80, animal husbandry had grown nearly 40% faster than arable farming. Thus the problems of the alleged low productivity of arable land were due not so much to technical backwardness, as to government food pricing policy which made it more profitable to produce meat and dairy products. Paradoxically, as the government reacted by trying to cut back on meat supplies and by removing consumer subsidies, the possibility of sale through commercial and black market outlets made such production more profitable to the producer. Productivity in agriculture was thus affected by the relative growth in animal husbandry and was further aggravated by the fact that too much good grain was used as animal feed instead of going direct to the consumer. As a consequence, food imports were necessary to keep pace with demand.[28]

As if the material intensity of industrial production, low labour productivity of agriculture, and the imbalance of foreign trade did not have serious enough implications for standards of living in Poland, there were also grave balance of payments problems, as the strategy of import-led growth aided by massive borrowing of hard currency had been impeded by the world recessions of 1974–5 and 1978 onwards. This meant that not only would many of the loans have to be renegotiated, but the cost of servicing them under conditions of high interest rates would take up a large percentage of foreign currency earnings from exports.[29]

The effect of all of this upon living standards was devastating. In terms of individual incomes, a government Decree of June 1980, although it did not change the principles on which the Wages Fund was to be paid out, permitted the NBP to exert greater control over the ministries and industrial associations to ensure that guidelines were observed.[30] The government had naively attempted to curb personal expenditure, and hence wage demands, by restricting market supplies. Average rates of increase of wages had fallen from 11–13% in the years 1972–5, to around 5.8% in 1978,[31] but the increases in real disposable income since 1976 had been negligible as there was an inflationary situation of too much money chasing too few goods for which the cost was either queueing or the payment of higher prices in commercial shops or on the black market. By the end of the first half of 1980, the situation was extremely grave as actual wage rises had exceeded the plan target increase by 17 billion zł., but the supply of goods and services was 50 billion zł. less than planned.[32] Turning to social consumption, this had already been under attack since 1977 when efforts began to 'rationalise' its provision between place of work and local authorities. While the avowed aim was the same standard of provision in health, housing, recreation, etc., with a lower level of expenditure this proved impossible to achieve, and with the exception of 'socio-political activists' most people were made substantially worse off.[33]

Thus the workforce in the shipyards in Gdańsk, Gdynia and elsewhere in Poland faced a cut in wages, shortages of (and hence queues for) basic food items, and longer waiting lists for housing, holidays, medical treatment, etc. At the same time as their Party was talking about improved communication, trust, honesty and frankness with people, it was permitting certain people to live a very privileged lifestyle. Such a discrepancy could only appear in the popular eye as duplicity. The attempt to restrict wage increases in June 1980 and the ending of meat subsidies a month later were too much to bear. A groundswell of protest arose from within the grass-roots organisations of the PZPR, expressing itself in factory committees, who demanded independent means of representing workforce interests.

The political developments that took place in the four months after the signature of the Gdańsk Protocol up until late December 1980, are breathtaking. Solidarność has succeeded in achieving official registration without being forced to accept the leading role of the Party within its ranks, but insisting on its identity as a non-political organisation. Similarly, the demand for freedom of the Press and an amnesty for political prisoners have been pursued as civil rights and not as political demands. At the same time the PZPR is still reeling from the shock and has considerable difficulty in containing this. With tired inevitability, the government appointed a Commission on Economic Reform in November 1980, to investigate a route out of the economic crisis. The only difference from those that have ever preceded it is that representatives of Solidarność are included in their own right.[34] The pathetic claim made at the second session that it was working on a new economic plan to be introduced just over one month later in January 1981 was not only symptomatic of a lack of realism, but also of the anxiety felt about the length of time needed to work out a solution acceptable to all.[35]

Clear policy options, though, remained elusive. While the economic mechanism underpinning the WOGs was theoretically abandoned, a distinct alternative was not visible. While some felt that the reform introduced in early 1971 had been sound in principle and some required greater restraint upon central government intervention and a more effective form of worker participation,[36] others came out in favour of a contractual approach to planning, management resource allocation and marketing that was redolent of Liberman's ideas but with a larger 'helping' of workforce control over social consumption services and wages.[37] The Polish Economics Society also prepared a 'blueprint' for discussion by the new Commission on Economic Reform. The major objective was to increase economic 'effectiveness' by confining the planning process to a strategic as opposed to operational role (i.e. to a five-year as opposed to an annual horizon), by reducing the central planning and management apparatus by one-third to one-half of its former size, and by restricting central management control over production units to the subject of investment, foreign trade and co-operation. The major function of central authorities was to act as an 'intelligence' unit and institutions that engaged in a 'particularistic' approach to policy-making (the branch ministries) should be abolished.[38] Their proposals for the status of the industrial enterprise were ambiguous: it should not automatically become swallowed up in a conglomerate on the lines of the WOGs, yet, on the other hand, a return to small-scale decentralised production would not automatically follow. Rather, there should be no organisational blue-print for industry, and the structure of production was to depend very much on the technical and economic conditions of particular branches of industry.

Many of these proposals are depressingly familiar, and policy seems to be emerging in an eclectic fashion. Talk of a new economic model is superfluous if no attempts are made to cope with the serious disequilibria in the economy. Historical experience should warn the Poles against introducing an economic reform at a time of economic stress. It is sufficient that attention be diverted to a three-year stabilisation plan to raise the standard of living, to bring industrial supplies and output back into equilibrium, and to cope with the balance of payments problems.[39] While it could be argued that nothing short of a miracle is needed to cure the ills of the Polish economy, divine intervention may also be required to prevent the extraordinary Ninth Congress of the PZPR to be held before July 1981 from being the excuse for Soviet intervention to 'defend' the sovereignty of the Polish socialist order from 'revisionist' or even 'counter-revolutionary' elements. Democratic centralism has already been disturbed by the resolution of the VII Central Committee Plenun in early December 1980 to permit a more open election of delegates to the Ninth Congress, indicating how much grass-roots support there was for the open election of Party officials at all levels and for limits upon their tenure of office.[40] Furthermore, in one Party organisation in Toruń, an unprecedented initiative has taken place without the prior sanction of the Central Committee: the creation of a Consultative Commission on Party Organisation by the Institute of Social Sciences at Toruń University and eight large industrial plants. Membership of the Commission is open to any organisation that wishes to send elected delegates, and it will specifically focus on regional needs as it works out its proposals for the discussions at the Ninth PZPR Congress.[41] Even with a Politburo on which the armed and security forces are highly represented, the leadership of Stanisław Kania will need more than the political skills normally associated with these two apparats if it is to contain within the framework of Marxism–Leninism the new social forces whose latent presence for the last ten years has now become manifest in Polish political life.

Notes

1. Advanced industrialisation, the division of labour and the growth of bureaucratic power

1 The Moscow-dominated Union of Polish Patriots (formed in 1941) and the more nationalistic Polish Workers' Party (PPR) (formed later 1941–2) were the main partners in the Provisional Government.
2 M.K. Dziewanowski, *The Communist Party of Poland*, Cambridge, Ma., 2nd edn, 1976, pp. 162, 176, 184–5 and 204.
3 National income statistics show an index of growth rising from 48 in 1950 to 195 in 1971 (in terms of prices for 1960 held constant).
4 *Rocznik statystyczny*, Warsaw, 1972, p. 21. Whereas in 1950 industry contributed 37% and agriculture 40% to national income, by 1971 the relative proportion had been dramatically reversed to 58% for industry and 13% for agriculture.
5 M. Lavigne, *The Socialist Economies of the Soviet Union and East Europe*, London, 1974, pp. 127–8.
6 D. Bell (ed.) *Towards the Year 2000: Work in Progress*, Boston, 1968.
7 H. Kahn & A.J. Wiener, *The Year 2000: A Framework for Speculation on the next 33 Years*, New York, 1968.
8 R. Richta, *Civilisation at the Crossroads: Social and Human Implications of the Scientific-Technological Revolution*, Prague, 1969.
9 Ibid., pp. 38–9.
10 Ibid., pp. 72, 76–8, 83, 92, 98–101, 110–12, 232.
11 Ibid., pp. 239, 248–9.
12 Ibid., pp. 251, 254.
13 Komitet Badani, *Prognoz "Polska 2000"*, Warsaw, 1971.
14 M. Kaser and J. Zieliński, *Planning in East Europe*, London, 1970, pp. 12–14; J.G. Zieliński, *Economic Reforms in East European Industry: Poland*, London, 1973, pp. 278, 283, 308–18; P.T. Wanless, 'Economic reform in Poland 1973–79', *Soviet Studies*, Vol. XXXII, No. 1, January 1980, pp. 28–57.
15 P. Wiles, *Economic Institutions Compared*, Oxford, 1977.
16 Hannah Arendt *The Origins of Totalitarianism*, New York, 1958; L. Shapiro, *Totalitarianism*, London, 1972, pp. 13–15; R. Orr, 'Reflections on totalitarianism', *Political Studies*, Vol. XXI, No. 4, pp. 481–9.

17 C.J. Friedrich and Z.B. Brzeziński, *Totalitarian Dictatorship and Autocracy*, 2nd edn, New York, 1966.
18 Orr, 'Reflections'.
19 C.J. Friedrich, M. Curtis, B.R. Barber, *Totalitarianism in Perspective: Three Views*, London, 1969; Shapiro, *Totalitarianism*, pp. 20, 124, '... all this suggests that totalitarianism is not a final and immutable 'model' of government, but more in the nature of a spectrum with varying degrees of intensity and totality' (p. 124).
20 F. Fleron, Jr (ed.), '*Communist Studies and the Social Sciences: Essays on Methodology and Empirical Theory*', Chicago, 1969. This volume is a collection of some of the following articles: R.C. Tucker, 'On the comparative study of Communism' (Research Note), *World Politics*, Vol. XIX, No. 2, January 1967, pp. 242–57; F. Fleron, 'Soviet area studies and the social sciences: some methodological problems in Communist studies', *Soviet Studies*, Vol, XIX, No. 3, January 1968, pp. 313–39; J.A. Armstrong, A.G. Meyer, J.H. Kautsky, D.N. Jacobs, 'Symposium on comparative politics and Communist systems', *Slavic Review*, Vol. XXVI, March 1967, pp. 1–27.
21 V. Bunce & J.M. Echols III, 'From Soviet studies to comparative politics: the unfinished revolution', *Soviet Studies*, Vol. XXI, No. 1, January 1979, pp. 43–55.
22 I. Weinberg, 'The problem of the convergence of industrial societies: a critical look at the state of a theory', *Contemporary Studies in Society and History*, Vol. II, January 1969, pp. 1–15, esp. pp. 2–3.
23 For example, James Burnham's, *The Managerial Revolution*, (London, 1945), aims both to challenge the natural superiority of capitalism as a social system, and to reject the inevitability of it being superseded by a classless socialist society. Government intervention in the economies of Western capitalist societies removes the economy from the sphere of capitalist economic relations of production and replaces this by managerial relations of production. The class power of the managers is also exercised in the Soviet economy by virtue of their crucial function in the production process. The managerial economy is neither state capitalist nor state socialist: rather it is a form of corporate exploitation composed of a fusion of state and economy that will most likely be directed towards rational and efficient employment, growth, technology, investment, and planning. Either way, managerial power is exploitative, resting on preferential access to the distribution of the social product. See Burnham, pp. 26–37, 64, 70–2, 92–5, 103–15.

Another more recent example is J.K. Galbraith's, *The New Industrial State*, (London, 2nd edn, 1974), which has as its central themes the argument that it is the changing nature of the process of production that provides the basis for a change in the relationship between business and state, and that modern technology defines a growing function of the modern state (costs and risks associated with technological innovation for industry can be greatly reduced if the state pays for more exalted technical development, or guarantees a market for the technically advanced product) by harnessing the division of labour and making planning and large-scale organisation essential. Market uncertainty is further eliminated by the emergence of the large corporation and gradually consumer behaviour becomes controlled through a process of demand management. Galbraith is able to argue that, paradoxically, monopoly, far from inhibiting innovation can actually encourage it, and the enemy of the market is not socialist ideology but advanced technology. It is the modern corporation that allows the adaptation of an individual organisation to the needs of the 'technostructure': a group consisting not only of managers but of highly technically skilled people who are not motivated by profit maximisation, but by goals of corporate security, organisational success and survival. The balance of power between corporation and state is an equilibrium where neither can assert supremacy and is reflected in a co-operative co-ordination (rather than aggressive entrepreneurial individualism) with the 'technostructure' acting as the guiding intelligence of the industrial system. See pp. 31, 41–3, 49–51, 72–4, 75–86, 91–5, 174–7, 179–84, 261–2.

For Galbraith 'the modern large corporation and the modern apparatus of socialist planning are variant accommodations to the same need' and the technostructure is equally powerful in publicly owned enterprises and in socialist economies. In the former case the denial of autonomy by a public authority produces an immature organisation which hinders the development of the technostructure and results in operation at a loss. In the Soviet firm the need for autonomy is somewhat smaller, as it performs comparatively fewer functions than the American enterprise of the same size: planning, labour recruitment and resource allocation are all carried out by the state. For Galbraith, the Soviet firm is a simpler unit all round as there are no marketing, sales, nor product departments, and, as nearly all top personnel are engineers, technical and managerial problems rather than planning are the major concern (ibid., pp. 117–20).

Although the concept of a socially cohesive technostructure with non-pecuniary and non-instrumental motivation is one of the weakest points in the whole of the 'New Industrial State', the exposition of convergence is sophisticated. While the corporation is seen as central to the industrial system of a Western economy, the state carries out these functions in the Soviet Union and acts as a 'corporate umbrella' over the various industrial enterprises. In both cases the need for corporate autonomy either involves the exclusion of the capitalist from power, or of control by official bureaucrats. There is a convergence but it is incorrect to assume that this must take place via the market mechanism: it will arrive through the act of planning carried out by the symbiosis of large-scale corporate organisation and the state (ibid., pp. 120, 365–6, 372–83).

24 The well-known 'non-Communist manifesto' of W.W. Rostow (*The Stages of Economic Growth*, London, 1971, 2nd edn), abstracted five

stages of growth that take place in the transition from a traditional to a modern society (the emerging preconditions for take-off; take-off; the drive to maturity; the age of high mass consumption; and post-maturity). Rostow argues that the five states can be isolated by an examination of both aggregate growth rates of GNP, and disaggregated sectoral development. In addition, changes in elasticities of demand and social choices over the allocation of resources can be 'stimulated' by extraneous factors such as political revolution, international environment, technological change and social stratification. When *The Stages of Growth* was first published, it was criticised for being an extreme form of economic reductionism based on an inaccurate extrapolation of economic trends. This makes Rostow's comparative evaluation of Marx and 'stage theory' appear to be fairly ridiculous and his conclusions seem more than a little ideologically hide-bound: societies which have claimed to be undergoing the transition to a state of abundance (i.e. Communist societies) will not reach that stage because of problems in sectoral growth, and also because revolution-ary ideology will wither away, as in the case of the Soviet Union, when it approaches the stage of high mass consumption reached by the USA (pp. 4–16, 37, 118–21, 145–53, 157–8, 133, 163).

In contrast, Joseph Schumpeter's monumental work *Capitalism, Socialism and Democracy* (4th edn, London, 1954) presents a much more coherent anti-Marxist argument. Unlike Burnham or Galbraith, Schumpeter is not so much concerned with charting the rise of a new elite as with examining the process of enterprise management. Indeed, he takes issue with Karl Marx for failing to provide an adequate theory of enterprise in his analysis of capitalism. Schumpeter sees capitalism as a process of 'creative destruction': entrepreneurial capitalism is being destroyed from within by the emergence of monopoly and restrictive practice in order to forestall its collapse. It is the rationalist spirit that both precedes and is modified by capitalism which is responsible for the demise of this innovative, risk-taking entrepreneu-rial function and its supersession by routine specialist bureaucratic management. This determining economic and technological logic causes the disintegration of the entrepreneurial spirit through the extension of the division of labour, and the consequent change in values. Hence the transition from capitalism to socialism comes about not by means of a political act of a politically conscious proletariat led by a vanguard political party, but through the rational extension of the capitalist mechanism and the extension of bureaucratic co-ordination: the smashing and withering away of the bourgeois state is but a delusion, and the superiority of socialism rests not on moral grounds, but on logic. In his famous passage on democracy, Schumpeter is able to demonstrate that because socialism does not permit competition, it cannot be democratic, and is unlikely to be achieved unless the transition to socialism occurs at a mature stage of capitalism (pp. 22, 87–106, 132–4, 181–5, 195–6, 202, 221, 269, 300–2).

This forceful repudiation of Marx draws heavily on the inspiration of Max Weber and expands not so much a theory of convergence as a teleology of industrial development: in their true economic essence, capitalism and socialism are not such polar opposites as they claim to be, and such state socialist societies as exist, are a logical outcome of underlying economic trends.

25 In his early work *The End of Ideology* (Glencoe, 1960), Bell charted the decline of acutely differentiated value systems in an emerging mass society brought about by increased communication, interdependence and a more sophisticated division of labour. Human motivation changes from sympathy to rational self-interest.

In his more recent work *The Coming of Post-Industrial Society*, (London, 1974) he criticises what he perceives as the over-concentration by Karl Marx on class antagonisms in the productive sphere. In industrial society the forces of production (meaning essentially technology) replace social relations based on property ownership as the main 'axis' of social development. What is emerging is a 'post-industrial' society in which theoretical knowledge around which develops the new technology, growth and social stratification, is of central importance. Bell shies away from suggesting that industrial societies are directly converging. He is rather at pains to show how the economic infrastructure of industrial society has changed from being dominated by the production of goods in a rationalised, planned and bureaucratic production process where the engineer and the semi-skilled worker prevail, to the infrastructure of a 'post-industrial' society dominated by service industries for which the collection and dissemination of information is essential, and where the 'professional' has replaced the engineer and unskilled worker. Bell backs up his argument with empirical evidence on the changing occupational profile of the USA which he sees as on the threshold of transition to a 'post-industrial' society. Knowledge rather than bureaucracy is the medium of power, and there will not be a dominant cohesive technocratic class so much as a highly differentiated grouping with low class consciousness, in which the leading role will be taken by an enlightened research elite, divorced from the world of business, (pp. 55–62, 80, 111, 114, 12–30, 126–31, 70, 365).

Bell's arguments have a rather ethereal quality which owes more to imagination than solid empirical research. While his analysis of the 'post-industrial' society is certainly original, the concept is not, being coined in the early twentieth century and employed recently as the title of a book by Alain Touraine.

The subject of Touraine's work (*The Post-Industrial Society*, London, 1974) is distinguishable from capitalist and socialist society by the fact that economic decisions and conflict in the economic sphere are no longer of such importance. However, economic growth is itself both the precondition to, and dependent upon, the generation of scientific knowledge. Unlike any of the aforementioned theorists, with the possible exception of Daniel Bell, Touraine does not see the arrival of the 'post-industrial' society as heralding the eclipse of social class conflict. Social class conflict in the production process may well have been eroded by the excessive social integration of the individual into participation within a regulated hierarchy. However, social alienation arising from this 'dependent participation' rather than from direct economic exploitation, expresses itself in protest which arises, not in the conflict between capital and labour, nor from the marginal lumpen-proletariat, but out of the most enlightened forces which constitute the central social elements oriented towards change. Students, youth and the highly technically skilled, rather than trade unionists, are the backbone of the New Working Class (pp. 5–8).

26 Ralph Dahrendorf writes in *Class and Class Conflict in an Industrial Society* (Stanford, 1959), of a 'post-capitalist' society, where what counts is not ownership but authority. Conflicts between bourgeoisie and proletariat become institutionally isolated and the occupational determination of human behaviour is attenuated. As the relation to the means of production no longer decides either power or privilege in society, the ruling class can only be located amongst those at the head of bureaucratic hierarchies, amongst several elites including managers and a governing elite. Conflict becomes institutionalised, in both capitalist and Communist societies (where it is articulated through the Party). Raymond Aron (*Eighteen Lectures on Industrial Society*, London, 1967) is more concerned to examine Marx's analysis of accumulation in capitalist society and to adopt a concept of 'industrial society' that permits him to differentiate different models of social growth.

27 D. Lane, '*The Socialist Industrial State: Towards a Political Sociology of State Socialism*, London, 1976, p. 58.

28 Weinberg, 'Convergence', pp. 2–3.

29 Ibid.

30 K. Kumar, 'Industrialism and post-industrialism: reflections on a putative transition', *Sociological Review*, Vol. 24, No. 3, August 1976, pp. 439–78, esp. pp. 445–52.

31 A.G. Meyer, 'Theories of convergence', in A. Chalmers Johnson (ed.), *Change in Communist Systems*, Stanford, Ca., 1972.

32 Kumar, 'Industrialism'.

33 S. Huntingdon & Z.B. Brzeziński, *Political Power: USA/USSR*, New York, 1965, pp. 419–21, 430. M. Crozier, *The Bureaucratic Phenomenon*, London, 1964; J.A. Armstrong, 'Sources of administrative behaviour: some Soviet and West European comparisons', *American Political Science Review*, Vol. LXIII, September 1965, pp. 643–55.

34 'Were Marx or de Tocqueville, Weber or Durkheim to return today, what might give them cause for despondency would not be the insufficiency of their original analysis, but its continuing relevance. The surprise might be that the tendencies they observed had been of such long duration – coupled in some cases with a sorrowful reflection that they had been unduly optimistic about the capacity of industrial society to initiate radically new patterns of social development' (Kumar,

'Industrialism', p. 461), See also ibid., pp. 463, 464 and K. Kumar, *Prophecy and Progress: The Sociology of Industrial and Post-Industrial Society,* London, 1978.

35 S. Tellenback, 'The logic of development in Socialist Poland', *Social Forces,* Vol. 57, No. 2, 1978, pp. 436–56.

36 Lane, *Socialist Industrial State,* pp. 60–2. Peter Wiles has similar reservations with respect to sectoral economic development: P. Wiles, contribution to a symposium on 'Technocracy, politics and the post-industrial society', *Survey,* Vol. 17/1, 1971, pp. 1–27; P. Wiles, 'Will Capitalism and Communism spontaneously converge?', in M. Boornstein and D. Fusfeld (eds.), *The Soviet Economy: A Book of Readings,* Homewood, Ill., 1966.

37 Lane, *Socialist Industrial State,* 1976.

38 T. Cliff, *Russia: A Marxist Analysis,* London, 1964.

39 L. Trotsky, *The Revolution Betrayed,* New York, 1957: E. Mandel, *The Inconsistencies of State Capitalism,* (IMG), London, 1969; E. Mandel, 'Ten theses on the social and economic laws governing the society transitional between Capitalism and Socialism', *Critique,* No. 3, Autumn 1974, pp. 5–23.

40 Paul M. Sweezy, 'The transition to socialism', *Monthly Review,* Vol. 23, No. 1, 1971, pp. 1–16; Charles M. Bettelheim, 'Dictatorship of the proletariat, social class and political ideology', *Monthly Review,* Vol. 23, No. 6, 1971, pp. 55–76.

41 H.H. Ticktin, 'Towards a political economy of the USSR', *Critique,* No. 1, 1973, pp. 20–41; H.H. Ticktin, 'The political economy of the Soviet intellectual', *Critique,* No. 2, 1974, pp. 5–22. For Ticktin the Soviet Union is an atomised society resting on the production of waste and sustaining an elite that does not control the mode of production, but controls the appropriation of surplus.

42 S. Mallet, *The New Working Class* (Spokesman), 4th edn, Nottingham 1975. 'It is on the contrary these workers, technicians and cadres profoundly 'integrated' into industrial society in the most 'sensitive' and decisive sectors who are in a position to formulate possibilities for a human liberation which does not reject technological progress, and which rises against its distortion' (p. 12).

43 A. Gorz (ed.), *'The Division of Labour: The Labour Process and Class Struggle in Modern Capitalism',* Brighton, 1976. See especially the Preface and chapter 2 by S.A. Marglin, 'What do bosses do? Origins and functions of hierarchy in Capitalist production'.

44 A. Gorz, 'Technology, technicians and the class struggle', in Gorz, *The Division of Labour,* pp. 159–79.

45 S. Mallet, *Bureaucracy and Technocracy in the Socialist Countries* (Spokesman), Nottingham, 1974.

46 J. Kuron and K. Modzelewski, 'An open letter to members of the University of Warsaw sections of the United Polish Workers' Party and the Union of Young Socialists', in *Revolutionary Marxist Students Speak Out, 1964–68,* New York, 1968.

47 R. Bahro, *The Alternative in Eastern Europe*, London, 1978; R. Bahro, 'The alternative in Eastern Europe', *New Left Review*, No. 106, November–December 1977, pp. 3–37.
48 Bahro, 'Alternative', p. 25.
49 M. Rakovski, *Towards an East European Marxism*, London, 1978; G. Konrad and I. Szelenyi, *The Intellectuals on the Road to Class Power*, Brighton, 1979.
50 Konrad and Szelenyi, *Intellectuals*, p. 222.
51 Decree, 26 October 1950, cited in *Prawo przedsiębiorstw*, Warsaw, 1971, pp. 24–36.
52 W. Kuczyński, 'The state enterprise under Socialism', *Soviet Studies*, Vol. XXX, No. 3, July 1978, pp. 313–35.
53 F.M. Scherer, *Industrial Market Structure and Economic Performance*, Chicago, 1970. More sophisticated calculations of cross-elasticities of demand and the assessment of substitutability of factors of production to establish identity of the market are necessary before market concentration ratios and Gini coefficients can be established.
54 The 'others' include: A.A. Berle and G.C. Means, *The Modern Corporation and Private Property*, New York, 1932; Carl Kaysen, 'The corporation: how much power, what scope?', in A. Pizzorno (ed.), *Political Sociology*, London, 1971, pp. 136–54. A summary of different positions on the 'corporation' is found in R. Marris (ed.), *'The Corporate Society: Growth, Competition and Innovative Power'*, London, 1974.
55 R.J. Barber, *The American Corporation: Its Power, its Money, its Politics*, London, 1970. The power of 'ownership alliance' is evident in the recent proliferation of mutual funds, pension funds, interlocking directorates, merchant banks and the general internationalisation of finance. The repeated failure of anti-trust legislation in the United States is cited to demonstrate that the state is unable to impose its hegemony over the corporation, which in many cases, because of its multi-national structure, is able to employ international finance capital to its advantage.
56 R. Vernon, *Sovereignty at Bay: The Multi-National Spread of U.S. Enterprises*, London, 1973; R. Barnet and R.E. Muller, *Global Reach: The Power of the Multi-Nationals*, London, 1973; D. Kavanagh, 'Beyond autonomy? The politics of corporations', *Government and Opposition*, Vol. 9, No. 1, 1974, pp. 42–60. Kavanagh isolates four relevant features for the study of corporations within the discipline of Political Science: size; specialisation; the symbiosis of state and industry; the autonomy of the technostructure or specialist staff.
57 A. Shonfield, *Modern Capitalism: The Changing Balance of Public and Private Power*, London, 1965; D. Coombes, *State Enterprise: Business or Politics?*, London, 1971; J. Hayward and M. Watson, *Planning, Politics and Public Policy*, London, 1975; P. Naville, J.P. Bardou, P. Brachet, C. Levy, *L'Etat entrepreneur: le cas de la regie Renault*, Paris, 1971; M.V. Posner and S.J. Woolf, *Italian Public Enterprise*, London, 1967; S. Holland, *The State as Entrepreneur*, London, 1972.

58 Galbraith, *New Industrial State*, pp. 117–20; W. Brus, *Socialist Ownership and Political Systems*, London, 1975; Rakovski, *East European Marxism*, pp. 77–9.

59 An old debate within the confines of conventional sociology centred on whether the intelligentsia or the working class was in the ascendant. It is cited in: Lane, *Socialist Industrial State*, pp. 92–100, and rests on whether one chooses to see conflict as vertically aligned such as Parkin (between the political elite and the administration and the intelligentsia) or horizontally aligned between the workers and the bureaucracy (Giddens). Lane is dissatisfied with Parkin for failing to distinguish between the type and function of state apparatus and with Giddens for exaggerating demands for workers' control.

2 The building of a socialist economy: social and political limits to growth

1 J. Zieliński, *Economic Reforms in East European Industry: Poland*, London 1973., pp. 308–18. This eclecticism is seen to express itself in five types of irreconcilable objectives:

   (i)   The simultaneous use of administrative orders and economic parameters

  (ii)   The simultaneous use of annual plan targets and long term financial norms

 (iii)   The simultaneous decentralisation of authority both to the enterprise and to the industrial association with resultant friction

 (iv)   The preservation of the basic features of the traditional economic system with changes in enterprise behaviour

  (v)   The preservation of taut planning with simultaneous changes in the management mechanism

2 S. Mallet, *Bureaucracy and Technocracy in the Socialist Countries* (Spokesman), Nottingham, 1974, pp. 14–16, pp. 20–2; G. Konrad, I. Szelenyi, *The Intellectuals on the Road to Class Power*, Brighton, 1979, pp. 85–92, 101–16.

3 T.P. Alton, *The Polish Post-War Economy*, New York, 1955, p. 6; F. Zweig, *Poland Between the Two Wars*, London, 1944, pp. 102–6; J. Taylor, *The Economic Development of Poland 1919–1950*, Ithaca, NY, 1952, p. 92–3.

4 Taylor, *Economic Development*, pp. 57, 93–94.

5 D. Douglas, *Transitional Economic Systems: The Polish–Czech Example*, London, 1953, pp. 20–21; Taylor, *Economic Development*, p. 29; Alton, *Post-War Economy*, p. 14; Zweig, *Between the Two Wars*, p. 108.

    Zweig estimated the share of state ownership in the following industries during the 1930s to be:

Railroads	90%
Merchant marine	95%
Commercial aviation	100%
Iron and steel	70%

Local industry	30%
Forestry	37%
Potash	100%
Metallurgy	50%
Armaments	100%

6 Z. Rybicki, *Administracyjno – Prawne Zagadnienia Gospodarki Planowej*, Warsaw, 1971, p. 10.

7 Douglas, *Transitional Economic Systems*, 'Altogether many of the characteristics of an eighteenth century Mercantilist State may be seen, flowering belatedly in the new Poland' (pp. 21–2); Taylor, *Economic Development*, 'If we exclude the USSR, we may say that state capitalism was developed in Poland to a greater extent than in any other European country during this period' (p. 33), see also p. 91.

8 J. Szczepański, 'Materiały do charakerystyku ludzi Polskiego Swiatu', in *Odmiany czasu teraźniejszego*, Warsaw, 1971, pp. 17–57.

9 J. Chałasiński, *Przeszłość i przyszłość inteligencji polskiej*, Warsaw, 1958; M. Hirszowicz, 'Intelligentsia versus bureaucracy? The revival of a myth in Poland', *Soviet Studies*, Vol. XXX, No. 3, July 1976, pp. 336–61, 339–42.

10 J. Szczepański, 'Inteligencja a pracownicy umysłowi', in *Odmiany czasu*, pp. 58–78.

At the same time the size of the industrial manual working class was small. Although in 1931 the working class covered about 15.6% of the economically active population, the numbers working in medium- and large-scale industry only reached about 5.5% in 1937. K. Zagorski, 'Changes of socio-occupational mobility in Poland', *Polish Sociological Bulletin*, No. 2, 1976, p. 20.

11 Douglas, *Transitional Economic Systems*, pp. 15–16.

12 Alton, *Post-War Economy*, pp. 15–16; Douglas, *Transitional Economic Systems*, p. 16; Taylor, *Economic Development*, p. 69.

13 Alton, *Post-War Economy*, pp. 21–2; Douglas, *Transitional Economic Systems* p. 33.

46% of the territory had been lost in the East and 26% was gained in the West.

14 For a fuller account of developments within the PZPR at this time see: M.K. Dziewanowski, *The Communist Party of Poland*, 2nd edn, Cambridge, Mass., 1976, pp. 183–222.

15 J.M. Montias, *Central Planning in Poland*, New Haven, Conn., 1962, pp. 53–5; G.R. Feiwel, *The Economics of a Socialist Enterprise: A Case Study of the Polish Firm*, New York, 1965, p. 4. These arguments reflect very much the exchanges between the Left and Right opposition in the Soviet Union during the 1920s.

16 Douglas, *Transitional Economic Systems*.

17 Douglas, ibid, pp. 50–1; Alton, *Post-War Economy*, p. 62; D. Lane, 'Structural and social change in Poland', in D. Lane and G. Kolankiewicz, *Social Groups in Polish Society*, London, 1973, p. 13.

Since the 1950s, about 95% of farms are between 2 and 15 hectares.

T. Toivanen and S. Widerszpil, 'Changes in socio-economic and class structure', in E. Allardt and W. Wesołowski (eds.), *Social structure and change: Finland and Poland*; Warsaw, 1978, p. 105; M. Lavigne, *The Socialist Economies of the Soviet Union and East Europe*, London, 1974, p. 18. While they cover only a small area, these state farms have been more productive in Poland than in most other East European economies. In 1966 they accounted for 13.5% of the cultivated land compared with 5% to 10% elsewhere, and their contribution to the gross agricultural product rose from 10.8% in 1960 to 13.3% in 1967. Many of these farms were situated in the Western territories, where land redistribution was facilitated by the emigration of many of the original land owners both during the Nazi occupation and afterwards.

18 Their numbers fell sharply from 9,076 units in 1955, to 1,668 in 1960 and 1,214 in 1968. Lane, 'Structural and social change', p. 13; Lavigne, *Socialist Economies*, p. 24; A. Korbiński, *The Politics of Socialist Agriculture in Poland, 1945–1960*, New York, 1965.

19 P. Lewis, 'The peasantry', in Lane and Kolankiewicz, *Social Groups*, p. 54–5.
Toivanen and Widerszpil, 'Changes in socio-economic and class structure', pp. 96–7, 40.

20 *Dziennik ustaw*, 3/1946; *Dziennik ustaw*, 2/1946.

21 Rybicki, *Administracyjno*, pp. 10–11.

22 Douglas, *Transitional Economic Systems*, pp. 53–6; Alton, *Post-War Economy*, p. 55. Douglas argues that after the passage of the 1946 law considerable numbers of industrial properties, hitherto in the hands of public authority, had to be handed back into private possession, and that the policy of support for private enterprise continued during the Three Year Plan of Reconstruction 1947–9. Alton, on the other hand, sees the year 1947 as the inauguration of a more stringent policy of discrimination against the private sector.

23 Alton, *Post-War Economy*, pp. 50–76.

24 Ibid., p. 7; Rybicki, *Administracyjno*, p. 14; Douglas, *Transitional Economic Systems*, pp. 57–68; Feiwel, *Socialist Enterprise*, p. 3.

25 Rybicki, *Administracyjno*, p. 13.

26 In early 1947 there were 14 such boards in the ministry of industry.

27 Rybicki, *Administracyjno*, pp. 20–1. The new ministries were for mining, heavy industry, light industry, agriculture and food processing, domestic trade and foreign trade. A further three ministries were set up in 1953 and by 1956 there were twelve. Alton, *Post-War Economy*, pp. 78–81; Montias, *Central Planning*, pp. 75–80.

28 For example, financial institutions and banks had been placed under state supervision in 1938, and this structure was used by the Provisional Government to provide credit and investment finance for both state and private sectors, and there was no reform until 1948. Taylor, *Economic Development*, p. 180. Alton, *Post-War Economy*, pp. 98–100.

29 G. Feiwel, *Poland's Industrialisation Policy: a current analysis*, Vol. I: *Sources of Economic Growth and Retrogression*, New York, 1971, pp. 230–6.

30 Industrial Production Index

(1948=100)

1929–36	1937– 69
1932–39	1939– 74
1934–49	1948–100
1935–57	1949–122
1936–58	1950–162

Source: United Nations Statistical Yearbook, 1952, p. 30.
There are, of course, problems concerning the basis for calculation of such figures, but they definitely indicate a rapid growth, especially during 1949–50.

31 A. Zauberman, *Industrial Progress in Poland, Czechoslovakia and East Germany, 1937–62*, London, 1964, pp. 2–7.

32 Montias, *Central Planning*, pp. 63–4. The phrase 'half-war economy' was coined by B. Minc.

33 O. Lange, 'Rola planowania w gospodarcze socjalistyczny', in *Pisma ekonomiczne i spoleczne: 1930–1960*, Warsaw, 196, pp. 137–47.

34 Ibid. Other economists have not been so generous in rationalising the necessity of a war economy in the first stage of constructing socialism. Feiwel, *Socialist Enterprise*: 'In a "sui generis war economy" the concern with scarcity relations, rational allocation of resources and economic calculation, is not deemed to be of primary importance. The planners' primary task seems to be that of assuring compatability between requirements and availability of products; hence the importance of material balances. At best, the method of balances will show internal consistency of requirements and availability, but it will not indicate the optimal solution, as there is a multitude of theoretically possible ones' (p. 16).

35 *Rocznik statystyczny 1972*, Warsaw, 1973, p. 121; Feiwel, *Industrialisation Policy*, pp. 76–90.

36 M. Jaroszińska, J. Kulpińska 'Czynniki polożenia klasy robotniczej', in W. Wesolowski (ed.) *Ksztalt struktury spolecznej*, Warsaw, 1978, pp. 107–69; W. Bielicki, S. Widerszpil, 'z problematyki przemian spolecznych w Polsce ludowej', *ND*, 7/1979, pp. 74–85.

37 G. Kolankiewicz, 'The industrial manual working class', in Lane and Kolankiewicz. *Social Groups*, p. 90; J. Zielińki, *Economic Reforms in East European Industry: Poland*, London, 1973, p. 9.

38 J.M. Montias, 'Planning with material balances in Soviet-type economies', in A. Nove and D.M. Nuti (eds.), *Socialist Economics*, London, 1972, pp. 223–51.

39 Feiwel, *Socialist Enterprise*, pp. 238–41.

40 J. Whalley, 'Polish post-war economic growth from the view point of the Soviet experience', *Soviet Studies*, Vol. XXIV, No. 4, April 1973, pp. 533–49.

41 Feiwel, *Industrialisation Policy*, pp. 228–41, 253–4; Montias, *Central Planning*, p. 62.

42 Feiwel, *Industrialisation Policy*, p. 256.

43 In June 1956 Edward Ochab replaced Bolesław Bierut as First Secretary of the PZPR, and in October 1956 the former was in turn replaced by Władysław Gomułka who made a blistering attack on past abuses of power. See the report of the VIII Plenum of the PZPR Central Committee. *ND*, 10/1956.

44 Montias, *Central Planning*, pp. 264–70.

45 Uchwała Nr. 704 RM 10 (10 November, 1956), *MP*, 94/1956, item 1047. These 8 directive indices included:
the value of total output
the limit in the wages fund
the ratio of profit to loss
payments to the central state budget
limits on the central budgetary grants for investment
financial limits for capital repairs
norms for the use of and replacement of working capital.

46 W. Dobierski, 'Ankieta rady ekonomistów', *ZG*, 31/1961, pp. 1, 5.

47 M. Misiak, 'Racje nieufności', *ZG*, 48/1961, p. 1.

48 W. Dudziński, 'A jednak rynek nabywcy?', *ZG*, 11/1959, p. 3.

49 O. Lange, 'Niektóre zagadnienia centralizacji i decentralizacji w zarządzaniu', *ZG*, 13/1971, pp. 1, 4.

50 Feiwel, *Industrialisation Policy*, pp. 16–21.

51 Montias, *Central Planning*, pp. 276–9.

52 Feiwel, *Industrialisation Policy*, pp. 274–87.

53 Zieliński, *Economic Reforms*, p. 2. The official Polish estimate is however higher, averaging 8.7% for the period 1959–68: A. Karpiński, *Polityka uprzemysłowienia Polski w latach 1958–1968*, Warsaw, 1969, p. 23.

54 Whalley, 'Post-war economic growth', pp. 533–49, especially pp. 537–8, 549.

55 H. Flakierski, 'Polish post-war growth', *Soviet Studies*, Vol. XXVII, No. 3, July 1975, pp. 460–76. 'High growth rates have been achieved owing to substantial increases in prime inputs, mainly capital, with a marked deterioration in the growth of total factor productivity, and in the rate of improvement in the efficiency of capital and labour' (p. 469).

56 'This is because Poland has a smaller reserve of labour and land, a slightly lower growth rate of population and a faster decline of this growth rate, a bigger dependence on foreign trade, and a stronger resistance to low consumption patterns' (ibid., p. 470).

57 Karpiński, *Polityka uprzemysłowienia*, pp. 2–27, 70–9.

58 Ibid., pp. 81–3, 116–18.

59 Feiwel, *Industrialisation Policy*, pp. 291, 297–8, 302–5, 305–10.

60 Karpiński, *Polityka uprzemysłowienia*, pp. 139–53, 160–3.

61 M. Gamarnikow, 'Poland', in P. Wiles (ed.), *The Prediction of Communist Economic Performance*, London, 1971, pp. 213–15. Between 1961 and 1966 employment in the socialised sector had risen from 7.3 million to 8.5 million. Gamarnikow estimates that there were around 300,000 people unemployed in late 1966, but only one-fifth of these were actually registered as unemployed.

62 Feiwel, *Industrialisation Policy*, pp. 291–6, 316.

63 Karpiński, *Polityka uprzemysłowienia*, pp. 165, 207.
64 Feiwel, *Industrialisation Policy*, pp. 305–10.
65 Gamarnikow, 'Poland'; Zieliński, *Economic Reforms*, pp. 310–11; Feiwel, *Industrialisation Policy*: '...despite the intricacies of concrete reform solutions (systems of indexes, incentives, prices) the key role undoubtedly is played by the concept of the plan... Poland's experience has shown that excessive plan tautness is paid for by under-fulfilment of planned increases of consumption, and in the last analysis, by a reduction in the long term rate of growth' (pp. 331–2).
66 The publication of Liberman's article marked the acceptance by the CPSU of the introduction of some market phenomena into a planned economy. It paved the way for parametric models of planning and management to be introduced. In the model, prices are used to convey information about scarcity which will be used by managers in advance of planning output, as opposed to information gleaned by ex-post accounting procedures. These parameters or performance indicators which include success indicators (regulators of resource allocation, purchase and sales) and technical norms and indices, must all be linked to the incentive or bonus system in order to be effective. E.G. Liberman, 'The Plan, profits and bonuses', in A. Nove and D. Nuti (eds.), *Socialist Economics*, London, 1972, pp. 309–18.
67 Zieliński, *Economic Reforms*, pp. 16–17, 86.
68 Ibid., pp. 86, 194–5, 209–13, 233.
69 Fifth Congress PZPR (11–16 November 1968), *Podstawowe materiały i dokumenty*, Warsaw, 1968; J.K. 'W kierunki nowoczesności', *Polityka*, 15/1969.
70 Zieliński, *Economic Reforms*, p. 18; Feiwel, *Industrialisation Policy*, pp. 415–42. Investments were reclassified into branch, enterprise and state-budget categories, and branch investment mainly financed by bank credit was to be the key to the 'intensive selective development' strategy. The financial reform involved encouraging greater Bank supervision and control of enterprise activity through the application of preferential and penalty interest rates.
71 Feiwel, *Industrialisation Policy*, pp. 344–6.
72 By 1967 agricultural output only contributed 17% of the national income compared with 40% in 1950: but, whereas in 1950 57% of the Polish population derived their income from agriculture, this had only fallen to 42% in 1967. P. Lewis, 'The peasantry', in Lane and Kolankiewicz, *Social Groups*, p. 85.
73 Gamarnikow, 'Poland', p. 221.
74 Feiwel, *Industrialisation Policy*, (1971), pp. 333–4, 394.
75 Gamarnikow, 'Poland', p. 226.
76 N. Bethel, *Gomułka: His Poland and His Communism*, London, 1972, chapter 16; W. Woods, *Poland: Phoenix in the East*, London, 1972, pp. 168–83.
77 T.P. Wanless, 'Economic reform in Poland 1973–79', *Soviet Studies*, Vol. XXXII, No. 1, January 1980, pp. 28–57.
78 Ibid. Amongst the constraints mentioned are the general level of

economic strain; the ambitious programme of economic growth financed increasingly by foreign debt; the failure to change the planning process away from a bureaucratic annual cycle; the incomplete implementation of the reform (domestic price changes did not cover retail and wholesale prices; direct access to foreign exchange was abandoned; and the whole reform co-existed with the old principles of economic and financial management elsewhere in the economy) and the failure to encourage competitiveness despite the emphasis on introducing market forces and incentives. See also 'Zmodyfikowany system WOG', Interview with J. Pajestka, in *ZG*, 14/1977, p. 1.

79 'Co powiedzieli ekonomisci o gospodarce', *ZG*, 26/1971.

80 Ibid.

81 'Doskonalenie procesu planowania i zarządzania i kierowania gospodarką narodową', materiały z plenarnego posiedzenia komisji partyjno–rządowej dla unowoczessnienia systemu funkcjonowania gospodarki i państwa', 12 April 1972, Warsaw. See also Decree No. 122 of the Council of Ministers (May 1972) on the principles for the construction of the 1973 plan.

82 M. Gronicki, 'Polish economic policy in the nineteen seventies', *National Westminster Bank Review*, 1979.

83 While during 1971–8 the productivity of land under cultivation only rose by 1.7%, this was higher for animal husbandry (4.1%) but was only achieved through higher imports of fodder. T. Wrzaszczyk, 'Rozwoj społeczno–gospodarczy a postęp naukowo–techniczny w latach osiemdziesatych', *ND* 1/1980, pp. 14–58, especially p. 34.

84 T. Wrzaszczyk, 'Podstawowe kierunki rozwoju kraju w 1979 roku', *ND* 1/1979.

85 During the period 1971–8, 450 foreign licences to produce were purchased of which 90% came from the West (especially in the field of electrical engineering and chemicals). T. Wrzaszczyk, 'Podstawowe', p. 22.

86 In 1976 Poland owed the West an estimated $10 billion, and the cost of servicing this debt for 1976 alone was estimated to be between $2 billion and $2.5 billion. *Guardian*, 11 January 1977. Unofficial estimates of the size of this debt in July 1980 placed it in the region of $20 billion!

87 Some scholars would argue that this is considerably overstated: a centrally planned economy such as Poland stands as an example to the West on the control of inflation, as even under conditions of taut planning, prices on the domestic market can be insulated from foreign trade prices. R. Portes, 'The control of inflation: lessons from the East European experience', *Economica*, Vol. 44/1976, p. 130, '...it is clearly possible to run a modern economy under high pressure with rapid growth and virtually no inflation, even with significant foreign trade dependence on an inflating capitalist world.'

88 By 1975, 47.5% of Polish foreign trade was with non-CMEA countries, and imports from the West had increased from 26% in 1970 to 49% in 1975. W. Morawski and P. Seppanen, 'Industrialisation and mod-

ernisation', in E. Allardt and W. Wesołowski, *Social Structure and Change: Finland and Poland*, Warsaw, 1978, p. 48.

89 These price rises were eventually rescinded. *ZG*, 29/1976, p. 15.

90 J. Dzieciołowski, 'W sieci wskazników', *ZG*, 13/1972, pp. 1, 6; S. Jakubowicz, 'Granice eksperymentu', *Polityka*, 1/1974.

91 It has been forecast that the size of the workforce which had been growing rapidly since 1970 would undergo a slower growth rate from between 3 to 6 times less after 1980. (The working population had expanded by 1.9 million from 1971–5; 0.6 million from 1976–80; and the forecast for 1980–5 was 0.3 million) Much of this is the result of demographic factors, especially the coming-of-age of the post-war baby boom, and a large number of workers reaching the retirement age. Misiak, 'Ogniwo procesu', *ZG*, 13/1976, p. 7.

92 A. Szpilewicz, 'Problemy lepszego gospodarowania surowcami', *ND*, 1/1977, pp. 84–92; Gronicki, 'Economic Policy', pp. 68–70.

93 The central problem is that food needs increase by about 3% p.a. but the net product of agriculture only rises by about 1.9% p.a. 'Guidelines for the Eighth PZPR Congress', called for an annual increase of between 2.2% to 2.4% from 1981 to 1985; L. Kłonica, 'Rolnictwo w latach osiemdziesiątych', *ND*, 1/1980, pp. 59–68.

94 As many farmers are reaching retirement age (one third are over 50 and 50% of all farmers are women) and as there is a low level of mechanisation, much land is going out of use. Kłonica, 'Rolnictwo'.

95 The housing programme for the period 1976–80 has not kept up with demand and by late 1978 there were 337,000 dwellings still to be built by 1980. Although between 1971 and 1978 965,000 new homes had been built which was more than the total for 1956–70, waiting lists were very long and were probably pushed up by the higher number of marriages taking place. Report of the XIII Plenum of the KC PZPR (13, 14 December 1978), *ND*, 1/1974; St. Kukuryka, 'Mieszkania – bariery i mozliwośći', *ND*, 2/1980, pp. 65–73.

96 Zieliński, *Economic Reforms*, (1973), p. 39.
The exceptions are the relatively slack years of 1954, 1963 and 1968, when plan targets were revised downwards as investment ceilings were reached.

97 *The Intellectuals on the Road to Class Power*, Brighton, 1979.

3 The emergence of corporate structure in Polish industry, 1958–68

1 O. Lange, 'Niektóre zagadnienia centralizacji i decentralizacji w zarzadzaniu', *ZG*, 13/1971.

2 M. Crozier, *The Bureaucratic Phenomenon*, London, 1964; J. Child, *The Business Enterprise in Modern Industrial Society*, London, 1969; D. Silverman, *The Theory of Organisations*, London, 1970.

3 J. Staniszkis, *Patologie struktur organizacyjnych*, Warsaw, 1972; J. Stanisz-

kis, 'On remodelling the Polish economic system', *Soviet Studies*, Vol. XXX, No. 4, 1978, pp. 547–52; W. Narojek, *Społeczeństwo planujące: próba socjologii gospodarki socjalistycznej*, Warsaw, 1973.

4 See above, pp. 16–18.

5 See above, pp. 28–9, 30–2.

6 A. Nove, *An Economic History of the USSR*, London, 1969.

7 Ibid., pp. 89–97, 143; E.H. Carr & R.W. Davies, *Foundations of a Planned Economy 1926–29*, London, 1969.

8 Nove, *Economic History*, pp. 263–5. For example, the reform of credit and banking in 1930 which put an end to the ability of the 'trusts' to make credit agreements between one another and which was followed by strictly controlled planning, reduced both the trusts and the *'ob'edinenie'* to an administrative function, with little economic influence over enterprises.

9 Ibid., pp. 266, 294; M. Dobb, *Soviet Economic Development since 1917*, London, 1966, 6th edn, p. 364.

10 B. Gliński, 'Problemy usamodzielnienia przedsiębiorstw prsemysłowych', *ND*, 3/1958, pp. 32–44; Czesław Bobrowski, 'Przed zmianą modelu gospodarczego's, *ZG*, 19/1957, pp. 1, 2.

11 B. Gliński, 'Problemy, *ND*, 3/1958. For example in the sugar processing industry, it was only necessary for the Central Board to supervise a common investment, sales and supplies policy; whereas the Central Board in the engineering industry tended to be more directly involved in product design and the production process.

12 S. Frenkiel, 'Zjednoczenia: nowa jednostka gospodarcza', *ZG*, 10/1958, pp. 1, 6.

13 'Rada ekonomiczna w sprawie dotychczasowego przebiegu zmian modelowych', *ZG*, 30/1958, p. 2; B. Gliński, *Teoria i praktyka zarządzania przedsiębiorstwami przemysłowymi*, Warsaw, 1964, pp. 180–2.

14 W. Brus, 'Zysk, ceny i zjednoczenia', *ZG*, 9/1958, pp. 1, 3. Brus stressed that it was necessary to avoid fixing uniform internal prices for goods produced by different enterprises as there were tremendous variations in profitability. It was necessary to fix a uniform sales price for all goods produced by enterprises within the association, but at the same time to allow the association to fix clearing prices according to the particular conditions of production of individual enterprises.

15 Uchwała Nr 128, RM (18 April 1958).

16 B. Gliński, *System zarządzania w przemyśle kluczowym*, Warsaw, 1960 Chapter 6, p. 69; B. Gliński, 'W kwestiach wielkich organizacjiach gospodarczych', *ND* 3/1973, p. 66.

17 Gliński, *System zarządzania*, pp. 71–2. In the association of the machine tools industry, employment fell from 100 in 1955 to 87 in 1959 and was accompanied by a redistribution of staff between departments. New posts and offices for the chief mechanic, chief energy engineer, and exports were set up.

18 It was estimated that in 1959 there were 44 ministries, central offices and committees that were directly responsible to the Council of

Ministers with the number of industrial ministries totalling 15 (see the abstract of details from 'Rocznik polityczny i gospodarczy' 1958), *ZG*, 8/1959.

19 A. Jakubowicz, 'Funkcje zjednoczeń przemysłowych w nowym systemie planowania w Polsce w latach 1956–1958', SGPiS, manuscript, Warsaw, 1970, p. 58.

20 A. Płocića 'Na co czekają zjednoczenia?', *ZG*, 21/1959. The statute for the industrial association in the cement industry was finally approved in April 1959 although the association has been conducting business since January 1959. J.L. Toeplitz, 'Szkodliwy schematyzm', *ZG*, 32/1958, pp. 1, 6, cites the example of the association for food concentrates where the only differences in its statute related to the powers of the chief director over appointments of all senior management and over approval of all norms for labour and production.

21 'Nie obcinąć głowy', *ZG*, 40/1958, p. 8. Toeplitz, 'Szkodliwy schematyzm', cites the example of the ministry of food and provisions that insisted that all industrial associations pass on to the enterprises as an obligatory directive, the index of production of basic commodities fixed by the ministry.

The association of the heavy engineering industry received 100% more binding indices in 1958 in comparison with the Central Board in 1957!

J.L. Toeplitz, 'Co z samodzielnosci?', *ZG*, 18/1959, pp. 1, 2; W. Dudziński, 'Zjednoczenie czyli rozdzielnia niedoskonała', *ZG*, 45/1961, p. 5; Z. Madej, 'O zjednoczeniu inaczej', *ZG*, 49/1961, p. 7.

22 Gliński, 'W kwestiach', p. 67. In the early 1960s, about 25% of enterprise investment was controlled by the industrial association; only 30% by the enterprise; and the rest by the ministry.

A study carried out by the CRZZ in 1962 and 1963 which investigated 85 industrial associations run by 9 ministries, found that in 1963, 41 associations received the same number of directive indices as they did in 1962; 28 received more and 16 received less; and that 36 received the same number of information indices and 24 more and 25 less. In 1963 the association of the cables and electrical equipment industry received 83 directive indices; the association of the sugar industry received 38; and the association for iron ore mining received 61. 'Wskazniki dyrektywne', *ZG*, 44/1963, p. 9.

23 Ibid. Of the 7 industrial associations in the coal industry, 5 had to fulfil more than the statutory 8 DIs and the number ranged from 11 to 25. Also 78% of the enterprises in the 85 industrial associations received the DIs for the plan year 1963, as late as December 1962.

24 'Samorządowe przemiany', *ZG*, 21/1963, p. 6.

25 M. Misiak, 'Zjednoczenie o sobie: wskazniki dyrektywne', *ZG*, 14/1965. The association for the fishing industry received 467 directive indices annually, and then passed on between 30 and 150 to its component enterprises, when only 20 of these were considered to be essential.

222   *Notes to pages 59–63*

26 Z. Saldak & W. Woznićko, 'Sródła trafnośći inwestycyjnych', *ZG*, 9/1964, pp. 1, 8, 9; B. Gliński, 'O zadaniach i formach organizacyjnych zjednoczeń', *ND*, 12/1964, pp. 128–36; B. Gliński, 'O roli zjednoczenia i przedsiębiostwa', *ND*, 6/1964, pp. 94–7; J.C. Toeplitz, 'Na co czekają przedsiębiorstwa?', *ZG*, 20/1959, pp. 1, 4.

27 J. Toeplitz, 'Działać nie urzędować', *ZG*, 47/1959, pp. 1, 7.

28 Gliński, *Teoria i praktyka*, pp. 181–87.

29 H. Sadownik, 'Kontrola w zarządzaniu zjednoczeniom przemysłowym', Doctoral thesis, SGPiS, Warsaw, 1972. Sadownik estimated that 20% of the reports and requests for information received by the association originated in the Central Statistical Office.

30 'Zjednoczenia i integracja', *ZG*, 10/1962, pp. 1, 5.

31 Gliński, *System zarządzania*, p. 67. See also the contribution by the same author to 'O roli zjednoczenia i przedsiębiorstwa', *ND*, 6/1964, pp. 63–126.

32 Uchwała RM 611/1965 *MP*, 91 item 1027.

33 Sl. Glowacki, *Zjednoczenie państwowych przedsiębiorstw terenowych w systemie organów rad narodowych*, Warsaw 1972, pp. 31–3; B. Gliński, *Teorie i praktyka*, pp. 348–9. In 1959 locally controlled industrial enterprises contributed 20% of national industrial production and 30% of the construction industry output. In 1963 the percentage of state production derived from local industry was 29% in metallurgy; 9% in chemicals; 6.8% in textiles and clothing; 9.3% in leather; 13.6% in forestry and timber; and 22.7% in food. By 1964 the output of locally controlled industry had fallen to only 10% of the global value of production in the socialised sector.

34 Glowacki, *Zjednoczenie państwowych*, pp. 33, 59–61; Gliński, *Teorie i praktyka*, pp. 259–65.

35 Nove, *Economic History*, pp. 342–4, 359–69; M. Lavigne, *The Socialist Economies of the Soviet Union and East Europe*, London, 1974.

36 M. Doroszewicz, 'Zjednoczenie – główne ogniwo zarządzania', *ZG*, 44/1965.

37 Ibid.; K. Zimniewicz, 'Funkcjonowanie przedsiębiorst patronackich', *ZG*, 5/1979, p. 4.

38 Doroszewicz, 'Zjednoczenie'. 50% of the votes were to be cast by the leading association and major industrial enterprise management, while the other 50% were divided proportionately between the other participants in the Branch Commission including the accounting, research and development and other service units. Z. Rybicki, *Administracyjno – prawne zagadnienia gospodarki planowej*, Warsaw, 1971, pp. 234–5; W. Liniewicz, 'Organizacja zjednoczeń i kombinatów', (Master's thesis), Warsaw SGPiS, 1970.

39 M. Misiak, 'Koordynacja branżowej – ciąg datszy', *ZG*, 34/1964, pp. 1, 2.

40 M. Doroszewicz, 'Zjednoczenie'; Z. Rybicki, *Administracyjno*.

41 J. Kwejt, 'Niektóre problemy ko-ordynacji branżowej i terenowej', *Przegląd Organizacji*, 7/1965.

42 See Chapter 2, pp. 41–2.

43 It was also agreed that the number of directive indices to be fulfilled by the industrial association was too many; and that they should be able to have greater powers to independently set for their enterprises the following targets and parameters: development policy; credit policy; and foreign trade. The possibility of having foreign trade offices located in the association headquarters was also considered. Gliński, 'O roli zjednoczenia', pp. 65–9, 72.

44 Doroszewicz, 'Zjednoczenie'. While in 1960 there were 6,800 enterprises in existence in which the average number of plants was 5.6, by 1965 this had risen to 7.9. See G. Blazyca, 'Industrial structure and the economic problems of industry in a centrally planned economy: the Polish case', *Journal of Industrial Economics*, Vol. 28, No. 3, 1980, p. 321.

45 *ND*, 6/1964, 'O roli zjednoczenia, pp. 79, 104–6.

46 For example the massive Cegielski Engineering Works in Poznań would fit in best with the amalgamated plant structure according the horizontal integration prevailing there; but the association-combine was seen as a much more suitable model for the needs of vertical integration in the chemical industry.

47 J. Pajestka, *Kierunki doskonalenia systemu planowania i zarządzania w Polsce Ludowej*, Warsaw, 1965, pp. 28–33; 'Resolution of the Fourth Congress of the PZPR', *ND*, 7/1964, pp. 144–204, especially, p. 184.

48 A. Skowroński, 'Problemy amalgamacji przemysłowej zjednoczenia i kombinaty', *Ruch Prawniczy Ekonomiczny i Socjologiczny*, 4/1971, pp. 81–94; B. Gliński, 'O zadaniach i formach organizacyjnych zjednoczeń', *ND*, 12/1964, pp. 128–36. Responses to the second questionnaire were rather surprising as they revealed that fewer associations than previously anticipated would prefer increased powers over enterprise development policy. (Although responses were divided upon questions concerning association investment, the financing of new projects etc.)

49 Gliński, 'O zadaniach'. The smallest industrial association in the orthopaedic industry employed only 800 employees, while the largest in the iron and steel industry employed 150,000.

50 Ibid. The number of research institutes attached to associations varied: while the association of the iron and steel industry had two research institutes, industrial associations in light industry, forestry and timber, and the food industry rarely possessed such resources. Also where they existed the numbers employed in this work fluctuated. In the association of the oil refining industry 17.6% of staff worked in research institutes; while this was 8.8% in the association of mining machinery and only 3.3% in the association of iron and steel metallurgy.

51 Ibid. In general, association management was frequently very keen to make changes in the enterprises or production profile, and in the case of multi-branch industrial associations, they were more keen to increase their control over enterprises than relinquish it.

52 See Chapter 5, p. 147.

53 'Zjednoczenia i integracja', *ZG*, 10/1962. Gliński, 'O roli zjednoczenia', p. 107.

54 B. Fick, 'Reforma systemu plac w zjednoczeniach', *ZG*, 31/1964, pp. 1,

7. This author constructed an index of average wages. If that for association management was held at 100, then the index for the enterprise director was 155; 162 for the deputy enterprise director for technical development; 156 for the chief interprise accountant; 155 for the manager of the enterprise economics unit; and 183 for the manager of the enterprise technical unit.

55 Ibid. Wage differentials between senior association management and economic staff tended to widen considerably and in the association of the iron and steel industry, although the official differentiation between the senior economist and chief director was 100:95, in practice it reached 100:400.

56 L. Braiter, 'Uprawnienia administracyjne', *ZG*, 6/1965, p. 2.

57 Gliński, 'O zadaniach', p. 132; Z. Lewandowicz, 'Uprawnienia zjednoczeń, *ZG*, 2/1967, pp. 1, 6; E. Murawski, 'Zjednoczenie przemysłu cukierniczego', Doctoral thesis, SGPiS, Warsaw, 1973.

58 Uchwała IV Plenum KCPZPR, 'O kierunkach zmian w systemie planowania i zarządzania gospodarką narodową', *ND*, 8/1965.

59 B. Gliński, 'Niektóre problemy rozwoju systemu zarządzania przemysłem', *ND*, 4/1966, pp. 99–109. See also Resolutions Nos. 276, 277, 280, and 281 of the Council of Ministers passed on 28 October 1965 and quoted in 'Nowe zasady dotychczące gospodarki finansowej zjednoczeń i przedsiębiorstw państwowych', *ZG*, 50/1965, pp. 7, 8.

The five funds controlled by the industrial association were: the association Head Office Fund; the association Investment Fund; the Reserve Fund; the Fund for Economic Enterprise; and the Branch Fund. The five funds controlled by the enterprise were: the Enterprise Head Office Fund; the Development Fund; the Repair Fund; the Wages Fund and the Factory Fund.

60 Uchwała KCPZPR, 'O kierunkach'; M. Doroszewicz, 'Kilka uwagi i wniosków', *ND*, 2/1965, pp. 96–103.

61 E. Winter, 'Nowy system finansowy przemysłu', *ZG*, 1/1966, p. 4.

62 M. Misiak, 'Reforma na co dzień: wskaźniki dyrektywne 1966', *ZG*, 2/1966, pp. 1–2.

63 'Pierwszy statut Ministerstwa', *ZG*, 37/1965, pp. 1, 6.

64 Uchwała RM Nr 383 (7 December 1966), 'w/s zasad organizacji i funkcjonowania zjednoczeń przemysłowych', *MP*, 64/1966, item 197.

65 Z. Lewandowicz, 'Uprawnienia zjednoczeń', *ZG*, 2/1967.

66 Ibid. B. Gliński, *Zjednoczenie i przedsiębiorstwo*, Warsaw, 1968, p. 30.

67 H. Weber, 'Przedsiębiorstwo: sztuka zarządzania – pierwszy komisji zakładowych', *ZG*, 9/1967, p. 4; J. Niedzwiecki, 'O systematyczne doskonalenia organizacji produkcji i zarządzania', *ND*, 5/1967, pp. 3–14.

68 G. Leptin, 'The G.D.R.', in H.H. Höhman, M.C. Kaser & K. Thalheim (eds.), *The New Economic Systems of Eastern Europe*, London, 1975. Michael Keren, however, does not consider the New Economic System to have been an unreserved success and claims that after 1970, there was little to distinguish the GDR from other States with

command economies: M. Keren, 'The New Economic System in the G.D.R.: an obituary', *Soviet Studies*, Vol, XXIV, No. 4, 1972/3, pp. 554–87.

69 M.C. Kaser and J.G. Zieliński, *Planning in East-Europe*, London, 1970, p. 94; H. Boehme, 'East German price formation under the NES', *Soviet Studies*, Vol. XIX, No. 3, 1967/8, pp. 340–58.

70 Kaser and Zieliński, *Planning*, pp. 89–90; Keren, New Economic System, p. 561.

71 P.C. Ludz, *The Changing Party Elite in East Germany*, Cambridge, Ma., 1972.

72 T.A. Bayliss, *The Technical Intelligentsia and the East German Elite*, London, 1974.

73 After the V Plenum of the PZPR Central Committee in 1965, the directive index on employment was relaxed (although Wages Funds were still limited) for selected enterprises in the food, catering, clothing, footwear and railway industries and in some other areas of domestic and foreign trade. Later, after the VI Plenum of the PZPR Central Committee in 1966, an 'Exporters Club' was set up to facilitate co-ordination and exchange of ideas between all enterprises who directed more than 50% of their output to export; and after July 1966 a special bonus system was introduced for certain employees in such enterprises. M. Misiak, 'Reforma na co dzień'; Z. Zawadski, 'Premiowanie pracowników umysłowych, po trzech latach doswiadczeń', *ZG*, 46/1967.

74 Zjednoczenie przemysłu stolarki budowlanej (ZPSB)
Zjednoczenie przemysłu farmaceuticznego (ZPF 'Polfa')
Zjednoczenie przemysłu azotowego (ZPA)
Zjednoczenie przemysłu okrętowego (ZPO)

75 T. Baumberger, 'Stani i perspektywy rozwoju eksperymentalnego zarządzania w przemyśle okrętowym', in 'Konferencja n.t. doswiadczenia zjednoczeń eksperymentujacych', PTE papers, Warsaw, 1968. The directive indices were labour productivity, the product assortment, an index of deductions from profit to the central state budget, the index of the apprentices Wages Fund, the general Wages Fund and the maintenance costs of the association.

76 Ibid. Overtime rose from 8% to 10.4% of the total hours worked during 1965–7.

77 M. Cybulska, 'Eksperyment zjednoczenia przemysłu okrętowego i zjednoczenia przemysłu stolarki budowlanej w swietle observacji Narodowego Banku Polskiego', in 'Konferencja' (PTE Warsaw, 1968).

78 E. Wiewińska, 'Analiza eksperymentu zjednoczenia przemysłu stolarki budowlanej w zakresie nowych form planowania i organizacja produkcji', Warsaw, 1970, p. 41.

79 Uchwała Nr 48, RM 8 March 1967; Zarządzanie, Przesa RM Nr 21, 31 March 1967.

80 See Chapter 6 pp. 153–85.

81 Wiewińska, *Analiza*, pp. 46–9.

Although workforce representatives were chosen by the enterprise Conference of Workers' Self-management (KSR), had to be approved by the association director and could only attend one full session of the 'kolegium' per annum, it was argued that by February 1969 they were involved in making important decisions on the distribution of the Factory Fund.

82 Zarządzanie Nr 21, Przesa RM 1 March 1966. (This statute was not finally applied until August 1966). J. Olszewski, 'Eksperyment gospodarczy zjednoczenia przemy*l*su ażotowego', in 'Konferencja', (1968).

83 The major directive indices were: the value of commodities produced (in factory prices), the share of costs in the value of output (in factory prices), the basic product assortment in terms of the value of sales; and the value of exports. The limits included: the value of imports, the size of the Wages Fund, the size of employment, investment, and the distribution of centrally listed commodities. The norms included the index of payments from profits to the central state budget and the index of payments into the Factory Fund. See E. Nędzowski, *Funkcjonowanie dużych organizacjach przemysłowych na przykładzie przemysłu ażotowego*, Kraków, 1972.

84 Ibid. On average the ministry requested 15 reports a day on various activities of the association.

85 Sz. Jakubowicz, 'Eksperyment i reforma', *Polityka*, 18/1968. Jakubowicz disagreed quite strongly with the popular presentation of Polfa as an industrial association that was conceding greater independence to its enterprises. See Sz. Jakubowicz, 'Integracja przedsiębiorstw w zjednoczeniach eksperymentujących', in L. Bar (ed.), *Grupowanie przedsiębiorstw państwowych: zagadnienia prawne*, Warsaw, 1972 p. 112.

86 H. Tarcha*l*ska, 'Eksperyment gospodarczy zjednoczenia przemy*sl*u farmaceuticznego Polfa', in 'Konferencja' (PTE Warsaw, 1968); J. Sidorowicz, 'Polfa–jak cienie?', *ZG*, 46/1968, p. 5; S. Bukowski, 'Zjednoczenie trzeba rozwijać', *ZG*, 14/1969, p. 3.

87 Materia*l*y z konferencją naukową n.t. 'Doswiadczenia zjednoczeń eksperymentujących', Zarząd Główny PTE, Warsaw, 1968.

88 Jakubowicz, 'Integracja przedsiębiorstw', p. 97.

89 Ibid., pp. 98–100. Also Sz. Jakubowicz, 'Sytuacja przedsiębiorstw w zjednoczeniu eksperymentujacym', Materialy dyskusyjne Instytut Planowania, Warsaw 1970, pp. 9–11. The reduction in the total number of directive indices received by enterprises in each association was as follows:

	ZPA	Polfa	ZPSB
1966	63	35	35
1968	30	17	9

90 Jakubowicz, 'Integracja przedsiębiorstw', p. 101.

91 Ibid., pp. 111–12.

92 Ibid., pp. 116–18.

93 Jakubowicz, 'Sytuacja przedsiębiorstw', pp. 11–38; 'Uwaga na

zjednoczenia', *ZG*, 12/1967, p. 1; 'Reforma i ludzie', *ZG*, 31/1967, p. 1.

94 Jakubowicz, 'Sytuacja przedsiębiorstw'; Jakubowicz, 'Integracja przedsiębiorstw', p. 122.

95 Jakubowicz, 'Integracja przedsiębiorstw', pp. 110–11. '...realizacja zasad koncentracji i specializacji produkcji prowadzi do integracji przedsiębiorstw w większych organizacjach gospodarczych'.

96 'Zjednoczenie', *ZG*, 50/1966, p. 1; Z. Sołdak, 'Pierwsze doswiadczenia nowego systemu inwestycji', *ZG*, 22/1966, pp. 1, 4, 5; Murawski, 'Zjednoczenie przemysłu', p. 164. Of 1,000 investment projects examined by the NBP between January and April 1966, most were considered to be inadequately documented and some showed that enterprises were being accorded preferential treatment on non-economic grounds.

97 Ibid. Also, A. Teter, 'Dyrektór i kolegium w zjednoczeniu przemysłowym', Master's thesis, SGPiS, Warsaw, 1970. In the association for household chemicals between 1967 and 1969, there had been an average of three or four kolegium sessions a year, but their convocation, the agenda, documentation and implementation of resolutions were all settled by the association central office. The director could veto certain resolutions, and representatives of workers' self-management organisations could attend certain sessions in an advisory capacity only.

98 T. Wolski, 'Czy zjednoczenia przedskadzają przedsiębiorstw?', *ZG*, 40/1967, p. 5.

One 'horror' story that was quoted involved the truck factory in Starachowice where the director claimed that he had to engage in protracted bargaining with the industrial association over the plan for 1968 after having been presented with a plan requiring the fulfilment of 70 directive indices issued three months late by the association and without any prior consultation. A. Bober, 'Zarządzanie w oczach przedsiębiorstwa: Samodzielność a inicjatywa', *ZG*, 27/1968, p. 3.

99 These commissions were set up after November 1966 and were charged, in particular, with improving inter-factory co-operation, and encouraging the arrangement of branch agreements between leading associations. (The administrative barriers between branches of industry inhibited co-operation, rendering problems in cost accounting.) S. Stefański, *Organizacja i metody zarządzania w przedsiębiorstwach i zjednoczeniach oraz funkcje gospodarcze zjednoczeń*, PTE, Katowice, 1967.

However, the activities and recommendations of these factory commissions were often ignored by industrial association management. H. Weber, 'Przedsiębiorstwo sztuka zarządzania, Pierwszy etap komisji zakładowych', *ZG*, 9/1967, p. 4, T. Niedźwiećki, 'O systematyczne doskonalenie organizacji produkcji i zarządzania', *ND*, 5/1967, p. 3–14; K. Krauss, 'Porządek i nieporządek', *Polityka*, 18/1967.

100 Sadownik, 'Kontrola w zarządzaniu', pp. 142–8, 153–81.

This requirement for resorts also placed a tremendous burden upon industrial enterprises. The director of the truck factory in Starachowice complained that he had to send 200 different reports to the industrial association each month, and nearly 90 were sent to GUS. Bober, 'Zarządzanie w oczach'.

101 J. Pajestka, 'Doskonalenie planowania i funkcjonowania Gospodarki w Polsce Ludowej', Materiały dyskusyjne, Instytut Planowania, Zeszyt 7, Warsaw, 1967, p. 30.

102 S. Paradowski, 'Administracyjne dylematy', *ZG*, 10/1968, p. 5. A government regulation of 1966 limited the percentage growth of office workers within the total number of employees in the association. However there was evidence that this was achieved by regarding some office staff as manual workers!

4 The emergence of a corporate structure in Polish industry, 1968–80

1 See Chapter 2, pp. 43–4. It must not be forgotten that the years 1967–8 were characterised by less than full employment.

2 Zarządzanie Nr 125, RM, 1968. This resolution granted certain privileges to these exporting firms including an overall reduction in the number of DIs, priority in allocation of raw materials and investment finance, flexibility in the limits on wages and employment, special bonus funds for those producing for export and for those management staff with knowledge of a foreign language. D. Fikus, 'Kto weźmie?', *Polityka*, 11/1969.

In the electrical engineering industry, 90% exports were to be manufactured in specialised enterprises enjoying priority treatment.

3 G. Blazyca, 'Industrial structure and the economic problems of industry in a centrally planned economy: the Polish case', *Journal of Industrial Economics*, Vol. 28, No. 3, 1980.

4 B. Gliński, 'O mozliwości w prowadzenia koncernowe formy zjednoczenia', *ZG*, 25/1965, p. 2. The 'koncern' would be most suitable for the food, construction, mining and energy industries but was seen as less suitable for the chemical industry and other branches of heavy industry. Other economists such as J. Pajestka and E. Lipiński were less favourably disposed to concentrating all major management decisions at the level of the industrial association, as they feared the development of monopoly powers in industry.

5 These proposals varied from leading enterprises, branch unions (*zreszenie*), the fusion of factories into a single-enterprise combine, to the grouping of enterprises around a 'mother' enterprise (a regional branch centre that provided specialised marketing facilities). W. Zastawny, 'Zjednoczenie – przedsiębiorstwo – zarząd robotniczych', in *'Symposium poswięcone usprawnienia funkcjonowania przedsiębiorstw i zjednoczeń'*, PTE Katowice, 1968.

6 Uchwała Nr 193, RM (23 October 1969), w/s 'Kombinatów przemysłowych i budowlanych', *MP*, 46/1969, item 362.

7 Report of the V Plenum KCPZPR, 19–20 May, 1970. 'Kierunki

usprawnienia systemu bodzców, materialnych w gospodarce uspolecznionej'.

8 M. Kaser and J. Zieliński, *Planning in East Europe*, London, 1970, pp. 50–62; Sz. Jakubowicz, 'Kombinaty w NRD (2): zasady dzialania', *ZG*, 16/1970, p. 1; Sz. Jakubowicz, 'Integracja przedsiębiorśtw w przemysle kluczowym Węgier i NRD', Manuscript, Warsaw, 1971.

9 M. Kaser and J. Zieliński, *Planning*; M. Keren, 'The New Economic System in the G.D.R.: an obituary', *Soviet Studies* Vol. XXIV, No. 4 1972/3 pp. 554–87.

10 Sz. Jakubowicz, 'Dylematy kombinatów', *ZG*, 27/1972, p. 10.

11 B. Gliński, 'O Kwestii W.O.G.', *ND*, 3/1973, pp. 68–9.

During 1958–60 a sulphur combine was built at Machów in S.E. Poland to process raw sulphur. Its rural location was seen as an important factor in helping to solve unemployment and encouraging the emergence of 'peasant workers'. H. Siwek, 'Studia na przeobrazenjami swiadośći spolecznej w zapleczu wiejskim, Kombinatu Tarnobrieskiego', Master's thesis, Kraków, 1965.

A combine for smelting copper was built in Lubin in 1961. By late 1968 it had expanded to include copper mines, and produced 45% of Polish requirements. By 1972 it had the distinction of being one of the very few combines based on vertical integration embracing the whole of the production process from mining to sheet copper. R. Jelenek, 'Organizaćja i efektywność ekonomiczna funkcjonowania dużej organizacji przemyslowej na przykladu kombinatu Górniczo – Hutnicznego Miedzi w Lubinie', Master's thesis, Kraków, 1970.

Other combines in existence in the 1960s could be found in nitrates, petrochemicals and steel (of which the best known example was the Lenin Steel Foundry at Nowa Huta near Kraków).

12 L. Zelchak, 'Kombinaty przemyslowe', in L. Bar (ed.), *Grupowanie przedsiębiorstw państwowych*, Warsaw, 1972, p. 90; B. Byrski, 'Nowe i tradycyjne kombinaty przemyslowe', *ZG*, 21/1970, p. 7.

13 L. Bar, 'Roziwiązanie administracyjno – prawne w kombinatach w swietle badań ankietowych', in *Funkcjonowanie rozwiązań prawnych w kombinatach przemyslowych*, Warsaw, 1972, pp. 5–6.

14 Ibid., p. 6; M. Kula, 'Przeslanki twórżenia kombinatów i rola kolegium i ich zarządzania (na przykladzie kombinatu przemyslu lożysk tocznych w Kielcach)'. Master's thesis, Kraków, 1973.

15 Zelczak, Kombinaty przemyslowe, p. 68. These were:
production of a final product, its components and semi fabricates
production of a group of products destined for a single customer
production of goods via a special technical process
production of goods relying upon the use of a particular raw material goods produced by different industries which nevertheless meet a specific regional demand.

16 Bar, 'Roziwiązanie administracyjno', p. 8. The actual number varied between 4 and 9.

17 Ibid., pp. 14–17.

18 Ibid., pp. 22–3.
19 In 1968 the engineering industry contributed to about 19% of general industrial production, 40% of exports and employed 1.1 million people. The industrial associations varied in size from 8,000 employees in textile machinery to 150,000 in iron and steel metallurgy. It was thus a very important industry to the Polish economy. T. Kleszcz, 'Kombinaty przemysłowe a zjednoczenia', *Problemy Organizacji*, 4/1969, p. 146; M. Mrela, L. Sajkiewicz, Z. Wisniewski, 'Kombinaty Przemysłowej', (artykul dyskusyjny), IOPM and *EiOP*, 5/1969, p. 220.
20 In the association of machine tools, 39 out of the 52 units were production enterprises employing around 38,000 people.
21 The reasons given were under-investment, limitations upon the growth of supplies from ancillary factories, difficulties in obtaining raw materials, the relatively high proportion of output destined for export and the limited foreign currency available for importing machine tools. W. Liniewicz, 'Organizacja zjednoczeń i kombinatów w rekonstrukcji branżowej i terenowej', Master's thesis, SGPiS, Warsaw, 1970, pp. 74–5, 78–81.
22 Ibid., pp. 83–90. The combines were:
      (i)   Kombinat Obrabiarek do Części Tocznych
      (ii)   Kombinat Obrabiarek do Części Korpusowych
      (iii) Kombinat Obrabiarek Ciężkich
      (iv)   Kombinat Obrabiarek i Narzędzi do Obróbki Ściernej
      (v)   Kombinat Obrabiarek i Narzędzi do Obróbki Plastycznej
      (vi)   Kombinat Narzędzi Pomiarowych i Tnących
      (vii) Kombinat Przyrządów i Uchwytów
      (viii) Kombinat Narzedzi Zmechanizowanych i Rzemieslniczych.
    This left only 8 independent cost-accounting units in the industrial association (2 production enterprises, 1 scientific research institute, 1 repair enterprise, 2 technical drawing offices and 2 trade units).
23 'Kombinaty w przemysłe maszynowym jako najefektywniejsza forma koncentracji i specjalizacji produkcji', *EiOP*, 5/1970, p. 197. These were:
      (i)   Kombinat Przemysłu Teletechnicznego (in Warsaw)
      (ii)   Kombinat Zródeł Światła (in Warsaw)
      (iii) Kombinat Przemysłu Kablowego (in Kraków)
      (iv)   Kombinat Typowych Elementów Hydrauliki (in Wrocław)
      (v)   Kombinat Przemysłu Łozyskowego (in Kielce)
24 Zarządzanie Przesa RM Nr 43, 15 May 1972, w/s 'wdróżeń inicujących kompleksowe zmiany w metodach planowania i zarządzania gospodarką'.
25 T. Gorzkowski, 'Kombinaty budowlane w Warszawie', *ZG*, 4/1971, p. 4; Z. Sekułowicz, 'Zasady gospodarowania w fabryce domów', *ZG*, 20/1972, p. 5.
26 Much of the material for these studies of combines in the ball bearing and sulphur processing industry, arose out of reports from a joint

research project conducted during 1972–3 by the Instytut Nauk Prawnvch and the Instytut Filosofii i Socjologii Polska Akademia Nauk; the Instytut Organizacji Przemysłu Maszynowej and the Instytut Planowania in Warsaw. This was supplemented by information from Master's theses (notably from SGPiS in Warsaw and the Jagellonian University in Kraków).

In 1972 nine combines in the engineering and chemicals industries had begun to function. Thirteen factories were selected for a preliminary investigation and four factories from two combines were chosen for intensive study: the factories in Poznań and Kielce from the ball bearings combine, and the factories in Grzybów and Machów from the sulphur processing combine.

27 J. Błazejewski, 'Funkcjonowanie kombinatów przemysłowych', Warsaw, 1972; E. Oskarol, 'Ankieta dla zakładu wiodącego kombinatu Przemysłu Łozysk Tocznych "Predom" F.L.T.', Kielce, 1972; M. Kula, 'Organizacja wewnętrzna zakładu wiodącego w kombinacie', Diploma thesis, Kraków, 1972.

28 Oskarol 'Ankieta', pp. 14–15.

29 L. Kolarska, 'Sprawozdanie z socjologicznych badań relacji zakład – Kombinat – zjednoczenia', Manuscript (PAN), Warsaw, 1973.

30 Oskarol, Ankieta; M. Kula, 'Przesłanki twórżenia kombinatów i rola kolegium i ich zarządzania na przykładzie kombinatu przemysłu łożysk tocznych w Kielcach', Master's thesis, Kraków, 1973.

31 Błazejewski, 'Funkcjonowanie'.

32 Ibid.

33 Ibid., p. 3; Oskarol, 'Ankieta' pp. 16–17.

34 Kolarska, 'Sprawozdanie'.

35 Ibid.

36 Błazejewski, 'Funkcjonowanie', pp. 38–9, 49. For example in 1972, when the Poznań factory was supposed to be observing a two-year plan it was not issued with financial norms on a two-year basis. They were subject to frequent adjustment along with a growth in the number of directive indices up to a total of 32.

37 See p. 95.

38 Błazejewski, 'Funkcjonowanie'.

39 Oskarol, 'Ankieta'.

40 Zełczak, 'Kombinaty przemysłowe', pp. 88–90.

41 Oskarol, 'Ankieta'.

42 Uchwała Prezydium ZGZZ Metalowców w/s 'dalszego doskonalenia zasad i form działania organizacji związkowych i samorządu robotniczego w kombinacie i zakładach wchodzących w jego skladu', Warsaw, December 1971.

43 Oskarol, 'Ankieta'.

44 J. Stefaniak, 'Funkcjonowanie rozwiązań prawnych w kombinacie kopalń i zakładów przetwórczych śiarki "Siarkopol" w Tarnobrzegu', Machów, 30 March 1971.

45 H. Siwek, 'Studia na przeobrażeniami świadomośći społecznej w zapleczu wiejskim kombinatu Tarnobrzeskiego', Master's thesis, Kraków, 1965.

46 Stefaniak, 'Funkcjonowanie rozwiązań, pp. 3–7. The mines and sulphur processing factories in Machów consisted of a combine management unit, two factories and a construction–repairs unit.

47 'Kombinat Kopalń i zakładów przetwórczych śiarki "Siarkopol", im. M. Nowotki w Tarnobrzegu', Warsaw, 1972, pp. 14–29; Stefaniak, 'Funkcjonowanie rozwiążań'.

48 Ibid., p. 19.

49 'Kombinat Kopalń', p. 26.

50 Kolarska, 'Sprawozdanie'.

51 L. Bar, *Funkcjonowanie kombinatów przemysłowych*, Tarnobrzeg, 1972.

52 Kolarska, 'Sprawozdanie'.
   Others would argue that the factory at Grzybów and other units further away from the Machów plant had greater freedom in decision-making than those immediately proximate to the combine administration. Stefaniak, 'Funkcjonowanie rozwiążań'.

53 Ibid. The plant at Grzybów was situated in Kielce, the poorer region, while only 40 kilometers away, the Machów plant was to be found across the border in nearby Rzeszów. The latter plant was larger and boasted a higher amount of fixed capital, yet the Grzybów factory (as we noted above) was more profitable. Thus it was important for the local authority of Kielce to maintain their level of revenue from taxation (which would be lost if the plant was deprived of its status as an enterprise and became swallowed up in a combine whose head office was elsewhere beyond reach). As Rzeszów was the richer of the two authorities and able to provide a better standard of social services and housing, and the largest plant was situated in Machów, it seemed obvious that the combine administration should have its headquarters there.

54 Stefaniak, 'Funkcjonowanie rozwiążań'. This situation was totally different from the fate of worker representation in the ball bearing combine, where each constituent factory had an independent workers' council and representation for the whole combine was by means of delegates from factory KSRs attending a special all-combine committee.

55 'Kombinat Kopalń'.

56 Staniszkis, *Patologie struktur organizacyjnch*, Warsaw, 1972; Narojek, *Społeczeństwo planujące*.

57 L. Kolarska, 'Cele kombinatu a cele zjednoczenia: analiza socjologiczna', Instytut Filosofii, Sociologii, Warsaw, 1973.
   In respect of financial transactions, either the ministry or the industrial association would set norms, directives and control the distribution of profits. However, tremendous confusion arose between combine management and the industrial association; either the

industrial association would attempt to circumvent combine management in order to deal directly with factories to allocate plan targets and resources, and to set wages and bonuses; or the ministry would try to circumvent the industrial associations in order to deal directly with combine management. Anomalies would arise whereby other enterprises outside the combine would be instructed to trade only through the association sales office, although some factories within combines could conduct their sales policy independently.

A large combine controlled directly from the ministry could also have similar powers to an industrial association, and a combine controlled by the association might, purely on account of its size, take a disproportionate share of investment funds. See: N. Gajl, 'Finansowo – prawne zagadnienia funkcjonowania kombinatów', *Państwo i prawo*, 11/1971, pp. 671–7.

58 Kolarska, 'Sprawozdanie'. For example, the association was usually viewed as a threat to the combine administration or leading factory, and an alliance between the other factories in the combine and the industrial association management was a means of reducing the influence of the combine administration in every day affairs. These factories also saw an advantage to them in encouraging intervention by the industrial ministry.

59 H. Kutner, 'Egsamin wstępny kombinatów przemysłowych', *Państwo i prawo*, 3/4, 1971, pp. 483–4.

60 J. Łaszcz, 'Niektóre problemy organizacji kombinatu przemysłowego', *EiOP*, No. 6, 1970.

61 Kutner, 'Egsamin wstępny, p. 485.
The converse situation confronted three combines in the engineering industry which were faced with co-ordinating their production with the needs of the giant engineering works 'Zakłady im. H. Cegielski', in Poznań. The factor of relative size meant that the combines had to follow the lead of the Cegielski works even though the latter was only classified as an enterprise, and it was the combines who should assume a leading role.

62 J. Kramarczuk, 'Doskonalenia organizacji i zarządzania w resorcie przemysłu maszynowego', *Przeglad Organizacji*, 11/1971.

63 Sz. Jakubowicz, 'Zjednoczenie przedsiębiorstw', *ZG*, 40/1974, p. 1.

64 M. Misiak, 'Funkcjonowanie organizacji przemysłowe', *ZG*, 31/1970; 'Wstępny zwiad', *ZG*, 14/1971, pp. 1, 4, 5.

65 Sz. Jakubowicz, 'Organizacja to nie schematy', *ZG*, 20/1971, pp. 1, 6. A similar observation had resulted from a survey of 12 individual associations conducted during 1965–6. W. Świderski, 'Z zagadnień grupowania przedsiębiorstw w zjednoczeniach przemysłowych', *EiOP* 10/1967.

66 Jakubowicz, 'Organizacja'. These were the fully integrated combine, and the more decentralised 'zreszenie' and another even looser clustering of enterprises.

67 O. Lange 'Niektóre zagadnienia centralizacji i decentralizacji w zarządzaniu', *ZG*, 13/1971.

68 A. Jędraszczyk, 'Duże organizacje przemysłowe', *ZG*, 35/1972, pp. 1, 9 and *ZG*, 36/1972, p. 7.

69 M. Rakowski, Letter in *ZG*, 13/1971, p. 5; H. Sadownik, 'Miejsce zjednoczenia', *ZG*, 17/1971, p. 8; E. Lipiński, 'Zjednoczenie zbędny organ gospodarki', *Przegląd Techniczny*, 16/1971, p. 3.

70 'Doskonalenie procesu planowania i zarządzania...', Komisji Partyjna Rządowej, Warsaw, 1972; K. Golinowski, 'Tryb i organizacja wdróżeń inicjujących kompleksowe zmiany w systemie funkcjonowania gospodarki', *OMiT*, 7/1972, p. 3.

71 Zarządzanie Prezesa RM, Nr 43, 15 May, 1972 w/s 'wdróżeń inicjujących kompleksowe zmiany w metodach planowania i zarządzania gospodarką'.

72 B. Gliński, 'W kwestii W.O.G.', *ND*, 3/1973, pp. 70–1; K. Golinowski, 'Interpretacja hasła W.O.G.', *ZG*, 3/1973, p. 8; Sz. Jakubowicz, 'Zjednoczenie przedsiębiorstw', *ZG*, 40/1974.

73 J. Pinkowski, 'Wyniki i zadania J.I.', *ZG*, 30/1974, p. 6. There were 29 Pilot Units throughout the whole of the Polish economy at the end of 1973. These included 10 in the chemical industry; 7 in engineering; 2 in food processing; 1 in furniture; 1 in heavy industry; 6 in construction; 1 in shipbuilding and 1 in foreign trade. 'Po dziewięcu miesiącach', *ZG*, 51–2/1973, p. 12.

The project for 1974 was to bring the whole of chemicals, almost all of construction, and a considerable part of the machine tools industry within the new system. This implied that 4 Pilot Units would be set up in food processing; 2 in shipping; 7 in light industry; 7 in engineering; 3 in forestry and timber and also 5 from the local industrial sector. K. Szwarć, 'Dobry początek', *ZG*, 36/1973, pp. 1, 4; B. Gliński, (interview), *ZG*, 12/1974; Z. Długośćz, 'A zadanie ciężkie', *ZG*, 3/1974. Slightly different figures were presented in a later article reviewing the progress of these Pilot Units: 'Ile ich jest', *ZG*, 8/1975. In 1974, JIs provided work for 38% of those employed in socialised industry and produced 44% of the total value of products and services. During 1974, 46 new units were formed (of which 38 were in industry). In 1975, three industries (chemicals, engineering and light industry) were completely operating through Pilot Units, and it was estimated that by the end of 1975, their share in the value of industrial production sold would be around 62% and that they would employ over half of the industrial workforce.

74 Report of the Central Committee of the PZPR for the period from sixth to seventh Congress, *ND*, 1/1976, p. 17.

75 Interview with J. Pajestka (Chairman of the Planning Commission), 'Zmodifikowany system W.O.G.', *ZG*, 14/1977, p. 1.

76 The six types included two types of association, 2 types of combine (with monopoly over a production or without) an independent multi-plant enterprise, and a loose grouping of relatively independent enterprises. Gliński, 'W kwestii W.O.G.'; Sz. Jakubowicz, 'Organizacja

przemysłu w warunkach nowego systemu ekonomiczno – finanswego', *PO*, 10/1974.

77 B. Gliński, 'Jak Interpretować hasło W.O.G.?', *ZG*, 10/1973, p. 3.
78 T. Baumberger, Zarządzanie wielkimi organizmami gospodarczymi na przykładzie przemysłu okrętowego', PTE, Warsaw, 1973.
79 A. Sledziński, 'Nowa forma organizacja zarządzania zjednoczenia – typu koncernowego', *Finanse*, 5/1972, pp. 19–27.
80 M. Kaser and J. Zieliński, *Planning*, pp. 44–5, 96; Jakubowicz, 'Integracja przedsiębiorstw; E. Wilcsek, 'Miejsce i rola przedsiębiorstw państwowych w gospodarce narodowej w warunkach nowego systemu zarządzania', in I. Friss (ed.), *Reforma mechanizmu gospodarczego na Węgrzech*, Warsaw, 1971, pp. 232–44.
81 Wilcsek, 'Miejsce i rola', pp. 246–7; A. Lipowski and A. Zawisłak, 'Bezpłatny polygon', *Polityka*, 44/1973, p. 5.
82 Ibid.
83 O. Kyn, 'Czechoslovakia', in H.H. Höhman, M.C. Kaser and K. Thalheim, *The New Economic Systems of Eastern Europe*, London, 1975, pp. 105–54.
84 A. Gorlin, 'The Soviet economic associations', *Soviet Studies*, Vol. XXVI, No. 1, January 1974, pp. 3–27.
85 Ibid., pp. 10–11; Sz. Jakubowicz, 'Reorganizacja przemysłu w Z.S.S.R.', *ZG*, 17/1973, p. 13; D. Strazenew, 'Radieckie firmy', *ZG*, 27/1970, p. 11.
86 These included the extension of co-operation between enterprises on the basis of increased concentration and specialisation of production; more rational use of material and financial resources; a reduction in enterprise administrative machinery; centralisation of planning, research and development, investment allocation, production and sales. However, Gorlin also notes apparent contradiction that such concentration was seen as conducive to a decentralisation of management decision-making in industry. A. Gorlin, 'Soviet economic associations'.
87 Ibid., pp. 9, 19–26.
88 See Chapter 2, pp. 46–9.
89 Interview with W. Bień (Deputy Minister of Finance), *ZG*, 3/1973:
90 K. Golinowski, 'System planowania jednostki inicujących kompleksowe zmiany planowania i zarządzania gospodarką narodową a rola planu centralnego', *OMiT*, 10/1972, pp. 8–9.
91 Interview with the chief director of 'Petrochemia', *Polityka*, 41/1973; V Konferencja naukowa 'Dyrektór w procesie kierowania przedsiębiorstw', TNOiK, Bydgoszcz, 1973, p. 16.
92 E. Nędzowski, Funkcjonowanie dużych organizacjach przemysłowych na przykładzie przemysłu ażotowego', Kraków, 1972, p. 10.
93 B. Gliński, 'Od limitu do normatywu', *ZG*, 9/1973. The Equation for determining the Wages Fund was:

$$Fn = Fu\ (1 + Pd.R)$$

Where Fn = annual disposable Wage Fund
Fu = Wage Fund of the previous year
Pd = index of growth of production added

R   = coefficient relating the growth of the Wage
      Fund to the growth of production added.

See also: 'Nowy reguły gry w Petrochemią', *ZG*, 46/1972; 'Dlaczego chemie pragnię zmiań?', *ZG*, 13/1975, p. 2. (A round-table discussion between ministry officials and Pilot Unit management in the chemicals industry.)

94 J. Dzięciołowski, 'Zjednoczenie wogów', *ZG*, 6/1973.
95 B. Witek, 'Polifarb startuje', *ZG*, 5/1973, p. 7.
96 Jakubowicz, 'Organizacja przemysłu'.
97 A. Chadziński, 'Przełom w Delcie', *ZW*, 13 March, 1973, p. 3.
   During early 1973 the economic and financial principles were worked out for three Pilot Units in the engineering industry (The associations in electrical engineering – EMA; electronic engineering – UNITRA; and automatic machinery and measurement apparatus – MERA). Interview with J. Pińkowski, *ZG*, 7/1973, pp. 1, 2.
98 T. Karpiński, 'Nowy system w przemyśle cukierniczym', *ZG*, 49/1972, p. 7.
99 Komisja ekonomiczna przemyslu lekkiego ZGPTE, Lodz, 1973, p. 5.
100 R. Dolczewski, 'Doswiadczenie jednostek inicujących przemysłu chemicznego', *ND*, 9/1975, pp. 208–9. It was in fact easier to make annual revisions of coefficient 'R' than for the ministry and the Planning Commission to issue directives limiting payments to be made out of the Wages Fund.
101 H. Błaszak, 'Tak ale o dwóch parametrach', *ZG*, 19/1973, p. 11. J. Szafraniec, 'Parametr R – zamiast podatku', *ZG*, 21/1973.
102 'Kształt zmiań', *ZG*, 27/1973, pp. 1, 4, 5, 6; R. Bączak, 'Współczynnik 'R' a inwestycje', *ZG*, 50/1973, p. 5; M. Mieszczanowski, 'Czy zmodyfikować produkcje dodana?', *ZG*, 17/1974, p. 7; A. Topiński, 'Z podatkiem bez podatku?', *ZG*, 19/1974, p. 7.
103 Ibid.; J. Mujzel, 'Problemy motywacji', *ZG*, 5/1975, p. 11; A. Cmieliewski, 'Przymiarka do nowego', *ZG*, 37/1973, p. 5.
104 M. Mieszczanowski, 'Problemy wdrażania reformy', *ZG*, 18/1974, p. 7; H. Błaszak, 'A jednak dwa parametry', *ZG*, 25/1973; B. Pierzchałowa, 'Na modyfikacje za wczesnie?', *ZG*, 20/1974, p. 7.
105 Interview with B. Gliński, *ZG*, 12/1974; J. Pinkowski, 'Doswiadczenia i zadania jednostek inicujących', *ND*, 2/1975, pp. 30–9; M. Misiak, 'Aktualny problemy wzrostu wydajnosci pracy', *ND*, 8/1975.
106 Ibid.
107 Interview with E. Meisner (Deputy Minister of Engineering): 'Nowy system finansowo – ekonomiczny w przemyśle maszynowym', *ZG*, 47/1975, pp. 1, 2; 'Klub jednostek inicujących', *ZG*, 6/1976, p. 11; H. Błaszak, 'Kierunki modyfikacji formuły płacowej', *ZG*, 42/1974, p. 22; 'Zmodyfikowany system W.O.G.', *ZG*, 14/1977, p. 1; 'Pracują juz

według zmodyfikowanegu systemu', *ZG*, 20/1977, p. 2; J. Szydlak, 'Dla osiągniecią strategicznych celów Partii' (Speech to Party–Government Commission), *ZG*, 28/1977 (10 July), pp. 8, 9. See also P.T. Wanless, 'Economic reform in Poland 1973–79', *Soviet Studies*, Vol. XXXII, No. 1, January 1980, pp. 43–50.

108 Uchwała Nr 49, RM 18 February 1972 w/s 'rozszerzenie uprawnień dyrektorów przemysłu kluczowego i dyrektorów ich zjednoczeń', *MP*, 13/1972, item 90; Interview with J. Olszewski (Minister of the Chemical Industry) *ZG*, 11/1972, pp. 1, 2.

109 T. Grzeszyk, 'Samodzielność kierownictwa przedsiębiorstwa', *DKK*, 3–4/1972, p. 18; Z. Lewandowicz, 'Problemy struktur organizacyjnych zarządzania jednostkami organizacyjnymi przemysłu', PTE Sosnowieć, November 1972, pp. 19–21.

110 In 1972 a series of books in the Biblioteka Dyrektóra appeared, including a translation of John Humble's *Management by Objectives*: J.W. Humble, *Zarządzanie przez cele*, Warsaw 1972; A.K. Kozmiński, '*Zarządzanie systemowe*', Warsaw, 1972.

111 B. Gliński, 'Przedsiębiorstwo socjalistyczne i jego ewolucja', *ND*, 6/1977, pp. 92–101.

112 'Klub jednostek inicujących', *ZG*, 14/1976, p. 4; 'Status przedsiębiorstw', *ZG*, 16/1978, pp. 1, 8, 9; Blazyca, 'Industrial Structure', p. 319; L. Stepniak, 'Status węgierskich przedsiębiorstw', *ZG*, 25/1978, p. 13.

113 B. Gliński, 'Ranga organizacji', *ZG*, 2/1978, pp. 1, 2.
Even in the highly advanced engineering industry, management structure was seen to be top heavy and inflexible. A. Kopeć, 'Racjonalizacja struktur zarządzania w przemysłe', *ND*, 4/1978, pp. 64–9.

114 J. Kordaszewski, 'Służby pracownicze i doskonalenie systemu pracy w przedsiębiorstwach', *ND*, 3/1979. This referred to a new Decree in November 1973 which aimed to keep control of the growth of administrative personnel.

115 W. Dziewiałtowski and Z. Szeliga, 'Fabryki coraz większe', Polityka Statystyka Nr 11, *Polityka* 47/1972, pp. 13–15.

Industrial enterprises

	1960	1965	1970	1971	1975
State-run	3,514	3,252	3,058	2,916	2,454
Co-operative	3,301	2,780	2,489	2,413	2,000

Sources: Rocznik statystyczny 1972, p. 193. B. Gliński, 'Ranga organizacji'. *Rocznik statystyczny 1976*, p. 179.

116 *Industrial plants in state-owned industry according to % of numbers employed*

Nos. employed	1965	1971	1975
up to 4	20.6	21.7	13.1
5– 10	17.3	15.5	16.6
11– 15	7.2	7.7	7.8
16– 50	23.0	21.0	22.5
51– 100	10.6	11.1	12.0
101– 200	8.0	8.5	10.1
201– 500	6.6	7.1	8.6
501–1,000	3.5	3.8	4.7
1,001–2,000	1.8	2.0	2.6
2,001–5,000	1.0	1.2	1.5
over 5,000	0.4	0.4	0.5

Sources: Dziewałtowski and Szeliga, 'Fabryki'; G. Blazyca, 'Industrial Structure', pp. 314–15; *Rocznik statystyczny 1972*, p. 195, *1976*, p. 184.

117 On average each enterprise had 7.9 plants in 1965, 9.1 in 1970 and 11.8 in 1975. Whereas in 1960 each enterprise had an average 5.6 plants, by 1976 this had risen to 12.2 factories, of which 80.9% employed less than 50 people. Blazyca, 'Industrial structure'; P. Stefaniak, 'Struktury organizacyjne', *ZG*, 46/1978, p. 10; Gliński, 'Ranga organizacji'.

	Number of plants in state-owned industry	Number of enterprises in state-owned industry
1960	13,500	3,514
1965	14,600	3,252
1970	14,400	3,058
1975	12,500	2,454

Source: Rocznik statystyczny 1976, pp. 179, 182.

118 *The reduction in the number of enterprises according to branch of industry 1961–71*

Food industry	numbers fell by	679
Light industry	"	418
Construction industry	"	154
Wood and forestry	"	171

Source: Dziewałtowski and Szeliga, 'Fabryki'.

		1970	1977
119 Nos. of state enterprises			
employing	500	70%	51%
	100	20%	12%

Sources: Rocznik statystyczny 1972, pp. 193 (Table 38) and 195 (Table 4); S. Skowrónski 'Manowce koncentracji', *ZG*, 25/1979, p. 9.

120 Gorlin, 'Soviet economic associations'.

121 S. Jakubowicz, 'Integracja przedsiębiorstw w zjednoczeniach ekspery-

mentuiących, in L. Bar (ed.), *Grupowanie przedsiębiorstw państwowych*, Warsaw, 1972, pp. 110–11; Z. Leskiewicz and A. Szorć, *W.O.G.: Założenia i Problemy Organizacyjne*, Warsaw, 1975.

122 Gliński, 'Ranga organizacji'. The number of industrial associations has fallen from 121 in 1959; to 120 in 1965; to 107 in 1971 and 105 in 1977.

123 S. Jakubowicz, 'Zjednoczenie przedsiębiorstw', *ZG*, 40/1974.

124 See book review by J. Dąbrowski, 'Małe jest piękne', *ZG*, 47/1977, p. 13.

125 S. Skowroński, 'Granice koncentrajcji', *ZG*, 28/1976 (11 July), p. 8. Between 1970 and 1974 the number of enterprises employing over 5,000 people had risen from 23.6% to 33.5% of the total numbers employed in socialised industry. S. Skowroński, 'Manowce koncentracji', *ZG*, 25/1979.

126 Ibid.

127 T. Piętrzkiewicz, 'Szansa racjonalizacji', *ZG*, 13/1979, p. 10.

128 T. Wrząszczyk, 'Rozwój społeczno – gospodarczy a postęp naukowo – techniczny w latach osiemdziesiątych', *ND*, 1/1980, p. 50.

129 S. Skowroński, 'Warto rozwijać drobny przemysł', *ZG*, 19/1978, p. 10; Uchwała XIV Plenum of the KCPZPR, 11/April 1979; *ND*, 5/1979, p. 1.

130 (Małe czy duże?), 'Ważny jest rozsądek', *ZG*, 7/1979, p. 1.

131 K. Krauss, 'Potrzeba a nie przerost ambicji', in series 'Małe czy duże?', *ZG*, 12/1979 (25 March), p. 10; K. Krauss, 'Trzeba szanować miliony', *ZG*, 15/1979, (15 April), pp. 8, 9.

132. K. Krauss, 'Nie na jednej płaszczyznie', in series 'Małe czy duże?', *ZG*, 26/1979 (1 July), p. 3.

5 The political consequences of industrial integration and concentration: I

1 P. Nettl, *Rosa Luxemburg*, London, 1969; M.K. Dziewanowski, *The Communist Party of Poland*, 2nd edn, Cambridge, Ma., 1975, pp. 1–54.

2 Dziewanowski, *Communist Party of Poland*, pp. 97–115; R. Hiscocks, *Poland: A Bridge for an Abyss?*, London, 1963, pp. 60–75; I. Deutscher, 'The tragedy of the Polish Communist Party', in *Marxism in our Time*, 6th edn, London, 1971, pp. 113–60.

3 W. Wesołowski, 'Changes in the class structure in Poland', in J. Wiatr (ed.), *Studies in the Polish Political System*, Warsaw, 1967, pp. 33–80.

4 W. Bielicki and S. Widerszpil, 'Z problematyki przemian społecznych w Polsce Ludowej', *ND* 7/1979, pp. 74–85.

5 K. Zagórski, 'Changes in socio-occupational mobility in Poland', *Polish Sociological Bulletin*, 2/1976, pp. 17–30.

6 Bielicki and Widerszpil, 'Z problematyki'.

7 M. Jarosińska and J. Kulpińska, 'Czynniki położenia klasy robotniczej', W. Makarczyk and J. Błuszkowski, 'Przemiany warstwy pracow-

ników umysłowych'. Both in W. Wesołowski (ed.), *Ksztalt struktury spolecznej*, Warsaw, 1978, pp. 109, 179.

8 K. Zagórski, 'Robotnicy w strukturze spoleczno – zawodowej', in J. Szczepański (ed.), *Narodziny socjalistycznej klasy robotniczej*, Warsaw, CRZZ 1974, pp. 192–230.

9 Jarosińska and, Kulpińska, 'Czynniki polozenia' pp. 121–2.

10   Workers with above   Workers with below

Workers with above basic level education		Workers with below basic level education	
Engineering	41%	Engineering	7.2%
Chemicals	38.5%	Chemicals	9.3%
Construction	31%	Construction	21.2%

On the *Taryfikator* scale I–VII, the wage band most regularly encountered in industry was

III–IV	80% workers in textiles
IV–VII	72% workers in engineering
V	70% workers in chemicals

Source: M. Jarosińska, J. Kulpińska, 'Czynniki polozenia', p. 125.

11 Ibid.; W. Wesołowski, 'Perspektywy rozwojowe klasy robotniczej', in Szczepański (ed.), *Narodziny* pp. 59–75.

12 *Proportion of the economically active population who live in rural areas, but work outside agriculture*

1931	13%
1950	19%
1960	23%
1970	33.5% (2.9 million people)

Source: F. Kolbusz, 'Rezerwy w każdym gospodarstwie', *ZP*, 8/1978. Widerszpil, 'Przeobrażenia', p. 170.

13 Widerszpil, 'Przeobrażenia', 1973, pp. 172–3.

14 M. Dziewicka, *Chlopi-Robotnicy*, Warsaw, 1963; Zagórski, 'Robotnicy', pp. 197, 222.

15 M. Hirszowicz, 'Intelligentsia versus bureaucracy? The revival of a myth in Poland', *Soviet Studies*, Vol. XXX, No. 3, March 1976, pp. 336–65.

16 J. Szczepański, 'Intelligencja a pracownicy umyslowi' in J. Szczepański, *Odmiany czasu teraźniejszego*, Warsaw, 1971.

17 A. Gella, 'The life and death of the old Polish intelligentsia, *Slavic Review*, Vol. 30, No. 1, March 1971, pp. 1–27.

18 Bielicki and Widerszpil, 'Z problematyki'

19 J. Szczepański, 'Pracownicy administracyjno-biurowe', in J. Szczepański, *Przemysl i spoleczeństwo w Polsce Ludowej*, Warsaw, 1969.

20 W. Bielicki and S. Widerszpil, 'Z problematyki'.

21 Ibid. By 1969, of Higher Education graduates, 28% were of working-class, 18% were of peasant, and over 50% of intelligentsia/white-collar worker social origin. In 1970–1, 33% of day release and 50% of evening and correspondence-course students were of working-class social origin. Widerszpil, 'Przeobrażenia 1973, pp. 208–9; Zagórski, 'Robotnicy', K. Zagórski, 'Changes in socio-occupational mobility in Poland', *Polish Sociological Bulletin*, 2/1976, pp. 17–30.

Number of part-time graduates of Higher Education
Total graduates

1951–5	7.1%
1956–60	17.7%
1961–5	23.3%
1966–70	34.8%

Source: W. Makarczyk, J. Bʃuskowski, 'Przemiany warstwym pracowni-ków umysʃowych', in Wesoʃowski, *Ksztaʃt Struktury*, pp. 171–230.

22 Gella, 'Life and death'.
23 S.J. Rawin, 'The Polish intelligentsia and the socialist order: elements of ideological compatibility', *Political Science Quarterly*, Vol. 83/1968, pp. 353–77.
24 Z. Bauman, 'Economic growth, social structure, elite formation: the case of Poland', in R. Bendix and S.M. Lipset (eds.) *Class Status and Power*, New York, 1966, p. 534.
25 A.R. Evans Jr, 'Developed socialism in Soviet ideology', *Soviet Studies*, Vol. XXIX, No. 3, July 1977, pp. 409–28; D.R. Kelley, 'The Soviet debate on the convergence of the American and Soviet systems', *Polity*, Vol. 6/2, 1973/4, pp. 174–96.
26 S. Ossowski, *Class Structure in the Social Consciousness*, London, 1969.
27 Ibid., pp. 116, 182, 111, 176.
28 W. Wesoʃowski, *Klasy warstwy i wladza*, Warsaw, 1966.
29 J.H. Goldthorpe, 'Social stratification in industrial society', *Sociological Review Monograph* No. 8, *The Development of Industrial Societies*, Keele, 1964.
30 F. Parkin, *Class, Inequality and Political Order*, London 1972, p. 149.
31 W. Wesoʃowski, 'The notions of strata and class in socialist society', in A. Beteille (ed.), *Social Inequality*, London, 1969, pp. 122–45; W. Wesoʃowski and K. Sʃomczyński, 'Social stratification in Polish cities', in J.A. Jackson (ed.), *Sociological Studies*, No. 1, Cambridge, 1968; W. Wesoʃowski, (ed.), *Zróznicowanie spoleczne*, Warsaw, 1970.
32 Hirszowicz, 'Intelligentsia versus bureaucracy', pp. 355, 361.
33 S. Tellenback, 'The logic of development in socialist Poland', *Social Forces*, Vol. 57, No. 2, 1978.
34 S. Mallet, *Bureaucracy and Technocracy in the Socialist Countries* (Spokesman), Nottingham, 1974. S. Mallet, *The New Working Class* (Spokesman) 4th edn, Nottingham, 1975.
35 M. Rakovski, *Towards an East European Marxism*, London, 1978; G. Konrad, I. Szelenyi, *The Intellectuals on the Road to Class Power*, Brighton, 1979.
36 Z. Bauman, 'Social structure of the Party organisation in industrial works', in J. Wiatr (ed.), *Studies in the Polish Political System*, Warsaw, 1967, pp. 156–78.
37 Ibid.
38 K. Ostrowski and Z. Sufin, 'Problemy rozwoju Partii między IV a V Zjazdem', *ND*, 1/1969, pp. 30–6.
39 G. Kolankiewicz, 'The technical intelligentsia', in D. Lane and G. Kolankiewicz (eds.), *Social Groups in Polish Society*, London, 1973.

40 See citations under Table 2.
41 Source, Cz. Herod, in A. Dobieszewski (ed.) *Wiedza o Partii: wybrany problemy*, Warsaw, 1972, pp. 399–40; T.K. 'Portret Partii', pp. 12–14.
42 Ibid.; K. Ostrowski and Z. Sufin, 'Problemy rozwoju'.
43 Bauman, 'Social structure'.
44 While in 1975 28% of all white-collar workers and 15.3% of all industrial manual workers were PZPR members, by 1980 this reached 17% of all industrial manual workers and in particular 42% of all foremen. However, of 164 factories singled out for experimental activity by the PZPR, in 1968 42.6% engineers, 29.7% technicians and 59% foremen were PZPR members (and 17% of all manual workers). E. Babiuch, 'P.Z.P.R. przed VIII Zjazdem, *ND*, 1/1980, p. 9; J. Kubasziewicz, 'Rola organizacji partyjnych wielkich zakJadów pracy', *ZP*, 12/1978, p. 41–2.
45 There was a general increase of peasant members of the PZPR by 89,000 between 1975 and 1979 to reach 735,000 (i.e. an increase of 25%). Although PZPR membership among independent land-holders was 7.5% (out of a total of 3,146,200 in 1977), it was estimated that the PZPR had 27% of its total membership living in rural areas. 'Portret Partii', pp. 12–14; R. Czarnewski, 'O czym musimy pamiętac', *ZP*, 3/1978.

In 1978 in Częstochowa Wojewodztwa, 63% of all new members were of peasant origin. M. Przysucha, 'Lepsza praca z kandydatami dynamizuje rozwój Partii', *ZP*, 8/1978, pp. 3–4.
46 The increase in female membership of the PZPR was very marked after 1976. Women constituted 29.6% of new recruits in 1976 and 32.6% in 1977. As a proportion of total membership they rose from 23.5% in 1975 to 26.8% in 1979. T.K. 'Przejęcie do Partii w 1977', *ZP*, 4/1978, p. 10; T.K. 'Portret Partii'.
47 Z. Grudzień, 'O niektórych problemach praktyki partyjnego kierownictwa', *ND*, 10/1970, p. 118; Ostrowski and Sufin, 'Problemy rozwoju'. While the highest incidence of PZPR membership is found in the regions with the highest economic growth rates (such as Katowice which boasted 13.4% of the national total of PZPR members), the highest rates of increase were to be found in the new industrialising areas of Eastern Poland, while a fall in Party growth rates was witnessed in areas of industrial decline such as Lodz and Poznań. A. Szpotoń 'Codziennie z ludzmi', *ZP*, 6/1978, p. 9, reported a 20% increase in the PZPR membership for Tanobrzeg in 1976 and 1977.
48 J. Fastyn, 'Partyjna kontrola w terenie', *ZP*, 2/1978, p. 34; Z. Najdowski, 'Nigdy dość dyskusji o rozwoju partii', *ZP*, 5/1978, p. 2.
49 The basic organisational structure of a medium-sized factory would consist of the following hierarchy:
    Chief director
    Deputy directors/chief specialists
    Department managers
    Lower management
    Senior engineers/production engineers
    Foremen
    Supervisors

Senior technicians/technicians
Worker-technicians
Skilled workers
Unskilled workers

A. Preiss, 'Organizacyjne determinanty integracji kadry technicznej z przedsiębiorstwem', *SS*, 1/1972, pp. 213–43; Z. Niedbała, 'Zasada jedno-osobowego oraz kolektywnego podejmowania decyzji w przedsiębiorstwach państwowych i ich zjednoczeniach', *PO*, 12/1970, p. 108; Z. Niedbała, 'Jedno-osobowego kierownictwa a służbowa i karna odpowiedzialność dyrektóra przedsiębiorstwo państwowego', *PO*, 1/1973, p. 95.

50 A.K. Koźmiński, 'Rola zawodowa dyrektora przedsiębiorstw w aktualnym systemie zarządzania gospodarką socjalistyczną', *SS*, 1/1967, pp. 203–7.

51 R. Dudek, 'Płynność dyrektorów', in A. Sarapata (ed.), *Płynność załóg*, Warsaw, 1968.

52 Ibid.; H. Sadownik, 'Kontrola w zarządzaniu zjednoczeniom przemysłowyn', Doctoral thesis, SGPiS, 1972. The extent of these inspections of enterprise management activity continued unabated into the 1970s.

53 J. Tobera, 'Pożycia dyrektora przedsiębiorstwa przemysłowego a podejmowania decyzji', in J. Kulpińska (ed.), *Włókniarze w procesie zmian*, Warsaw, 1975.

54 W. Narojek, *System władzy w miejscie*, Warsaw, 1967; W. Narojek, 'The structure of power in a local community', in J. Wiatr (ed.), *Studies in the Polish Political System*, Warsaw, 1967, pp. 179–200. Narojek's study of seven small towns in the early 1960s had discovered an average of 29.9% of councillors to be employees of the local council; 29.4% were senior management from local industrial plants, trade offices, branches of the bank etc., and 16.7% were full-time employees of the local PZPR apparat.

See also R. Taras, 'The Local Political Elites', in Lane and Kolankiewicz (eds.), *Social Groups*; M. Kula, 'Przesłanki twórżenia kombinatów i rola kolegium i ich zarządzania na przykładzie kombinatu przemysłu łożysk tocznych w Kielcach', Master's thesis, Kraków, 1973.

55 A.K. Koźmiński, 'Czyńniki okreslające zachowania kierowników produkcji', in A. Matejko (ed.), *Socjologia kierownictwa*, Warsaw, 1969.

Concern at the extent to which bonuses were paid out 'privately' for a number of services for management was expressed in the Press in the early 1970s. A.K. Wróblewski, 'Remis', *Polityka*, 23/1977; A. Mozołowski', 'Czyje na wiezchu?', *Polityka*, 26/1977, p. 7.

56 H. Najduchowska, 'Dyrektórzy przedsiębiorstw przemysłowych'; J. Hoser, 'Inżynierowie w przemyśłę', both in J. Szczepański (ed.), *Przemysł i społeczeństwo w Polsce Ludowej*, Warsaw, 1969, pp. 81, 105.

57 Najduchowska, 'Dyrektórzy', p. 82.

58 Ibid. The number of PZPR members among factory directors rose rapidly from 61.5% in 1948 to 70.6% in 1949, and those with a working-class background rose from 33.3% in 1948 to 53.2% in 1949. This was accompanied by a simultaneous fall in the number with

higher technical education from 48.7% to 29.8% in 1949. By 1955, 95% of enterprise directors were PZPR members and 68% were of working-class origin.

59 J. Staskiewicz, 'Doskonalenie kadr kierowniczych', *ZG*, 4/1972, p. 1.

60 T. Grzeszczyk, 'Kwalifikacje kierownictwa przedsiębiorstwa i kryteria ich oceny', *Problemy Organizacji*, 3/1972.

61 Ibid. The qualifications of senior management in the engineering industry were as follows:

(1967) Deputy Directors for investment with higher technical education	95%
(1967) Deputy Directors for investment with higher economics education	3.6%
(1967) Deputy Directors for production with higher economics education	11.1%
(1968) Deputy Directors for economic affairs with higher technical education	7.2%
(1968) Chief Enterprise Directors with higher technical education	80%

62 H. Najduchowska, 'Dyrecktórzy', pp. 94, 100; J. Szczepański, 'Pracownicy administracyjno biurowej', in Szczepański (ed.) *Przemysl i Spoleczeństwo*, p. 142.

Out of a sample of 30–40 directors, the number with a higher education in economics only increased from 2.6% to 8.3%, as opposed to those with an engineering degree where the percentage increase was from 26% to 50%.

63 Ibid.:

Posts held prior to appointment as enterprise director (sample taken from five industries):

Deputy Director for technical affairs/chief engineer	22.8 %
Middle management within the technical and production departments of an enterprise	18.3 %
Managerial post outside industry	11.4 %
Employment in the ministry or industrial association	10.0 %
Deputy Director of trade, economic or administrative affairs	6.5 %
Middle management in economic and trade affairs	4.7 %
Plant Manager	3.9 %
Functionary in the PZPR or local government apparat	3.4 %
Middle management in the enterprise financial departments	3.1 %

64 L. Ługowski 'Kryteria oceny kadry kierowniczcj w kombinatach przemysłu maszynowego', Paper delivered at a conference on personnel management, Warsaw 1970; J. Idzikowski, Z. Dobruszek, K. Gęborski, A. Kisiel, 'Kursy doskonalenie dyrektorów naczelnych przedsiębiorstw przemysłowych w CODKK w okresie 1968–70', CODKK Warsaw, 1971.

65 W. Kosmala, 'Doskonalenie kadr kierowniczych wielkich organizacji

przemysłowych w Polsce', *DKK Biuletyn Informacyjny* 11/1971; 'Wytyczne Nr 23, 8 September 1970, Przewodniczącego Komitetu Pracy i Płac w/s przeprowadzenia kwalifikacji kadr w przemyśle'.

66 'Informacja o przebiegu realizacji kursów C.O.D.K.K.', Warsaw, 1971; R. Górski, 'Doskonalenie dyrektorów zjednoczeń przemysłowych w C.O.D.K.K.', *DKK*, 1/1970, p. 49; T. Gosciński, 'Doskonalenie kadr kierowniczych zjednoczeń i kombinatów', *GP*, 6/1971; W. Kosmała, Doskonalenie', *DKK*, 11/1971.

67 R. Ciesiećki, 'V Konferencja N.O.T.', *PT*, 2/1966; L. Pasieczny, *Inżynier w przemyśle*, Warsaw, 1968; B. Klapkowski, 'Przygotowanie ekonomiczne inżyniera', *ND*, 1/1970, pp. 103–13.

68 M. Misiak, W. Ochemiak, 'Społeczne współdziałanie inżynierów i ekonomistów', *ZG*, 50/1977, p. 10; B. Fick, 'Pozycia ekonomisty', *ZG*, 14/1976; 'Ekonomista w przedsiębiorstwie: płaszczyzny współpracy', *ZG*, 19/1976, pp. 1, 11.

69 W. Grochola, 'Test dla dyrektorów', *Polityka*, 37/1972.

70 In 1973 of all the graduates employed in finance, 54.3% were economists, in trade 33.3%, in transport 25.7% and in housing 19.1%, making a total of 17.2% of all graduates in industry and 15.5% in administration.

Year	Economists as a percentage of all employees with higher education
1958	12.7%
1964	11.6%
1973	11.4%

While in 1973 an economics degree was necessary for 13 types of job, by 1977 this reached 19. Economists tended mainly to be employed in industry but the numbers employed in foreign trade, transport construction and agriculture were 7–20 times less than the average, and even less frequent in areas of social policy such as housing. The feminisation of the profession had grown from 29.2% in 1958, to 33.5% in 1964, to 44.9% in 1973 and 51% in 1977. M. Olędzki, 'Ekonomisci Przyszłości', *ZG*, 15/1979, p. 11.

71 'Ekonomista w przedsiębiorstwie', pp. 1, 11; K. Moskowicz, M. Moskowicz, 'Sterować innowacjami czy doskonalić zarządzanie?'.

A study of managerial recruitment in lower Silesia noted that between 1970 and 1974 the proportion of senior management with a technical education rose from 46.8% to 54.8%, and those with an economics education fell from 22.6% to 20.6%.

72 G. Kolankiewicz, 'The technical intelligentsia', in Lane and Kolankiewicz, *Social Groups*, pp. 145–98.

73 Hoser, 'Inżynierowie', pp. 106–113.

74 'Racjonalna gospodarka kadrami inżynieryjno-technicznymi', NOT Warsaw, 1969; S. Boraszewska, 'Inżynier w przedsiębiorstwie', *ZG*, 32/1978, p. 8.

75 Ibid.; A. Litewski, 'W trosce o kwalifikacje kadr (z prac N.O.T.)', *ND*,

5/1977, pp. 165–72; J. Tobiasz, 'Jak rozwiązujemy problemy racjonalizacja zatrudnienia', *ZP*, 6/1978, pp. 21–2; A. Jedrzejczak, 'Zadanie mysléc', *ZG*, 29/1979, p. 6; C. Surowik, 'Zaplecze B.R. a praktyka', *ZG*, 33/1978, p. 11; W. Jaskiewicz, 'Pozycia spoŀeczna inżyniera wŀokieńnika a funkcja kierownicze', in J. Kuŀpińska (ed.), *Wlokniarże w procesie zmiań*, Warsaw, 1975. Textile engineers who entered management posts felt that their work did not receive sufficient acknowledgement from the rest of management, whilst workforce and technicians held it in higher regard. On the other hand, engineers found it difficult to handle a low-skilled, low-motivated and feminised workforce. During the 1970s, the number of people who entered R and D posts in industry increased, as did the numbers employed on research projects, but it was observed that the rate of project completion fell.

76 M. Bajer, 'Wedŀug zasŀug', *Polityka*, 28/1979, p. 6; L. Froelich, 'Specializaćja inżynierów', *ZG*, 28/1979, p. 2.

77 J. Szczepański, 'Pracownicy administracyjno–biurowej', in Szczepański (ed.), *Prżemysl*, pp. 141–48. Many of these low-qualified people worked in the accounts department of industrial enterprises, and in 1964 only 11.2% of chief enterprise accountants had higher education, and 20.6% were women.

78 A. Preiss, 'Organizacyjne determinanty integracji kadry technicznej z przedisębiorstwem', *SS*, 1/1972.

79 B. Gliński, 'Ranga organizacji', *ZG*, 2/1978, pp. 1 and 2; J. Kordaszewski, 'Sŀużby pracownicze i doskonalenie systemu pracy w przedsiębiorstwach', *ND*, 3/1979; 'Zatrudnienie w administracji państwowe i gospodarcze', *ZG*, 22/1977, p. 10.
    Although legislation had been introduced in the early 1970s to simplify the administrative structure of industrial enterprises, (Uchwaŀa Nr. 250 RM 9 November 1973 w/s 'sluzby pracowniczej w państwowych jednostkach organizacyjnych') the process of enterprise merger into WOGs had proceeded with little consideration for work efficiency and not until 1978 was there an attempt to tie wages and bonus payments to new work 'norms' and regularise payments out of the factory social fund.

80 Gliński, 'Ranga organizacji'.

81 J. Szczepański, 'Mistrzowie w zmieniające przemysŀe', in Szczepański (ed.), *Przemysl*, pp. 144–56; S. Karas, 'Problemy doskonalenia zawodowego mistrzów', *ND*, 3/1978. pp. 121–30.

82 Ibid. A study of 98 industrial enterprises in 1974/5 noted that 62.4% foremen had further educational qualifications, 12.7% had higher education and 60.5% were PZPR members.

83 J. Soboŀowski, 'Praca z mistrzami po nowemu', *ZP*, 7/1976, p. 21. This study of 578 foremen and senior foremen at the FSO car factory in Żerań, found that 80% had been working for over 10 years, and, while some were young people with a further or even higher technical education (often provided at the trade school at the Żerań works), many were still skilled workers.

84 S. Krzyskiewicz, 'Pożyćia społeczno zawodowa mistrza', *ND*, 8/1976, p. 108.

Since early 1972 there had been a conscious policy in the textile industry to encourage the appointment of young foremen with further education. Yet a survey a year later revealed that they felt the need for greater independence in decision-making over wages, planning and productivity, and felt more closely allied with the rest of the workforce than with management. Moreover, the workforce had a high degree of confidence that the foremen would defend their interests against management. E. Sobieszczańska, 'Obraz mistrza wsród robotników', in Kulpińska (ed.), *Wlokniarże w procesie zmiań*, pp. 112–22.

85 *Gierek face aux Grévistes de Szczeciń*, SELIO, Paris, 1971.

86 T. Sawczuk, B. Srenko, 'Mistrzowie o premiowanie zysku', *ZG*, 24/1976, pp. 10, 11.

87 'Problemy i dyskusji', *ND*, 11/1977, pp. 117; R. Deska, 'Mistrz – sojusznik i wychowawcza', *ZP*, 7/1978, p. 31; M. Surmaczyński, 'W poszukiwaniu modelu mistrza dyplomowanego' *ZG*, 25/1976, p. 5; J. Kubasziewicz, 'Organizatórzy i wychowawczy' *ZP*, 5/1976, pp. 31–2.

88 S.J. Rawin, 'The Manager in the Polish Enterprise; a study of accommodation under conditions of role conflict', *British Journal of Industrial Relations*, Vol. 3, 1965, pp. 1–16.

A marvellous case study illustrating this point is provided by an interview of the Director of the nitrates factory in Tarnów which employs over 12,000 people. In 1977 he had already held that post for 20 years and claimed to base his management knowledge on 'experience' (he did not have a degree), rather than scientific management. This meant leaving his specialist senior management to their own devices and devoting his attention to the relations of his plant with the external world. K.W. Kasprzyk and J. Zaręba, 'Każdy z nas robi swoje', *Polityka*, 28/1977, p. 6.

89 P.C. Ludz, *The Changing Party Elite in East Germany*, Cambridge Ma., 1972, sees SED recruitment policy as fostering competition for entry as it seeks to incorporate those groups with increasing functional importance to industrialisation. Of the two key groups within the East German political system, it is the 'institutionalised counter-elite' through its increasing penetration of the apparatus of industry and construction that is construed as presenting a threat to the 'strategic clique'. Although the latter succeeds in maintaining its domination, a form of 'consultative authoritarianism' is the consequence, with friction manifesting itself mainly over the issue of decision-making powers within industrial enterprises. Ludz holds that these developments can be traced in the changing patterns of recruitment into the SED Central Committee since 1963.

90 T.A. Bayliss, *The Technical Intelligentsia and the East German Elite*, London, 1974, is more concerned to illustrate the specific differences between the old and new technical intelligentsia and the different recruitment tactics adopted towards them by the SED. His study of a sample of technical and economic functionaries revealed that a

minimum period of Party membership was necessary to their careers. Unlike Ludz, Bayliss argues that the attitudes and activities of such middle level elites are more crucial for the exercise of economic power than are the deliberations of the Central Committee; and far from there being a conflict between SED functionaries and the new technicians 'they are partners in power rather than rivals for it' (p. 61).

91 Najduchowska, 'Dyrektórzy'. Turnover of enterprise directors sometimes was as much as 42% per annum in those years.

92 Ibid. The proportion of PZPR members among enterprise directors rose rapidly from 61.5% in 1948 to 70.6% in 1949, and those with working-class background increased from 33.3% in 1948 to 53.2% in 1949. This was accompanied by a simultaneous fall in the number of enterprise directors with a higher technical education from 48.7% in 1948 to 29.8% in 1949. By 1955, 95% of enterprise directors were Party members and 68% were of manual working-class origin.

93 Kolankiewicz, 'Technical intelligentsia', pp. 195–8.

94 Ibid., p. 206.

95 Najduchowska, 'Dyrektórzy', p. 95; Grzeszczyk, 'Kwalifikacje', pp. 97, 103–4. In 1968, 62.9% of all senior management in the engineering industry were PZPR members although this tended to be higher and subject to less fluctuation for enterprise directors (81.9%–90.9%) in comparison with the managers of enterprise technical departments (33.5% to 72.7%) and project officers (60% to 95%).

96 Kolankiewicz, 'Technical intelligentsia', pp. 209–17.

97 Najduchowska, 'Dyrektórzy', 1969, pp. 97–100; H. Najduchowska, 'Drogi Zawodowe kadry kierowniczej', *SS*, 3/1969, pp. 253–64. Of the sample, 32% had experienced a professional career, 29% an administrative career, 19% a managerial career and only 3.4% a political career.

98 Grzeszczyk, 'Kwalifikacje', p. 108.

99 Ibid; Najduchowska, 'Drogi zawodowe'.

100 W. Kata, 'Wiele do zrobeńia', *ZP*, 2/1974, pp. 4–5.

101 Ibid. Only 9 out of 20 heads of department in the construction industry association Bumar, and only 13 out of 28 in the electrical industry association, Ema.

102 A. Lubowski, 'Kierownicy jutra', *ZG*, 33/1977, p. 33.

103 K. Zagórski, 'Changes in socio-occupational mobility in Poland', *Polish Sociological Bulletin*, 2/1976, pp. 17–30.

104 J. Mażiarski, 'Drzwi do gabinetu', *Polityka*, 41/1978, p. 5.

105 'Młody aktywista Partyjna', *ZP*, 7/1978, p. 12.

106 J. Bołdok, 'Partnerży', *ZG*, 47/1977, p. 9.

107 J. Wasiłewski, 'Społeczne mechanizmy selekcji na wyższe stanowiska kierownicze', *SS*, 2/1978, pp. 181–206; J. Wasiłewski, 'Occupational careers of directors', *Polish Sociological Bulletin*, 3–4/1978, pp. 97–110; M.J. Kostećki, 'The managerial cadres of Polish industry: Research Report', *Polish Sociological Bulletin*, 2/1977, pp. 85–96.

108 Wasiłewski, 'Społeczne mechanizmy'; Wasiłewski 'Occupational careers'. The sample included all men aged 30–40 holding the post of

Director or Deputy in industrial ministries, associations, departments of the Wojewodztwo and city local government, and in all factories employing over 500 workers. Questionnaires and interviews were conducted in October/November 1972, to which there was a 96% response rate (270).

24% of directors came from intelligentsia families, 15% from white-collar families, and 20% from the peasantry. As many as 89% of directors had begun their careers in non-manual jobs. Although at the start of their careers directors did not experience a privileged position in wages, housing, etc., by the time of the survey wage differentials were very pronounced.

Net monthly earnings (zl.)	Directors (%)	White-collar workers (%)	Warsaw-citizens (%)
3,000		12.2	22.2
3,000–5,000	5.9	54.9	58.6
5,000–7,000	40.7	24.5	14.7
7,000–9,000	33.8	5.8	3.4
9,000	19.6	2.6	1.1
Average earnings (zl.)	7,609	4,645	4,062

Conspicuous consumption levels were high (60% of directors possessed a car) and access to spacious housing accommodation was favourable (8.8% of directors lived in houses with more than 1 room per member of the household) and, for many, such privileged consumption standards seemed to have been but a marginal improvement on their family circumstances when under the age of 14.

109

Socio-political involvement at beginning of career	Directors (%)	White-collar (%)	Warsaw citizen (%)
PZPR members and activists	12.8	3.9	1.9
ZMS members and activists	48.4	14.7	7.2
Trade union activists	32.9	—	—
Involvement in general	77.2	18.6	9.1
Socio-political involvement in 1972			
PZPR members and activists	88.6	35.5	22.8
PZPR activists	59.9	11.6	6.4
Trade union activists	34.2	13.5	10.6
Involvement in general	93.2	43.9	30.3

Sources: Wasilewski, 'Społeczne mechanizmy'; Wasilewski, 'Occupational careers'.

110 M.K. Kostećki, 'The managerial cadres of Polish industry: research report' Polish Sociological Bulletin, No. 2, 1977, pp. 88–96. K. Słomczyński, *Zróżnicowanie społeczno zawodowei i jego korelaty*, Warsaw, 1972.
Many bonuses were paid out on a 'private' basis to senior management; some staff jumped queues for housing, vacations, etc. Wróblewski, 'Remis'. A. Możołowski, 'Czyje na więzchu?', *Polityka*, 26/1977.

111 J. Kluczyński, 'Jak ksztalcić i gospodarować kadrami specjalistów', *ND*, 1/1970.

6 The political consequences of industrial integration and concentration: II

1 E. Olin Wright, *Classes, Crisis and the State*, London, 1978, pp. 181–230.
2 A. Dobieszewski, 'Partia kierownicza siła narodu', in *Wybrane zagadnienia ideologii i polityki P.Z.P.R.*, Warsaw, 1971, pp. 264–96.
3 Ibid. M.K. Dziewanowski, *The Communist Party of Poland*, 2nd edn, Cambridge, Ma., 1975, pp. 2–54.
4 See Clause 46 of 'The Statutes of the P.Z.P.R.', as outlined in *For the Further Development of People's Poland*, Warsaw, 1971, pp. 384–5.
5 Since 1948, four such exchanges of Party cards have taken place (1949, 1958/9, 1967 and 1974). This practice had not been used in the Polish Communist Party/Workers' Party before 1944, and since 1967 this process has had to be carried out by means of a systematic assessment of the ideological and moral attitudes and activism of members. B. Dubińska, 'Legitimacja Partyjna', *ZP*, 7/1974, pp. 22–3.
In the 1970s, most turnover in Party membership took place after the first National Conference of Party Activists in 1973. The level of withdrawal and dismissal reached 424,285 for the period 1971–5. 'Przed wymianą legitimacji P.Z.P.R.', *ZP*, 4/1974; T. Kołodziejczyk, 'Skreślenie – problem niepokójący', *ZP*, 8/1979, p. 7.
6 W. Grochola, 'Wątki bardzo aktualne', *Polityka*, 27/1977, pp. 1, 4. This included: the forging of links with the masses and a willingness to learn from the experiences of socialist development; the acceptance of responsibility for moral and ethical leadership; the recognition that membership should involve increased obligation and not increased privilege; vigilance against autocracy and extremism; the acceptance that conflict and difficulties are a natural element of social progress rather than just the survival of past epochs; and emphasis upon the importance of the lowest level of PZPR activists.
7 J. Staniszkis, 'On some contradictions of socialist society: the case of Poland', *Soviet Studies*, Vol. XXXI, No. 2, April 1979, pp. 167–87.
8 Z. Grudzień, 'O niektórych problemach praktyki partyjnego kierownictwa', *ND*, 10/1970, p. 118.
A. Dobieszewski, *Wiedza o Partii: wybrany problemy*, Warsaw, 1972 p. 402.

9 A. Dobieszewski, 'Węzłowe problemy struktury i zasad działania partii Marksistowski–Leninowskiej', *ND*, 6/1971, pp. 55–8.

The case study of the sulphur combine revealed considerable friction and competition in relations between the two Wojewodztwa Councils in Rzeszów and Kielce during 1970/1 over the location of the combine headquarters and hence revenue. L. Kolarska, 'Sprawozdanie z socjologicznych badań relacji zakład kombinat – zjednoczenia', unpublished manuscript, Warsaw, 1972.

10 R. Orzechowski (ed.), *Prawo przedsiębiorstw*, Warsaw, 1971, pp. 38–40.

11 Dobieszewski, 'Partia kierownicza siła', p. 313.

12 R. Dudek, 'Płynność dyrektorów', in A. Sarapata (ed.), *Płynność Zalog*, Warsaw, 1968, pp. 339–42.

13 Z. Niedbała, 'Tryb podejmowania i charakter prawny decyzji powołujących i odwołujących dyrektorów przedsiębiorstw państwowych', RPEiS, 1/1972, pp. 43–54.

14 Clause 17 of the Statutes of the PZPR, in *For the Further Development of People's Poland*, Warsaw, 1971.

15 'Wnioski sekretariatu K.C.P.Z.P.R. w/s umacnianiu roli wielkich zakladów i ich organizacji partynych w politycznym i ekonomicznym życiu kraju', Warsaw, 1971; Uchwała KCPZPR w/s ideowo-wychowawczej wsród załogi zakładu przemysłu metalowego H. Cegielski w. Poznaniu', August, 1972.

16 *Krajowa narada aktywu Partynego i gospodarczego*, Warsaw, 1973, p. 126.

A second such conference was held in 1978 but was more concerned with questions of economic and social policy (market output, agricultural output, housing, transport, communications) than with style of Party work. *ZP*, 2/1978, pp. 3–4; speech by E. Babiuch to IX Plenum KCPZPR, *ND*, 5/1972, pp. 181–2.

17 'Sprawozdanie K.C.P.Z.P.R. za okres od VI do VII zjazdu', *ND*, 1/1976, p. 37; K. Marszał, 'Ideowo-wychowawcze funkcje organizacji partyjnych w wielkich zakładach przemysłowych', *ND*, 4/1976, pp. 72–81; J. Kubasziewicz, S. Gajda, H. Starostka, 'Rola organizacji partyjnych w wielkich zakladach pracy', *ND*, 4/1976, pp. 64–5; B. Dubińska, 'Zdaniem sekretarzy KCPZPR', *ZP*, 1/1974; J. Kubasziewicz, 'Rola wielko-przemyslowej klasy robotniczej w zyciu Partii', *ZP*, 5/1977.

18 The Cegielski engineering works was the first plant in which both the Central Committee and local Wojewodztwo committee of the PZPR directly intervened. Uchwała KCPZPR w/s 'pracy ideowo-wychowawczej wsród załogi zakładu przemysłu metalowego H. Cegielski w Poznaniu', August 1972. See also the articles by: E. Michałczuk, *ZP*, 10/1973, p. 11; Z. Jaskowiak, *ZP*, 12/1976.

By 1976 in a total workforce of 16,000 there were 3,500 PZPR members (over 70% were manual workers) amounting to nearly 25% of all the staff organised into 14 POPs, 69 OOPs and 271 Party groups.

On the Ursus Tractor Factory see the article by S. Maczkowski, *ZP*, 5/1976, pp. 33–4, and *ZP*, 6/1974, pp. 20–1. Here, 2,400 PZPR members and candidates were organised into 20 POPs, 36 OOPs and 175 groups.

On the Stalowa Wola Steelworks see the article by J. Piłkuski ZP, 2/1976, p. 22. Here, amongst a total workforce of 20,000, 4,500 were PZPR members.

On the Northern Shipyard in Gdańsk see the articles by W. Wodecki, ZP, 6/1975, pp. 34–5 ZP, 10/1976, p. 12. It is interesting to note that of the 1,000 PZPR members here in 1975, over 50% were under 35 years of age and had not long been in their post. This was reflected in a high annual labour turnover of around 25% mainly among unskilled workers. On the other hand, over 75% of all PZPR members were skilled workers.

Other plants reported to be included in the experiments included the FSO Zerań Car Factory (ZP, 11/1975) and a textile factory in Łódz (ZP, 9/1977).

19 J. Kubasziewicz, 'Rola wielko'; 'Partia', ZP, 1/1976, pp. 14–19; A. Łopatka, J. Błuszkowski, 'Problematyka Partyjna w badaniach naukowych', ZP, 3/1978, pp. 13–14.

20 B. Dubińska, 'Zdaniem sekretarzy'; K. Konstański, 'Konferencja naukowa na tematu roli organizacji Partyjnych w wielkich zakładach pracy', ND, 3/1976, p. 201; A. Łopatka, J. Błuszkowski, K. Konstański, *Organizacja Partyjne wielkich zakładów pracy*, Warsaw, 1976.

21

	POPs	OOPs	Groups
At the VII PZPR Congress 1976	75,200	23,000	61,000
At the VIII PZPR Congress 1980	75,000	27,000	70,000

Sources: 'Partia', ZP, 1/1976, pp. 14–19; 'Sprawozdanie K.C.P.Z.P.R. za okres od VII do VIII Zjazdu', ND, 3/1980, pp. 38–9.

22 J. Kubasziewicz et al., 'Rola organizacji'; J. Wacławek', 'Rola zebrania w systemie pracy partyjnej', ND, 1/1975, pp. 98–103. See also the articles by S. Warpas in ZP, 5/1972 and I. Biel, ZP, 8/1972.

23 J. Suliga, 'Metody ksztaltowania za-angazowanych postaw', ZP, 4/1975, p. 19; P. Musiewicz, 'Wyższe wymagania – aktywniejsza praca', ZP, 10/1978, pp. 6–7; T. Fiszbach, 'Robotniczy aktyw propagandowy w Wojewodztwie Gdańskim', ND, 5/1973, pp. 143–8.

24 'Partia', ZP, 1/1976, pp. 14–19.

25 Statutes of the PZPR in *For the Further Development of People's Poland*, p. 383: 'Party organisations in ministries, offices, state economic and social institutions aim in their work at the constant improvement of the functioning of their administrative appratus, struggle against bureaucratism and malpractices, strengthen the state and professional discipline and shape socialist norms of human relationships. The organisations watch over the proper work of the executive apparatus and its responsibility for tasks entrusted to it, and evaluate the fulfilment of the Party's decisions in their own field of activity. These organisations conduct political and organisational work among the employees, evaluate the stand and fulfilment of duties by the Party members. They

analyse the situation in respect to the selection, placement and training of cadres, and transmit their conclusions to the proper Party authorities and the administrative heads of their institutions.'

26 In the ministry of agriculture, 30% of staff were full or candidate members of the POP. K. Racławski, 'Funkcje kontrolne najtrudniejśze', *ZP*, 10/1974.

In many industrial associations, Party membership amongst middle management was low, and fewer than half the section heads had secondary or incomplete higher education. (This applied to the association in the construction industry 'Bumar'; in the electrical industry 'Ema'; and in the agricultural machinery industry 'Agromet'.) W. Kata, 'Wiele do zrobienia', *ZP*, 2/1974, pp. 4–5.

27 'Co nam przeszkadza w dobrym gospodarowaniu', *ZP*, 10/1971, pp. 9, 11.

28 K. Małolepszy, 'Organizacji Partyjne instytutów resortowych', *ND*, 1/1976, pp. 33–42

29 T.K. 'Partia w ministerstwie i centralym urzędzie', *ZP*, 8/1974, pp. 8–10; Kata, 'Wiele do zrobienia'; J. Koniarski, 'Partia w centralnej administracji', *ZP*, 2/1976, pp. 10–11.

30 A. Dobieszewski, 'Wiedza o Partii', pp. 362–3; W. Kata, 'Organizacja Partyjne ministerstw i centralnych urzędow wobec nowych zadań', *ND*, 11/1975, pp. 148–54.

31 Kata, 'Wiele do zrobienia'; Koniarski, 'Partia w centralnej administracji'. A high turnover of staff working in industrial ministries took place between 1971 and 1976.

32 Dubińska, 'Zdaniem sekretarzy', pp. 12–14.

33 'Partia'.

34 SJ. Głowacki, *Zjednoczenia państwowych przedsiębiorstw terenowych w systemie organów rad narodowych*, Warsaw, 1972; R. Taras, 'Democratic centralism and Polish local government reforms', *Public Administration*, 53/1975, pp. 403–26. The 22 Wojewodztwo Councils controlled over one-third of the total expenditure of local authorities.

35 'O roli zjednoczenia i przedsiębiorstwa', *ND*, 6/1964, pp. 63–126; T. Dębowska-Romanowska, 'Oddziaływanie rad narodowych na gospodarkę przedsiębiorstw zarządzanych centralnie', *Finanse*, 9/1972, pp. 12–16.

36 See Chapter 5, and also W. Narojek, *System władzy w miejscie*, Warsaw, 1967, p. 274.

37 In 1960 the proportion of PZPR membership among Powiat councillors varied from 20% to 60%, but in the Wojewodztwo Councils it could be as high as 80%. By 1969, however, there was less of a disparity and Party membership could be found to fall between 49% and 56% at all levels. R. Taras, 'The local political elites', in D. Lane and G. Kolankiewicz (eds.) *Social Groups in Polish Society*, London, 1973, pp. 264–5; *Radni i czlonkowie prezydiów rad narodowych 1958–69*, GUS, Warsaw, 1972, p. 70.

38 Taras, 'Local political elites'; Taras, 'Democratic centralism'.

39 B.W. Olszewski, 'Operacja gminna', *Polityka*, 2/1973; Taras, 'Democratic centralism'; A. Zarajczyk, 'Reforma władz terenowych w praktyce pracy Partyjnej', *ND*, 12/1974, pp. 25–33.

40 J. Wieczórek, 'Reforma władzy terenowej: doswiadczeńia i wnioski', *ND*, 3/1975, pp. 84–91; J. Budziński, 'Rady narodowe w roku po reformie', *ND*, 5/1975, pp. 100–7. It was also claimed that as a result of the reform better-qualified council members were recruited.

41 J. Dzięciołowski, 'Dwa miesiące po reformie', *ZG*, 32/1975.

42 A. Karpiński, 'Planowanie makro-regionalne', *ZG*, 30/1975, pp. 1–2; J. Wieczórek, 'Reforma w toku', *ND*, 7/1975. Both the Regional Planning Units and Regional Development Commissions were made accountable to the Planning Commission in Warsaw and to a new ministry for regional development.

43 J. Kluczyński, 'Jak kształcić i gospodarować kadrami specjalistów', *ND*, 1/1970, pp. 18–31. This can be illustrated by the growth of employment in the socialised sector of the economy which had risen by 12.4% in 1964 (in comparison with 1958) but which by 1968 had reached 34.3% (in comparison with 1958).

44 Ibid., p. 25. Already in 1964, of the total number with Higher Education (310,000), 4,110 were working in jobs where only further education was required; and a full 3% of those with higher education were employed in manual posts.

45 Ibid., pp. 26–31. Of those with higher education, about 20% were employed in posts outside of their specialism, but in specific areas such as the humanities or exact sciences it could be as high as 50%.

In the case of further education although this lack of correspondence with employment was at a lower level (30% of those with further education employed in agriculture and 25% of those employed in technician posts) the trend was on the increase in the late 1960s (while correspondence between further education and job specification was 86.2% in 1964, by 1968 it had fallen to 83.4%).

46 By the mid-1970s, it was claimed that there were about 700,000 people in Poland who held a university degree, but that as many as 300,000 had acquired their degree since 1970! A. Lubowski, 'Kierownicy jutra', *ZG*, 33/1977, p. 33.

47 w/s 'dalszego doskonalenie polityki kadrowej i podnoszeńia poziomu pracy kadr kierowniczych', Warsaw, October 1972; w/s 'Partyjnego systemu doskonalenie kadr kierowniczych', Warsaw, June 1973. See also, 'Partia', pp. 14–19. The debate on a new conception of cadre policy was opened in the PZPR Journal *Nowe Drogi*: Z. Stępien 'Węzlowe problemy polityki kadrowej' *ND*, 4/1972, pp. 40–51.

48 J. Staskiewicz, 'Doskonalenie kadr kierowniczych', *ZG*, 4/1972, p. 1; L. Lugowski, 'Kryteria oceny kadry kierowniczej w kombinatach przemysłu maszynowego', IOPM, 1970.

49 Z. Prochot, 'O doskonalenia kadr kierowniczych', *ZP*, 2/1976, pp. 28–9.

Many courses were only of two weeks' duration and the time budget was as follows:

22 hours on ideological-political issues
24 hours on the PZPR's socio-economic strategy
32 hours on management techniques
24 hours on sport and recreation

50 W. Wodecki, 'Nowe spojrzenie na kadry', *ZP*, 4/1975, pp. 10–11.
51 These interviews included both Party members in leading positions (*ZP*, 11/1972, p. 3; *ZP*, 7/1973, pp. 18–20; *ZP*, 3/1975, p. 1.; *ZP*, 2/1976, p. 3.) and many non-Party members in posts of responsibility (especially the foremen) who it was hoped could be induced to join. B. Dubińska, 'W hucie Warszawie', *ZP*, 8/1973, pp. 13–14.
52 A. Banaszak, 'System pracy z kadrą Partyjną', *ZP*, 12/1978, pp. 24–5.
53 M. Dobrzyński, *Kierowanie kadrami*, Warsaw, 1977; Uchwała Nr 247, RM 5 November 1977 w/s 'twórczenia rezerwy kadrowej na stanowiska kierownicze w administracji panstwowej i gospodarce narodowej'.
   However, there was nothing new in the interest of creating a cadre reserve which had been proposed at the V PZPR Congress, J. Klasa 'Własciwy sens polityki kadrowei' *ND*, 5/1972, pp. 103–8.
54 W. Wodecki, 'Nowe spojrzenie'; E. Michałuk, 'Szkolenie i doskonalenie kadr', *ZP*, 4/1975, pp. 23–4; Z. Zandarowski 'Rola kadr i polityka kadrowa PZPR' *ZP*, 6/1980, pp. 1–5. Of the total number of 170,000 people in senior management, only 11,000 were aged under 29, although 37% of the Polish labour force were under the age of 30.
55 J. Maziarski, 'Drzwi do gabinetu', *Polityka*, 41/1978, p. 5.
56 J. Lęgowski, *Polityka kadrowa w zakładzie pracy*, Warsaw, 1976.
57 J. Cave, 'Local officials of the Polish United Workers' Party 1956–75', *Soviet Studies*, Vol. XXXIII, No. 1, January 1981, pp. 125–41.
   In 1980, half of the PZPR apparat of 500,000 members worked in offices in town, wojewodztwo and commune committees but there was a strong preference amongst those with higher education to work in urban centres (63%) rather than rural areas (8%), Z. Zandarowski 'Rola kadr i polityka Kadrowa PZPR', *ZP*, 6/1980, pp. 1–5.
58 The similarity of the Polish and Soviet experience in this respect is striking. T. Dunmore, 'Local Party organs in industrial administration: the case of the Ob'edinenie reform', *Soviet Studies*, Vol. XXXII, No. 2, April 1980, pp. 195–217.
59 G. Kolankiewicz, 'The Polish industrial working class', in Lane and Kolankiewicz (eds.), *Social Groups*; A. Babeau, *Les Conseils ouvriers en Pologne*, Paris, 1960; I. Deutscher, *Soviet Trade Unions: Their Place in Soviet Labour Policy*, London, 1950.
60 M. McCaulay, *Labour Disputes in Soviet Russia, 1957–1965*, London, 1969.
61 D. Douglas, *Transitional Economic Systems: The Polish–Czech Example*, London, 1953; H.T. Ludlow, 'The role of Trade Unions in Poland', *Political Science Quarterly*, Vol. 90, No. 2, 1975, pp. 315–24.
62 Although both Kolankiewicz and Babeau see these as having a forerunner in the brief-lived factory committees of 1944–46. Kolankiewicz, 'Polish industrial working class'; Babeau, *Les Conseils ouvriers*.
63 While the PZPR and the trade union apparat suggested the reform of

the trade union factory councils, and newly trained engineers (frustrated with their low status and by irrational management policies) suggested the creation of technical-advisory councils in enterprises, a government commission, realising the course that events were taking, proposed the creation of a separately elected body to fulfil both the functions of democratic participation and technical advice.

64 Babeau, *Les Conseils ouvriers*, p. 120; W. Morawski, *Samorząd robotniczego w gospodarce socjalistycznej*, Warsaw, 1973.

65 Morawski, *Samorząd robotniczy*. M. Błazejczyk, *Prawo samorządu robotniczego*, Warsaw, 1971, pp. 26–30.

After 1964 representatives of the Socialist Youth (ZMS) and Technicians Organisation (NOT) in the enterprise could also be included in quarterly sessions of the KSR.

66 See my unpublished paper delivered to the Annual NASEES Conference at Cambridge 29–31 March 1980, entitled 'Worker participation in Polish enterprises: some conceptual problems in the light of industrial concentration of Poland since 1958'. In this I argue that while the scepticism (conveyed by means of the theory of Democratic Elitism) towards the potential for participation by a conscious citizenry within the liberal democratic framework of capitalist society can be justified in terms of social survey analysis and in terms of the suitability of a balanced civic culture, the tolerance of a low incidence of participation in state-socialist societies in general is seen as a testimony to either the despotism of a Marxist–Leninist Party, or to the more insidious control of technocratic managerialism. Secondly, while I see it as facile to deny that worker participation should be judged by the standard set by the Polish state, there is a utopian quality in much of the East European and Radical Left literature which results in the dismissal of all exercises in worker participation which do not live up to this standard, and, as a consequence, contributes to a failure to perceive that partial participation can co-exist with non-democratic authority structures, and that lower-level participation may be of greater interest and relevance to workforce than at higher but more remote centres of power.

67 Błazejczyk, *Prawo Samorządu*, pp., 32–3.

68 L. Gilejko, 'Samorząd robotniczy a nadrzędna jednostki administracji gospodarczej', ZGPTE; 'Konferencja naukowa n.t. doswiadczeńie zjednoczeń eksperymentujących', Warsaw, 1968, p. 6.

69 Ibid.; M. Pruszak, 'Wspolpraca samorządu ze zjednoczeniem nad planem', *SR*, 6/1969, pp. 5–6. This description of the role undertaken by the KSR in the planning process in the construction industry, illustrated the lack of opportunity for detailed scrutiny, either of the guidelines issued in the preceding year, or of the various directive indices issued. Most of the exchange of information took place between the enterprise and association management, and so the limited access of the enterprise Workers' Council to information, fostered relations of mutual mistrust between them and the association. However, the

solution proposed by Pruszak involving regular meetings between enterprise, Party, trade union, Workers' Council leadership and enterprise and association management (with representatives from the investment bank) did not augur well for greater democratic involvement of the workforce in the planning and management process.

70 'Dyrektor wykonawca ponastowineń samorządu robotniczego', *SR*, 7/1966; K. Wierzbićki, 'Stała więz zjednoczenia z radą robotniczą siedlićkich zakładów 'Koro', *SR*, 1/1969.

71 J. Małecki, 'Współpraca zjednoczenia z samorządem robotniczym', *SR*, 1/1969, p. 35; A. Teter, 'Dyrektór i kolegium w zjednoczeniu przemysłowym', Master's thesis, SGPiS, Warsaw, 1970; Gilejko, 'Samorząd robotniczy', pp. 21–2.

72 W. Szyndler Głowacki, 'Bez samorządu trudno: Dylematy gospodarkiego planowania', *ZG*, 20/1968; Letter in *ZG*, 16/1969, p. 7.

73 Pismo okolne prezesa R.M. i przewodniczącego CRZZ May 1969. Even according to this regulation, enterprise KSR representatives were not to have full decision-making rights. They were to be consulted on all matters of social-welfare policy, but with respect to employment and wages policy all they were entitled to was a reply to their proposals within 30 days. Greater emphasis was placed upon consultation between KSR and enterprise management and direct communication between enterprise and association management, rather than workforce participation in association policy making. See also T. Jaworski, *Udział załóg w zarządzaniu*, Warsaw, 1976, pp. 148–50.

74 *ZG*, 10/1971, p. 3. This reported on legal investigation by the Warsaw Procuracy into enterprises in three industrial associations.

75 For a consideration of the criteria distinguishing industrial enterprises from other production units see B. Gliński, 'Przedsiębiorstwo socjalistyczne i jego ewolucja', *ND*, 6/1977, pp. 92–100.

76 Z. Niedbała, 'Samorząd w kombinacie', *SR*, 2/1971, p. 13; S. Podemski, 'Kapitał ze złych doswiadczeń', *ZG*, 23/1973, p. 5.

77 The arrangements in the combine 'Polam' in the electrical industry were held to be an unqualified success. B. Jańczyk, 'Zycie zebranie czekać, *SR*, 4/1972, p. 19; S. Łypaczewicz, 'Z duchem ustawy', *SR*, 4/1972, p. 21.

78 J. Michna, 'Z doswiadczeń Huty Pokój', *ZG*, 46/1968, p. 3.

79 L. Skorupski, 'Co z S.R. w kombinacie?', *SR*, 15/1970, p. 4; J. Fiólna (Letter), *SR*, 19/1970, p. 4; L. Skorupski, (Reply) *SR*, 19/1970, p. 4. The academic study of the sulphur and ball bearing combines was conducted by the industrial sociology unit of the Polish Academy of Sciences.
J. Błazejewski, 'Funkcjonowanie kombinatów przemysłowych', Instytut Nauk Prawnych, Warsaw, 1972, pp. 27–8, 34.

80 J. Stefaniak 'Funkcjonowanie rozwiązań prawnych w kombinacie kopalń i zakładów przetwórczych siarki "Siarkopol" w Tarnobrzegu', Machów, 1971.

81 The plant delegates to the Council of Representatives of factory self-management organisations would include the Chairmen of the

Workers' Council, and of the trade union Factory Council, the Secretary of the PZPR factory committee plus the factory director. Sessions were to be presided over by the Chairmen of the Workers' Council of the leading factory and were to serve as a means of ventilating issues already raised at the KSR in the plant and of discussing the plan profits and their implementation for the combine. The combine director was a central figure to all of this as he could send his representatives to individual KSR sessions in the plants and could attend the combine council. Although he was obliged to implement any resolutions taken at the latter, he could veto measures he considered to be contrary to the interests of the combine as a whole. E. Oskarol 'Ankieta dla zakładu wiodącego kombinatu przemysłu lozysk tocznych Predom', Kielce, 1972.

It is not surprising that these arrangements degenerated in practice into a series of *ad hoc* weekly meetings at the leading factory in Poznań attended by senior management and the leadership of PZPR, trade union youth organisations and Workers' Councils from all the units in the combine. J. Błażejewski, 'Funkcjonowanie kombinatów przemysłowych', pp. 27–8, 34.

82 Uchwała Prezydium ZGZZ Metalowców w/s 'dalszego doskonalenia zasad i form działania organizacji związkowych i samorządu robotniczego w kombinacie i zakładach wchodzących w jego skład', Warsaw, December 1971. Each session of the KPSRK was to last seven days and to take place once every quarter in a different factory, although the presidium of the Workers' Council in the leading factory aided by the secretaries of each plant's KSR would act as a secretariat. Decisions were to be made on the basis of simple majority voting (with a two-thirds majority necessary for a change in policy). Representatives of the plant ZMS, NOT and PTE branches could be invited to attend or to give advice, and the combine director was to attend all sessions, and make a report and implement KPSRK resolutions in all matters except social welfare which was the responsibility of the trade union and Workers' Council organisations. He could only veto a resolution of the KPSRK after due consultation with the industrial association, the ministry and the chief executive of the metalworkers' trade union, and had to supply any information on request to members of the KPSRK at least 14 days in advance. Finally, the KPSRK itself was also answerable for information from the industrial association, the local branch of the NBP and the metal workers' trade union.

83 Although there were self-management organisations in the ten individual plants in the combine which could meet to scrutinise annual and long-term plans, these had to receive approval from the whole combine. Plant representatives could also be invited to give advice to the combine 'kolegium'. B. Jańczyk, 'Zycie zebrania czekać', *SR*, 4/1972, p. 19; S. Łypaczewicz, 'Z duchem ustawy', *SR*, 4/1972, p. 21.

It is interesting to note that one dispute that had to be resolved at the first meeting concerned the use of a holiday centre built and financed by the largest factory. A. Sikórski, 'Kryterium prawdy', *ZG*, 42/1973, p. 10.

84 'Przy redakcyjnym stole', *SR*, 4/1972, pp. 12–17. Besides lamenting the ambiguity of the procedures and weakness of powers in the areas of employment policy, many participants cited the confusing terminology that could apply to production units of identical size and function (enterprise, factory, plant, department, unit, section, combine, etc.).

85 L. Gilejko and M. Kamiński, 'Samorząd robotniczy W.O.G.', *ZG*, 48/1973, p. 11.

86 T. Wasilewski, 'Może rada kombinatu?' *SR*, 4/1972; W. Rogowski, 'Społeczne funkcje samorządu robotniczego', *ZG*, 6/1977.

87 A seemingly genuine attempt to encourage manual-worker participation in a multi-factory enterprise where the creation of a single KSR structure was avoided as it was felt that it would end up being dominated by white-collar technicians and middle and lower management. Even though a 35-member Workers' Council was elected for the whole of the enterprise in November 1969, three years later its statutory two-thirds share of manual workers had fallen to about one half by 1972. J. Majewski, 'Portzeby i przepisy', *SR*, 4/1972, p. 18.

88 J. Maziarski, 'Partner', *Polityka*, 39/1973; J. Maziarski, 'W imieniu robotników', *Polityka*, 21/1978, p. 3. The second of these is a particularly interesting article which reviews the changing climate surrounding the issue of workers' self-management. With the extension of the bureaucratic–technocratic philosophy of management, but retention of the principle of one-man management, the 1958 law and concept of workers' self-management had become outdated. The discouragement of worker interest by formalistic procedure, the failure to include all production units in the scheme, the passage upwards of issues of most interest to workers and which could be solved at a lower level and above all the instrumental and manipulative approach to workers' self-management heralded danger. If the mechanism of plant democracy did not fulfil the expectations of the staff, then there was a growing likelihood that they would seek other means of so doing. See also: 'O nowe formy działanie S.R.', 11/1971, p. 20; A. Paszyński, 'Robotnicza samorządoność, *Polityka*, 33/1978, pp. 1, 4, 5; J. Bołdok, 'Bo to jest walka', *ZG*, 18/1977, p. 1.

89 J. Solarz, 'Samorząd robotniczy w jednostkach inicujących', *PT*, 24/1973, p. 3; M. Kamiński, 'Samorząd robotniczy w nowej sytuacji', *ZG*, 36/1973, p. 7; Jawórski, *Udział załog*.

90 Z. Wyczesany, 'K.S.R. w kombinacie', *ZG*, 22/1974, p. 8.

91 *Trybuna samorządu robotniczego*, 19/1973.

92 A. Nałęcz-Jawecki, Z. Wyczesany, 'Samorząd w kombinacie', *ZG*, 47/1972, p. 6. Senior combine management here had considerable powers of veto over KSR resolutions.

93 J. Sardykowski, 'Bez samouspokojenia', *ZG*, 14/1979, pp. 1, 4.

94 L. Gilejko, 'Presłanki rozwoju samorządu robotniczego', *ND*, 11/1979, pp. 122–7.

95 Politburo resolution, April 1973, w/s 'zadań związków zawodowych w rozwijaniu budownićtwa socjalistycznego', quoted in *ND*, 1/1976. See also J. Misiewicz, 'Udział związków zawodowych w realizacji programu partii', *ZP*, 12/1979, p. 31; M. Cynkier, 'Większe uprawnieńia – większe zadania', *ZP*, 12/1973, p. 28.

96 A. Bilska, 'Rola związków zawodowych w J.I.', *ZP*, 10/1973, p. 32; A. Bilska, 'Narady wytwórcze w nowym systemie gospodarowania', *ZP*, 6/1975, pp. 33–4.

97 A. Bilska, 'Górnicze zespoły współdziałania związkowego ze zjednoczeniami', *ZP*, 8/1975, pp. 36–7. The major theme for discussion at the group meetings was to be general branch development.

98 A. Bilska, 'Co należy do rad zakładowych?', *ZP*, 5/1976, pp. 35–6.

99 E. Grochal, 'Kodeks pracy', *ND*, 1/1975, pp. 63–73.

100 Politburo Guidelines (22 May 1978), quoted in 'K.S.R. – podstawowe ogniwo demokracji', *ZG*, 23/1978, p. 3. See also:
Z. Szeliga, 'Wspólne decyzji i wspólna odpowiedzialność'; *Polityka*, 28/1978, pp. 1, 6; T. Jawórski, 'Rozwój samorządu robotniczego', *ND*, 8/1978, pp. 48–55; L. Winiarski, 'Nowy etap rozwoju S.R.', *ZP*, 8/1978, p. 1.
By the end of 1978 over 900 multi-factory enterprises and combines were equipped with some form of workers' self-management institution, and the same applied to 11,000 single plant enterprises. K. Krauss, 'Przyjmując współodpowiedzialność', *ZG*, 3/1979, pp. 1, 4. T. Jaworski 'Rozwój demokracji, robotniczej' *ZP*, 1/1980, p. 10.

101 A. Bilska, 'Znać uprawnienia i umieć z nich korzystać', *ZP*, 4/1977, pp. 22–3; J. Kwiek, 'Ludzie uparcie', *ZG*, 30/1978, p. 3.
In many of the enterprises in the Płock oil refining and petrochemicals complex Workers' Councils had never met. 'Rola i funkcje samorządu robotniczego', *ND*, 5/1979, p. 143 (on the Stalowa Wola steel mill); L. Ożimina 'Samorządność w fabryce', *ZP*, 7/1977, p. 27.
Here in the ball bearings combine, the leading factory, Iskra, had decided in 1976 to cease convening a Workers' Council. A. Kuczyński, 'Rola sejmiku załogi', *ZG*, 49/1979, pp. 8, 9.

102 D. Żuk, 'Nowe Zasady finansowania zakłady działalnośći socjalnej', *ZP*, 1/1974, p. 35, and see also p. 33.

103 R. Tomaka, 'Udział załogi w zarządzaniu przedsiębiorstwem a bodźce materiolnego zainteresowania', *RPEiS*, 1/1978, pp. 119–37.
D. Żuk, 'Nowe zasady działalnośći socjalnej w zakładzie pracy', *ZP*, 6/1975, pp. 30–1.

104 Report of the KCPZPR for the period between VI and VII Congress, *ND*, 1/1976, pp. 9–11.

105 Total expenditure on the Social Fund in state-owned industry:

1970	10.14	billion zł.
1975	28.6	„ „
1977	34.6	„ „
1978	36.5	„ „.

of which employee contributions were:
1970   31.1%
1977   11.8%
Source: K. Podoski, 'Zakładowe czy wspólne?', *ZG*, 50/1979, p. 3.
106 J. Piwosz, 'Pojęcie i zakres zakładowej działalnośći socjalno–kulturalnej', RPEiS, 1/1978, pp. 235–49; 'Urlopowa wachta', *ZP*, 7/1976, p. 17.
107 Report of the VIII Plenum KCPZPR, *ND*, 1/1979.
108 The house-building programme for the Five Year Plan period 1976–80 was behind schedule by late 1977 and the shortage seemed to be felt most acutely in the big cities: Warsaw, Katowice, Wrocław and Gdańsk. B.C., 'Drugi front', *ZP*, 3/1978, p. 26; St. Kukruryka, 'Na drodzie do mieszkania dla kazdej rodziny', *ZP*, 5/1978, p. 13.
109 See the Guidelines for the VIII PZPR Congress. Reported in Podoski, 'Zakładowe czy wspólne'.
110 It was admitted that the trade union Factory Councils 'did not always uphold the principles of social justice' in distributing social welfare benefits, and gave little consideration to the fact that administrative and managerial staff might fare better than manual workers, and in particular that certain categories such as worker-peasants who have to spend their holiday period working on their small-holdings might be unduly discriminated against. S. Gajda, 'Obowiązuja kryteria społeczne', *ZP*, 8/1977, pp. 27–8; K. Krupa, 'Komu i jak służyć?', *ZG*, 4/1979.
111 I. Sledzińska, 'I w tych nerwach człowiek cos wymyśl', *Polityka*, 33/1978, pp. 4, 5.
112 E. Wróbel, 'Podział (w miare) słuszny', *ZG*, 35/1980, p. 7.
113 Sledzińska, 'I w tych nerwach'.
114 W. Rogowski, 'Zasada współdecydowania', *Polityka*, 1/1980, p. 3.

Summary and conclusion

1 M. Lavigne, *The Socialist Economies of the Soviet Union and Europe*, London, 1974, pp. 127, 141.
2 W. Wesołowski, 'Interesy klas i Warstw a jedność moralno – polityczna narodu', *ND*, 1/1980, pp. 99–112.
3 W. Morawski, 'Socialist industrialisation in Poland: the doctrine, system of decision making; uncontrolled phenomena', *Polish Sociological Bulletin*, 1/1978, pp. 33–45; J. Staniszkis, 'On some contradictions of Socialist Society: the case of Poland', *Soviet Studies*, Vol. XXXI, No. 2, 1979, pp. 167–87.
4 W. Bielicki and S. Widerszpil, 'Z problematyki przemiań społecznych w Polsce ludowej', *ND*, 7/1979, pp. 74–85.
5 J. Loch, 'Forum: wzmocniony głoś', *Polityka*, 8/1980, pp. 1, 4.
6 E. Skalski, 'Jej wysokość struktura', *Polityka*, 23/1980.

Postscript

1 *The Economist* 1980: 19 July, p. 43; 26 July, p. 50; 9 August, p. 40; 23 August, p. 38; 30 August, p. 37.

2 *ZG*, 35/1980, p. 2. *ZP*, 9/1980, p. 1. Edward Babiuch who had only been Prime Minister since he replaced Jaroszewicz at the VIII PZPR Congress in February 1980 was forced to resign in August to be replaced by Jozef Pinkowski.

3 See the national news section, 'W kraju', *Polityka*, 46/1980, p. 2.

4 'Odstępcy, samorządni i niezależni', *Polityka*, 39/1980, p. 7. By this date, 11 out of the total 23 official trade unions had left the CRZZ, including the sailors and dockers, construction workers, transport workers, steel workers, media and communications workers, academics and co-operative workers.

5 See the national news section, 'W kraju', *Polityka*, 40/1980, p. 2.

6 W.D. Connor, 'Dissent in Eastern Europe: a new coalition?', *Problems of Communism*, January–February 1980, pp. 1–17.

7 M.J. Woodall, 'New social factors in the unrest in Poland', *Government and Opposition*, Vol. 16, No. 1, Winter 1981, pp. 37–57.

8 'Protokoł porozumienia', *Polityka*, 36/1980, p. 3.

Of the 21 demands of MKS, the first was the acceptance of free trade unions in accordance with ILO Conventions 87 and 98 on the Right to Organise and the Right to Collective Action. The other 20 demands were:

  2 Amendments to articles 52, 64, 85 of the authoritarian Labour Code

  3 Freedom of the Press

  4 An amnesty for those who were dismissed from work or who became political prisoners as a result of involvement in the protest of 1970–1 and 1976

  5 Full publicity of MKS activities in the mass media

  6 Full accurate publicity of the real state of economic affairs, and an open discussion in the press on reform proposals

  7 Full payment of wages lost during strike activity in 1980

  8 Raising the minimum wage to 2,000 zł. per month

  9 Indexation of wage increases to price rises

10 Priority for the satisfaction of the domestic consumer goods market before the sale of goods for export

11 Rationing of meat and other basic food products in short supply

12 The principles for appointment of all leading cadres/management to be formal qualifications and not PZPR membership

13 All privileges hitherto granted to leading cadres and to the security police to be revoked

14 The retirement age to be reduced to 50 for women and 55 for men

15 Pension rights to be equalised across occupations

16 Health services to be improved

17 Kindergarten and nursery facilities to be expanded

18 Paid maternity leave to last up until the child's third birthday
19 The waiting lists for housing to be shortened
20 Improvements in allowances and maintenance payments on divorce
21 The guarantee of work-free Saturdays or, for those working the 'Four Brigade' shift system, extra holiday time to be allowed in lieu
9 J. Grochowski, 'Trudny egsamin dojrzałość', *ZP*, 8/1978, pp. 14–15; E. Skalski, 'Miejscie na dole', *Polityka*, 20/1980, pp. 1, 6.
10 T. Deutscher, 'Voices of dissent', *Socialist Register*, 1978 (London), pp. 21–43, esp. pp. 23–5; Connor, Dissent in Eastern Europe', p. 4.
11 Connor 'Dissent in Eastern Europe' pp. 7–8.
12 E. Babiuch, 'P.Z.P.R. przed VIII Zjazdu', *ND*, 1/1980, p. 9.
13 J. Fastyn, 'Partyjna kontrola w terenie', *ZN*, 2/1978, p. 34.
14 'Młody aktywista Partyjny', *ZP*, 7/1978, p. 12.
15 E. Skalski, 'Jej wysokość struktura', *Polityka*, 23/1980; L. Gilejko, 'Związki zawodowe wobec aktualnych zadán', *ND*, 8/1980; J. Loch, 'Forum wzmocniony głos', *Polityka*, 8/1980, pp. 1, 4.
16 See Conclusion, pp. 192–3.
17 J. Urban, 'Mamy karty w ręku', *Polityka*, 6/1980, pp. 1, 4, 14; T. Fiszbach, 'Klimat rozwoju Partii', *ZP*, 9/1978, pp. 1, 3.
18 J. Wacławek, *Socialistyczne stosunki w zakladzie pracy*, Warsaw, 1970, pp. 152–160.
19 T. Fiszbach, 'Robotniczy aktyw propagandowy w wojewodztwie gdańskim', *ND*, 5/1973, pp. 143–8.
20 W. Wodecki, 'Aktyw robotniczy', *ZP*, 2/1978, pp. 23–4.
21 W. Wodecki, 'Szczerze, rzeczowo, życliwie', *ZP*, 5/1978, p. 2; St. Kukuryka, 'Na drodze do mieszkania dla kazdej rodziny', *ZP*, 5/1978, p. 13.
22 Ibid. One example was the sending of carpenters from the Lenin Shipyards to the Adolf Warski yards in Szczecin, even though they were not short of work in Gdańsk where production was held up because of their absence.
23 Fiszbach, 'Klimat rozwoju Partii'.
24 D. Zagrodzka, 'Co wolno wojewoda?', *Polityka*, 16/1980, p. 3.
25 S.R. Lipiński, 'Cos za cos', *ZG*, 25/1980.
26 T. Wraszczyk, 'Rozwój społeczno – gospodarczy a postęp naukowo – techniczny w latach osiemdziesątych', *ND*, 1/1980, pp. 14–57; J. Urban, 'Życie na własny rachunek', *Polityka*, 30/1980, pp. 1, 4.
27 'Pierwsze półrocze 1980 roku', *ZG*, 29/1980, p. 2.
28 P. Kapusciński, 'Paszowe realia', *ZG*, 31/1980.
29 T. Checiński, 'Stawiać czoło trudnosciom', *Polityka*, 26/1980, pp. 1, 4. It was estimated that Poland would have to pay $5 billion in interest payments to the West during 1980.
30 'Zrozumieć konieczność', *Polityka*, 25/1980, p. 7. Management would risk losing their own bonuses if the total Wages Fund was exceeded.
31 W. Krencik, 'Za parawanem płać', *Polityka*, 17/1980, p. 5.
32 'Pierwsze półrocze', p. 2.

33 E. Wrobel, 'Podział (w miarę) słuszny', *ZG*, 35/1980, p. 7.
34 *ZG*, 46/1980, p. 9.
35 'W kraju', *Polityka*, 44/1980, p. 2.
36 T. Kierczyński, 'Reforma systemu funkcjonowania organizacji gospodarczej', *ZG*, 46/1980, p. 8.
37 J. Knapik, 'Propozycie na dziś', *ZG*, 46/1980, p. 1.
38 'P.T.E. o reformie', *ZG*, 46/1980 (special supplement).
39 M. Mieszczanowski, 'Założenia tryletniego planu stabilizacyjnego', *ZG*, 47/1980.
40 J. Loch, 'Decyzja Albina Terki', *Polityka*, 40/1980, p. 3. Uchwała VII Plenum KCPZPR 'Zadania Partii w walce o socjalistyczny charakter odnowy zycia społecznego' *ZP*, 12/1980. pp. 3–6.
41 W. Pawlowski, 'Weryfikacja', *Polityka*, 45/1980, p. 3.

Bibliography

English and non-Polish texts

Allardt, E. & Wesołowski, W., eds., *Social Structure and Change: Finland and Poland*, Warsaw, 1978

Alton, T.P., *The Polish Post-War Economy*, New York, 1955

Arendt, H., *The Origins of Totalitarianism*, New York, 1958

Aron, R., *Eighteen Lectures on Industrial Society*, London, 1967

Azrael, J., *Managerial Power and Soviet Politics*, Cambridge, Ma., 1966

'The managers', in R.B. Farrel (ed.), *Political Leadership in the Soviet Union and Eastern Europe*, London, 1970

Babeau, A., *Les Conseils ouvriers en Pologne*, Paris, 1960

Bahro, R., *The Alternative in Eastern Europe*, London, 1978

Baran, Paul A. and Sweezy, Paul M., *Monopoly Capital: An Essay on the American Economic and Social Order*, London, 1973

Barber, R.J., *The American Corporation: Its Power, its Money, its Politics*, London, 1970

Barnet, R. and Muller, R.E. *Global Reach: The Power of the Multi-Nationals*, London, 1973

Bauman, Z., 'Social structure of the Party organisation in industrial works', in J. Wiatr (ed.), *Studies in the Polish Political System*, Warsaw, 1967

'Economic growth, social structure, elite formation: the case of Poland', in R. Bendix and S.M. Lipset (eds.), *Class Status and Power*, New York, 1966

Bayliss, T.A., *The Technical Intelligentsia and the East German Elite*, London, 1974

Beetham, D. *Max Weber and the Theory of Modern Politics*, London, 1974

Bell, D. *The coming of Post-Industrial Society*, London, 1974

The End of Ideology, Glencoe, 1960

Towards the Year 2000, Boston, 1968

Bendix, R. 'Managerial ideologies in the Russian orbit', in R. Bendix (ed.), *Work and Authority in Industry*, Berkeley, 1956.

Berle, A.A. and Means, G.C. *The Modern Corporation and Private Property*, New York, 1932

Berliner, J.S. *Factory and Manager in the U.S.S.R.*, Cambridge, Ma., 1957

Bethel, N. *Gomułka: His Poland and His Communism*, London, 1972

265

Bettelheim, C.M. 'Dictatorship of the proletariat, social class and political ideology', *Monthly Review*, Vol. 23, No. 6, 1971, pp. 55–76

Boornstein, M. East European economic reforms and the convergence of economic systems, in L. Wagner and N. Baltazzis, *Readings in Applied Econometrics*, Oxford 1973, pp. 59–79

Bower, J.L. 'On the amoral organisation', in R. Marris (ed.), *The Corporate Society: Growth Competition and Innovative Power*, London, 1974

Brus, W. *The Economics and Politics of Socialism*, London, 1973
   The Market in a Socialist Economy, London, 1972
   Socialist Ownership and Political Systems, London, 1975

Burnham, J. *The Managerial Revolution*, London, 1945

Carr, E.H. and Davies, R.W. *Foundations of a Planned Economy, 1909–1929*, London, 1969

Child, J. *The Business Enterprise in Modern Industrial Society*, London, 1969

Cliff, T. *Russia: A Marxist Analysis*, London, 1964

Coombes, D. *State Enterprise: Business or Politics?*, London, 1971

Crozier, M. *The Bureaucratic Phenomenon*, London, 1964

Dahrendorf, R. *Class and Class Conflict in Industrial Society*, Stanford, Ca., 1959

Deutscher, I. *Soviet Trade Unions: Their Place in Soviet Labour Policy*, London, 1950
   'The tragedy of the Polish Communist Party', in I. Deutscher, *Marxism in our Time*, 6th edition, London, 1971

Dobb, M. *Soviet Economic Development since 1917*, 6th edition, London, 1966

Douglas, D. *Transitional Economic Systems: The Polish–Czech Example*, London, 1953

Durkheim, E. *The Division of Labour in Society*, London, 1969

Dziewanowski, M.K. *The Communist Party of Poland*, 2nd edition, Cambridge, Ma., 1976

Feiwel, G.R. *The Economics of a Socialist Enterprise: A Case Study of the Polish Firm*, New York, 1965
   Poland's Industrialisation Policy: A Current Analysis, (2 vols.), Vol. I *Sources of Economic Growth and Retrogression*, New York, 1971

Fleron, F. Jr, ed., *Communist Studies and the Social Sciences: Essays on Methodology and Empirical Theory*, Chicago, 1969

Friedrich, C.J., Curtis, M. and Barber, B.R. *Totalitarianism in Perspective: Three Views*, London, 1969

Friedrich, C.J. and Brzeziński, Z.B. *Totalitarian Dictatorship and Autocracy*, 2nd edition, New York, 1966

Galbraith, J.K. *The New Industrial State*, London, 2nd edition, 1974

Gierek face aux Grevistes de Szczecin, S.E.L.I.O., Paris, 1971

Goldthorpe, J.H. 'Social stratification in industrial society', Sociological Review, Monograph No. 8, *The Development of Industrial Societies*, Keele, 1964

Gorz, A., ed. *The Division of Labour: The Labour Process and Class Struggle in Modern Capitalism*, Brighton, 1976

Grannick, D. *The Red Executive: a study of the Organisation Man in Industry*, London, 1960

Hayward, J. and Watson, M. *The One and Indivisible Republic*, London, 1973

Planning, Politics and Public Policy, London, 1975
Hiscocks, R. *Poland: A Bridge for an Abyss?*, London, 1963
Höhmann, H.H., Kaser, M.C. and Thalheim, K.C., eds. *The New Economic Systems of Eastern Europe*, London, 1975
Holland, S. *The Socialist Challenge*, London, 1975
The State as Entrepreneur, London, 1972
Hough, J. *The Soviet Prefects: Local Party Organs in Industrial Decision-Making*, Cambridge, Ma., 1969
Huntingdon, S. and Brzeziński, Z.B. *Political Power: U.S.A./U.S.S.R.*, New York, 1965
Ionescu, G. *The Political Thought of Saint-Simon*, London, 1976
Kahn, H. and Wiener, A.J. *The Year 2000: A Framework for Speculation on the next 33 Years*, New York, 1968
Kaser, M. and Zieliński, J. *Planning in East Europe*, London, 1970
Kaysen, C. 'The corporation: how much power, what scope?', in A. Pizzorno (ed.), *Political Sociology*, London, 1971
Kolankiewicz, G. 'The Polish industrial manual working class', in D. Lane and G. Kolankiewicz (eds.), *Social Groups in Polish Society*, London, 1973
'The technical intelligentsia', in D. Lane and K. Kolankiewicz, *Social Groups in Polish Society*, London, 1973
Konrad, G. and Szelenyi, I. *The Intellectuals on the Road to Class Power*, Brighton, 1979
Korboński, A. *The Politics of Socialist Agriculture in Poland 1945–1960*, New York, 1965
Kornhauser, W. *The Politics of Mass Society*, London, 1960
Kuron, J. and Modzelewski, K. 'An open letter to members of the University of Warsaw sections of the United Polish Workers' Party and the Union of Young Socialists', in *Revolutionary Marxist Students Speak Out, 1964–68*, New York, 1968.
Kumar, K. *Prophecy and Progress: The Sociology of Industrial and Post-Industrial Society*, London, 1978
Lane, D. *Politics and Society in the U.S.S.R.*, London, 1972
The Socialist Industrial State: Towards a Political Sociology of State Socialism, London, 1976
Lane, D. and Kolankiewicz, G., eds. *Social Groups in Polish Society*, London, 1973
Lavigne, M. *The Socialist Economies of the Soviet Union and East Europe*, London, 1974
Lee, D.M. 'Scientific Liberalism: Ward, Galbraith and the Welfare State', in M. Donald Hancock and B. Sjoberg (eds.), *Politics in the Post-Welfare State: Responses to the New Individualism*, Columbia, 1972
Ludz, P.C. *The Changing Party Elite in East Germany*, Cambridge, Ma., 1972
McCaulay, M. *Labour Disputes in Soviet Russia, 1957–1965*, London, 1969
Mallet, S. *Bureaucracy and Technocracy in the Socialist Countries* (Spokesman), Nottingham, 1974
The New Working Class (Spokesman), 4th edition, Nottingham, 1975
Mandel, E. *The Inconsistencies of State Capitalism*, London, 1969

Marcuse, H. *Soviet Marxism, a Critical Analysis*, London, 1971

Marris, R., ed. *The Corporate Society: Growth, Competition and Innovative Power*, London, 1974

Meyer, A.G. 'Theories of convergence', in A. Chalmers Johnson (ed.), *Change in Communist Systems*, Stanford, Ca., 1972

Montias, J.M. 'Central planning in Poland', New Haven, Conn., 1962

Narojek, W. 'The structure of power in a local community', in J. Wiatr (ed.), *Studies in the Polish Political System*, Warsaw, 1967

Naville, P., Bardou, J.P., Brachet, P. and Levy, C. *L'Etat entrepreneur: le cas de la Regie Renault*, Paris, 1971

Nettl, P. *Rosa Luxemburg*, London, 1969

Nove, A. *An Economic History of the U.S.S.R.*, London, 1969
Efficiency Criteria for the Nationalised Industries, London, 1973

Nove, A. and Nuti, D.M., eds. *Socialist Economics*, London, 1972

Olin Wright, E. *Class, Crisis and the State*, London, 1978

Ossowski, S. *Class Structure in the Social Consciousness*, London, 1969

Parkin, F. *Class, Inequality and Political Order*, London, 1972

Pateman, C. *Participation and Democratic Theory*, Cambridge, 1970

Posner, M.V. and Woolf, S.J. *Italian Public Enterprise*, London, 1967

Rakovski, M. *Towards an East European Marxism*, London, 1978

Richta, R. *Civilisation at the Crossroads: Social and Human Implications of the Scientific-Technological Revolution*, Prague, 1969

Rostow, W.W. *The Stages of Economic Growth*, 2nd edition, London, 1971

Scherer, F.M. *Industrial Market Structure and Economic Performance*, Chicago, 1970

Schumpeter, J. *Capitalism, Socialism and Democracy*, 4th edition, London, 1954

Scotford Archer, M. and Giner, S., eds. *Contemporary Europe: Class, Status and Power*, London, 1971

Shapiro, L. *Totalitarianism*, London, 1972

Shonfield, A. *Modern Capitalism: The Changing Balance of Public and Private Power*, London, 1965

Sik, O. *Plan and Market Under Socialism*, Prague, 1967

Silverman, D. *The Theory of Organisations*, London, 1970

Skilling, G. and Griffiths, F. *Interest Groups in Soviet Politics*, New York, 1971

Sturmthal, A. *Workers' Councils: A Study of Workplace Organisation on Both Sides of the Iron Curtain*, Cambridge, Ma., 1964

Taras, R. 'The local political elites', in Lane and Kolankiewicz *Social Groups in Polish Society*, London, 1973

Taylor, J. *The Economic Development of Poland, 1919–1950*, Ithaca, NY, 1952

Touraine, A. *The Post-Industrial Society*, London, 1974

Trotsky, L. *The Revolution Betrayed*, New York, 1957

Tugendhat, C. *The Multinationals*, Harmondsworth, 1973

Vaughan, M. 'Poland', in M. Scotford-Archer and S. Giner (eds.) *Contemporary Europe: Class, Status and Power*, London, 1971, pp. 318–57

Vernon, R. *Sovereignty at Bay: The Multi-National Spread of U.S. Enterprises*, London, 1973

Wesołowski, W. 'Changes in the class structure in Poland', in J. Wiatr (ed.),

Studies in the Polish Political System, Warsaw, 1967
Wesołowski, W. 'The notions of strata and class in socialist society', in A. Beteille (ed.), *Social Inequality*, London, 1969
Wesołowski, W. and Słomczyński, K. 'Social stratification in Polish cities', in J.A. Jackson (ed.) *Sociological Studies 1*, Cambridge; 1968
Wiatr, J., ed. *Studies in the Polish Political System*, Warsaw, 1967
Wilczyński, J. *Socialist Economic Development and Reforms*, London 1972
Wiles, P. 'Will Capitalism and Communism spontaneously converge?', in M. Boornstein and D. Fusfeld (eds.), *The Soviet Economy: a Book of Readings*, Homewood, Ill. 1966
Economic Institutions Compared, Oxford, 1977
ed. *The Prediction of Communist Economic Performance*, London, 1971
Woods, W. *Poland: Phoenix in the East*, Harmondsworth, 1972
Zauberman, A. *Industrial Progress in Poland, Czechoslovakia and East Germany, 1937–62* London, 1964
Zieliński, J.G. *Economic Reforms in East European Industry: Poland*, London, 1973
Zweig, F. *Poland Between the Two Wars*, London, 1944

Articles in English language journals

Armstrong, J.A. 'Sources of administrative behaviour: some Soviet and West European comparisons', *A.P.S.R.*, Vol. LXIII, September 1965, pp. 643–55
Meyer, A.G., Kautsky, J.H. and Jacobs, D.N. 'Symposium: comparative politics and Communist systems', *Slavic Review*, Vol. XXVI, March 1967, pp. 1–27
Bahro, R. 'The alternative in Eastern Europe', *New Left Review*, No. 106, November–December 1977, pp. 3–37
Blazyca, G. 'Industrial structure and the economic problems of industry in a centrally planned economy: the Polish case', *The Journal of Industrial Economics*, Vol. XXVIII, No. 3, March 1980, pp. 313–26
Boehme, H. 'East German price formation under the N.E.S.', *Soviet Studies*, Vol. XIX, No. 3, 1967/8, pp. 340–58
Brown, A. 'Problems of interest articulation and group influence in the Soviet Union', *Government and Opposition*, Vol. 7, Winter 1972, pp. 229–43
Bunce, V. and Echols, J.M. III 'From Soviet Studies to comparative politics: the unfinished revolution', *Soviet Studies*, Vol. XXI, No. 1, January 1979, pp. 43–55
Cave, J. 'Local officials of the Polish United Workers' Party 1956–75', *Soviet Studies*, Vol. XXXIII, No. 1, January 1981, pp. 125–41
Connor, W.D. 'Dissent in Eastern Europe: a new coalition?', *Problems of Communism*', January–February 1980, pp. 1–7
Deutscher, T. 'Voices of dissent', *Socialist Register* (London), 1978, pp. 21–43
Dunmore, T. 'Local Party organs in industrial administration: the case of

the 'ob'edinenie' reform', *Soviet Studies*, Vol. XXXII, No. 2, April 1980, pp. 195–217

Flakierski, H. 'Polish post-war growth', *Soviet Studies*, Vol. XXVII, No. 3, July 1975, pp. 460–76

Fleron, F. 'Soviet area studies and the social sciences: some methodological problems in Communist studies', *Soviet Studies*, Vol. XIX, No. 3, January 1968, pp. 313–39

Gella, A. 'The life and death of the old Polish intelligentsia', *Slavic Review*, Vol. XXX No. 1, March 1971, pp. 1–27

Gomułka, S. 'Growth and the import of technology – Poland 1971–1980', *Cambridge Journal of Economics*, Vol. 2, No. 3, 1978, pp. 1–16

Gorlin, A.C. 'The Soviet economic associations', *Soviet Studies*, Vol. XXVI, No. 1, 1974, pp. 3–27

Gronicki, M. 'Polish economic policy in the nineteen seventies, *National Westminster Bank Review*, 1979

Hirszowicz, M. 'Intelligentsia versus bureaucracy? The revival of a myth in Poland', *Soviet Studies*, Vol. XXX, No. 3, July 1976, pp. 336–61

Kavanagh, D. 'Beyond autonomy? The politics of corporations', *Government and Opposition*, Vol. 9, No. 1, 1974, pp. 42–60

Kelley, D.R. 'The Soviet debate on the convergence of American and Soviet systems', *Polity*, Vol. 6, 1973/4

Keren, M. 'The New Economic System in the G.D.R.: an obituary', *Soviet Studies*, Vol. XXIV, No. 4, April 1973, pp. 554–87

Kuczyński, W. 'The state enterprise under Socialism', *Soviet Studies*, Vol. XXX, No. 3, July 1978, pp. 313–35

Kumar, K. 'Industrialism and post-industrialism: reflections on a putative transition', *Sociological Review*, Vol. 24, No.3, August 1976, pp. 439–78

Ludlow, H.T. 'The role of trade unions in Poland', *Political Science Quarterly*, Vol. 90, No. 2, 1975, pp. 315–24

Mandel, E., 'Ten theses on the social and economic laws governing the society transitional between capitalism and socialism', *Critique*, No. 3, Autumn 1974.

Orr, R. 'Reflections on totalitarianism', *Political Studies*, Vol. XXI, No. 4, pp. 481–9

Portes, R. 'The control of inflation: lessons from the East European experience', *Economica*, Vol. 44, 1976, pp. 109–30

Quarterly Economic Review 'Poland, East Germany', No. 4, 1973

Rawin, S.J. 'The manager in the Polish enterprise', *British Journal of Industrial Relations*, Vol. 3, 1965, pp. 1–16

'The Polish intelligentsia and the socialist order: elements of ideological compatibility', *Political Science Quarterly*, Vol. 83, 1968, pp. 353–77

Staniszkis, J. 'On remodelling the Polish economic system', *Soviet Studies*, Vol. XXX, No. 4, 1978, pp. 547–52

'On some contradictions of socialist society', *Soviet Studies*, Vol. XXXI, No. 2, 1979, pp. 167–87

Starrels, J.M. 'Comparative and elite politics', *World Politics*, Vol. 29, No. 1, 1976, pp. 130–42

Sweezy, P.M. 'The transition to socialism', *Monthly Review*, Vol. 23, No. 1, 1971, pp. 1–16
Taras, R. 'Democratic centralism and Polish local government reforms', *Public Administration*, Vol. 53, 1975, pp. 403–26
Tellenback, S. 'The logic of development in Socialist Poland', *Social Forces*, Vol. 57, No. 2, 1978, pp. 436–56
Ticktin, H.H. 'The political economy of the Soviet intellectual', *Critique*, No. 2, 1974
  'Towards a political economy of the USSR', *Critique*, No. 1, 1973, pp. 20–41
Tucker, R.C. 'On the comparative study of communism', (Research Note), *World Politics*, Vol. XIV, No. 2, January 1967.
Urban, G.R. 'A conversation with Ota Sik', *Survey*, Spring 1973, pp. 250–65
Wanless, P.T. 'Economic reform in Poland 1973–79', *Soviet Studies*, Vol. XXXII, No. 1, January 1980, pp. 28–57
Weinberg, I. 'The problem of the convergence of industrial societies: a critical look at the state of a theory', *Comparative Studies in Society and History*, Vol. II, January 1979, pp. 1–15
Whalley, J. 'Polish post-war economic growth from the view point of the Soviet experience', *Soviet Studies*, Vol. XXIV, No. 4 1973, pp. 533–49
Wiles, P. Symposium on 'Technocracy, politics, and the post-industrial Society', *Survey*, Vol. 17, No. 1, 1971, pp. 1–27
Williams, R. 'The technological society and British politics', *Government and Opposition*, Vol. 7, No. 1, Winter 1972, pp. 56–84
Winkler, J.T. 'Corporatism' *Archives europeénes de sociologie*, Vol. 17, 1976, pp. 100–36
Woodall, M.J. 'New social factors in the unrest in Poland', *Government and Opposition*, Vol. 16, No. 1, Winter 1981, pp. 37–57
Zagórski, K. 'Changes in socio-occupational mobility in Poland', *Polish Sociological Bulletin*, No. 2, 1976

Polish language texts

Bar, L., ed. *Grupowanie przedsiębiorstw państwowych:-zagadnienia prawne*, Warsaw, 1972
Beksiak, J. *Spoleczeństwo gospodarujące*, Warsaw, 1972
Blazejczyk, M. *Prawo samorzadu robotniczego*, Warsaw, 1971
Bratkowscy, S. and A. *Gra o jutro*, Warsaw, 1970
Chalasiński, J. *Przeszłość i przyszłość inteligencji polskiej*, Warsaw, 1958
Dobieszewski, A., ed. *Wiedza o Partii: wybrany problemy*, Warsaw, 1972
  Wybrane zagadnienia ideologii i polityki PZPR, Warsaw, 1971
Dobrzyński, M. *Kierowanie kadrami*, Warsaw, 1977
Dudek, A 'Plynność dyrektorów', in A. Sarapata (ed.), *Plynność zalog*, Warsaw, 1968
Dziewicka, M. *Chlopi robotnicy*, Warsaw, 1963
Friss, I., ed. *Reforma mechanizmu gospodarczego na Węgrzech*, Warsaw, 1971
  Funkcjonowanie Rozwidązań Prawnych w kombinatach Przemyslowych (PAN) Warsaw, 1972

272   *Bibliography*

Gliński, B. *System zarządzania w przemysle kluczowym*, Warsaw, 1960
    Teoria i praktyka zarządzania przedsiębiorstwami przemyslowymi, Warsaw, 1964
    '*Zjednoczenie i przedsiębiorstwo*', Warsaw, 1968
Głowacki, Sł. *Zjednoczenia państwowych przedsiębiorstw terenowych w systemie organów rad narodowych*, Warsaw, 1972
Hoser, J. 'Inżynierowie w przemyśle', in J. Szczepański (ed.) '*Przemysł i spoleczeństwo w Polsce Ludowej*', Warsaw, 1969
Jaworski, T. *Udzial zalog w zarządzaniu*, Warsaw, 1976
Kalecki, M. *Zarys teorii wzrostu gospodarki socjalistycznej*, Warsaw, 1963
Karpiński, A. *Polityka uprzemyslowienia Polski w latach 1958–68*, Warsaw, 1969
    Krajówa narada aktywu Partyjnego i gospodarczego, Warsaw, 1973
Kulpińska, J., ed. *Wlokniarze w procesie zmiań*, Warsaw, 1975
Lange, O. *Pisma ekonomiczne i spoleczne 1930–1960*, Warsaw, 1961
Lęgowski, J. *Polityka kadrowa w zakladzie pracy*, Warsaw, 1976
Leskiewicz, Z. and Szorć, Z. *W.O.G.: Zalożenia i Problemy Organizacyjne*, Warsaw, 1975
Łopatka, A., Bluszkowski, J. and Konstański, K. *Organizacja Partyjne wielkich zakladów pracy*, Warsaw, 1976
Matejko, A., ed. *Socjologia kierowniétwa*, Warsaw, 1969
Morawski, W. *Samorząd robotniczy w gospodarce socjalistycznej*, Warsaw, 1973
Najduchowska, H. 'Dyrektórzy, przedsiębiortstw przemyslowych', in J. Szczepański (ed.), *Przemysl i spoleczeństwo w Polsce Ludowej*, Warsaw, 1969
Narojek, W. *Spoleczeństwo planujące: proba socjologii gospodarki socjolistycznej*, Warsaw, 1973
    System wladzy w miejsicie, Warsaw, 1967
Orzechowski, R., ed. *Prawo przedsiębiorstw*, Warsaw, 1971
Pajestka, J. *Kieruńki doskonalenia systemu planowania i zarządzania w Polsce ludowej*, Warsaw, 1965
    Przedsiębiorstwo samodzielne w gospodarce planowej, Warsaw, 1957
Rybicki, Z. *Administracyjno – prawne zagadnienia gospodarki planowej*, Warsaw, 1971
Sarapata, A., ed. *plyńność zalog*, Warsaw, 1968
Staniszkis, J. *Patologie struktur organizacyjnych*, Warsaw, 1972
Szczepański, J. *Odmiany czasu terazniejszego*, Warsaw, 1971
    Narodziny socjalistycznej klasy robotniczej, Warsaw, 1972
    Prżemysl i spoleczeństwo w Polsce Ludowej, Warsaw, 1969
Szczepański, J. and Secomski, K. *Komitet Badań i prognóz Polska 2000*, Warsaw, 1971
Szyr, E. *Nowe Elementy w planowaniu i zarządzaniu*, Warsaw, 1958
Waclawek, J. *Socjalistyczne stosunki w zakladzie pracy*, Warsaw, 1970
Wesolowski, W. *Klasy warstwy i wladza*, Warsaw, 1966
Wesolowski, W. ed. *Ksztalt struktury spolecznej* (PAN), Warsaw, 1978
Widerszpil, S. *Przeobrażenia struktury spolecznej w Polsce*, Warsaw, 1973

Masters' and doctoral theses, conference papers and other documents

Jelenek, R. 'Organizacja i efectywność ekonomiczna funkcjonowania dużej organizacji przemysłowej na przykładu kombinatu Górniczo-Hutniczego Miedzi w Lubinie', Master's thesis, Kraków, 1970

Kula, M. 'Organizacja wewnętrzna zakładu wiodącego w kombinacie', Diploma thesis, Kraków, 1972

'Przesłanki twórżenia kombinatów i rola kolegium i ich zarządzania w Kielce', Master's thesis, Kraków, 1973

Liniewicz, W. 'Organizacja zjednoczeń i kombinatów w rekonstrukcji branżowej i terenowej', Master's thesis (SGPiS), Warsaw, 1970

Murawski, E. 'Zjednoczenie Przemysłu Cukierniczego', Doctoral thesis (SGPiS), Warsaw, 1973

Sadownik, H. 'Kontrola w zarządzaniu zjednoczeniom przemysłowym', Doctoral thesis (SGPiS), Warsaw, 1972

Siwek, H. 'Studia na przeobrażeniami swiadomośći spolecznej w zapleczu wiejskim kombinatu Tarnobrzeskiego', Master's thesis, Kraków, 1965

Teter, A. 'Dyrektór i kolegium w zjednoczeniu przemysłowym', Master's thesis (SGPiS) Warsaw, 1970

Wiewińska, E. 'Analiza eksperymentu zjednoczenia przemysłu stolarki budowlanej w zakresie nowych form planowania i organizowania produkcji', Warsaw, 1970

Bar, L. 'Funkcjonowanie kombinatów przemysłowych', Tarnobrzeg, 1972

Baumberger, T. 'Zarządzanie wielkimi organizmami gospodarczymi na przykładzie przemysłu okrętowego' (PTE), Warsaw, 1973

Błazejewski, J. 'Funkcjonowanie kombinatów przemysłowych' (INP), Warsaw, 1972

Jakubowicz, A. 'Funkcje zjednoczeń przemysłowych w nowym systemie planowania w Polsce w latach, 1956–58', Manuscript (SGPiS) Warsaw, 1970

Jakubowicz, Sz. 'Sytuacja Przedsiębiorstw w zjednoczeniu eksperymentujcym', Discussion papers (IP), Warsaw, 1970

'Integracja przedsiębiortw w przemysłe kluczowym Węgier i NRD', Manuscript, Warsaw, 1971

Kolarska, L. 'Cele kombinatu a cele zjednoczenia: analiza socjologiczna' Manuscript (IFiS), Warsaw, 1973

Kolarska, L. 'Sprawozdanie z socjologicznych badań relacji zakład kombinat-zjednoczeniu', Manuscript (PAN), Warsaw, 1973

Konferencja Naukowa 'Doswiadczenie zjednoczeń eksperymentujacuch' (Zarząd Główny PTE), Warsaw, 1968 (Papers by T. Baumberger, M. Cybulska, J. Olszewski, H. Tarchalska.)

Konferencja Naukowa n.t. 'Oceny Kadry Kiersowniczej: Metodologia i Praktyka', Instytut Organizacji Przemysłu Maszynowego (IOPM) 1970

V Konferencja Naukowa 'Dyrektor w procesie kierowania przedsiębiorstw' (TNOiK), Bydgoszcz, 1973

'Kombinat Kopalń i zakładów przetwórczych Siarki "Siarkopol" im N. Nowotki w Tarnobrzegu', Warsaw, 1972

Nędzowski, E. 'Funkcjonowanie dużych organizacjach przemysłowych na przykładzie przemysłu azotowego', Kraków, 1972

Oskarol, E. 'Ankieta dla zakładu wiodącego kombinatu Przemysłu Lozysk Tocznych Predom' (FLT), Kielce, 1972

Pajestka, J. 'Doskonalenie planowania i funkcjonowonia gospodarki w Polsce Ludowej', Materiały Dyskusyjne Instytut Planowania (IP), Warsaw, 1967

Stefaniak, J. 'Funkcjonowanie rozwiązań prawnych w kombinacie kopalń i zakładów przetwórczych siarki "Siarkopol" w Tarnobrzegu', Machów, 30 March 1971

Stefanski, S. Organizacja i metody zarządzania w przedsiębiorstwach i zjednoczeniach oraz funkcje gospodarcze zjednoczeń (PTE), Katowice, 1967

'Symposiom poswięcone usprawnienia funkcjonowania przedsiebiorstw i zjednoczen' (PTE), Katowice, 1968

Polish newspapers and weekly and monthly journals which are cited in the text

Doskonalenie Kadr Kierowniczych (DKK)
Ekonomika i Organizacja Pracy (EiOP)
Ekonomista
Finanse
Gospodarka Planowa (GP)
Monitor Polski (MP)
Nowe Drogi (ND)
Organizacja Metodia i Technika (OMiT)
Państwo i Prawo (PiP)
Polityka
Problemy Organizacji (PO)
Przegląd Organizacji
Przegląd Techniczny (PT)
Ruch Prawniczy, Ekonomiczny i Socjologiczny (RPEiS)
Samorząd Robotniczy (SR)
Studia Socjologiczny (SS)
Trybuna Ludu (TL)
Trybuna Samorządu Robotniczego (TSR)
Zycie Gospodarcze (ZG)
Zycie Partii (ZP)
Zycie Warszawie (ZW)

Statistical sources and official documents

United Nations Statistical Year Book, 1952
Rocznik statystyczny przemysl, 1971
Rocznik statystyczny, 1972, 1976, 1979
Radni i czlonkowie preżydiów rad narodowych 1958–69, GUS, Warsaw, 1972
Reports and Resolutions of Plenary Sessions of the Central Committee of the PZPR, and of the Council of Ministers

Index